Why Did You Stay?

Why Did You Stay?

A memoir about self-worth

Rebecca Humphries

SPHERE

SPHERE

First published in Great Britain in 2022 by Sphere
This paperback edition published in 2023 by Sphere

1 3 5 7 9 10 8 6 4 2

A CIP catalogue record for this book
is available from the British Library.

Paperback ISBN 978-0-7515-8481-3

*In order to maintain anonymity in some instances,
the author has changed the names of certain individuals.*

Typeset in Garamond by M Rules
Printed and bound in Great Britain by
Clays Ltd, Elcograf S.p.A.

Papers used by Sphere are from well-managed forests
and other responsible sources.

Sphere
An imprint of
Little, Brown Book Group
Carmelite House
50 Victoria Embankment
London EC4Y 0DZ

An Hachette UK Company
www.hachette.co.uk

www.littlebrown.co.uk

That love is all there is, is all we know of love

EMILY DICKINSON

My name is Rebecca Humphries and I am not a victim.

I wasn't sure whether to respond to events from the past week, but I feel the narrative has missed a couple of crucial elements that I would like to clear up.

It's incredibly good of Him and the dancer to apologise in the media. I have received nothing, other than the support of my family, friends, and a host of strangers on the internet who all wanted to make sure I was OK. What I have also kindly received are many offers to sell my side of the story, but I would prefer for it to be on my own terms.

Those pictures were taken on October 3rd. It was my birthday. I was alone at home when He texted at 10pm saying the two of them were going for one innocent drink. We spoke and I told Him, not for the first time, that His actions over the past three weeks had led me to believe something inappropriate was going on. He aggressively, and repeatedly, called me a psycho / nuts / mental. As He has done countless times throughout our relationship when I've questioned His inappropriate, hurtful behaviour.

But – this whole business has served to remind me that I am a strong, capable person who is now free; and no victim. I have a voice, and I will use it by saying this to any woman out there who deep down feels worthless and trapped with a man they love.

Believe in yourself and your instincts. It's more than lying. It's controlling. Tell some very close friends who, if they're anything like my wonderful network, will swoop in and take care of the logistics and of you.

It's important also to recognise that in these situations those who hold power over you are insecure and fragile, and their need for control comes from a place of vulnerability. I think it certainly does in His case. Despite everything, I hope He gets what He wants from this. I'm not sorry I took the cat though.

Love, Rebecca
8.18PM – Oct 8, 2018 – Twitter Web Client

♡ 4.7k comments   ↱ 15.7k retweets   ♡ 84.7k likes

Replying to @Beckshumps
If he was that bad, why did you stay eh?

Author's Note

I never wanted to write a book. All I ever really want to do, at any given moment, is dance about to gay songs. But I need to. I need to do it because several years after surviving a relationship (one that culminated in the bin-fire of all break-ups), I am still seeing with my own eyes some of the coolest, cleverest, sexiest women allowing their brilliance to be drained in the name of love. I need to do it because, as Jane Fonda says, 'Once you know what's wrong and you stay silent, you're part of the problem.'

And although no one *actually* has to answer a BS, victim-shaming question like 'Why Did You Stay?', I hope that my choice to reclaim it will empower anyone who feels as lonely in their story as I once did in mine.

But this is as much a story of how I left it behind me as why I stayed. Because what defines you in life isn't what happens to you, but how you deal with it. I'm sure anyone who has ever experienced difficulty will attest that in their darkest moment, a part of them – an astonishing, resilient, actually quite iconic part they never knew existed – stepped out of the shadows. This is a book about how to hold on to that part moving forward.

I fully acknowledge this is a story from my perspective, and that everybody else featured will have a perspective of their own. Some of the names in this book have been changed to protect identities, and some people's names I haven't mentioned but you're going to know who they are anyway. I will definitely, definitely piss some of them off with all this. When certain people read it and think, *She's written that bit about me*, not all of them will be right, but some will. To those of them who are right, and who aren't very happy about it, I do understand because I probably wouldn't be happy either. I hope, though, that they will at least accept my right to express my version of events (as some of them have done already).

Finally, to anybody that feels this book has been inspired by their actions, I would just like to say:

> I am sorry if what I've included makes you feel bad.
> But I humbly accept your gratitude
> for the things I have graciously opted
> to omit.

I Left

Because, finally, the truth

At around 11:30 p.m. on 6 October 2018, my worst nightmare came true while standing in a car park.

The date is easy to remember because it was three days after my thirty-second birthday. My friend Theo describes my energy as 'a Diva everybody said was washed up on a sold-out arena tour', which is to say, a total slag for attention. But this year my birthday went uncelebrated. And I hadn't seen Theo in months.

Anyway, I'm in this car park, which is outdoors, and it's raining dribbly 'neither here nor there' rain. My umbrella is *in*doors, specifically a gazebo 15 feet to my left that's fizzing over with revelry and mutual fluffing.

'You were AMAZING!'

'YOU were amazing!'

The light from inside it is bleeding on to the wet tarmac, making the puddles on the ground brighter than the sky. I think that they look like spotlights, and am quite pleased with myself for connecting the showbiz dots. I am not standing in a spotlight, of course. I'm barely visible here in a dark bit, which is deliberate but not my choice.

The car park in question is one of many inside BBC Elstree Studios. Growing up I had expectations of television studios. I used to imagine the BBC as somewhere I could saunter down the street from *EastEnders*, then turn a corner and dodge bullets from a cop show, then a gaggle of feathery showgirls would teeter past like flamingos while somebody yelled 'ACTION!' into a big cone. It isn't. The fact is it's functional – a vast network of giant metal sheds with people in North Face jackets bombing around. A place where television gets done, rather than where magic gets made. That said, I did once walk past Tom Jones by a Portaloo.

Stood directly opposite me is my boyfriend.

I'm always freezing even when it's hot, but especially tonight because I'm wearing a new dress, £200 give or take (it's give, it's always give), which is roughly the size of a cobweb and just as thin. In expensive shops the price tag is often attached with a safety pin, making it really easy to take things you can't afford back after the weekend, so long as you've avoided red wine, haven't been anywhere too sweaty and given it a good Febreze. I've taken to doing this for the last few weeks – returning things after wearing them at the weekend (or 'borrowing', as I prefer to call it). I haven't had a job in a very long time and am quite skint, and the thing is for the past few weekends I have been mingling with VIPs, each and every one of them dripping in opulence. I myself am no VIP, not even an IP. Just a P, and a fraud, but at least I'm well dressed.

I should explain.

Earlier tonight I was sitting in the audience at the studio of *Strictly Come Dancing*, and the boyfriend standing opposite me was one of the celebrities competing in it. *Strictly Come Dancing* is the biggest show on UK television. Forgive me if you already know this; rest assured, I know how you feel. I myself am reminded almost daily. Lots of the time it's when He staggers home from rehearsals after 10 p.m.

'It's the biggest show on television!' He goes.

The 'biggest show on television' part is spoken in italics, and it quite often feels as though the words are sweeties for

4

the speaker to have a good suck on rather than information for a recipient. Still, I got the message. The stakes are high, millions watch it live, no one wants to screw up. There's a good chance I'd be on the biggest show on television too if He referred to me in His thank-you address to the camera, which is something that the celebrities often do. 'I couldn't have done it without my wife/husband/partner', etc., camera cuts to a beaming face in the crowd. For the last four weeks it hasn't happened in my instance, but I've been wearing a new dress every time just in case. I have paired this one with flat black Chelsea boots. I toyed with sharp stilettos, which are less 'me' but more feminine. In general, though, I always try to avoid anything that gives me more length or girth at *Strictly*, as around the women who appear on the show I often feel like the only manatee at Mermaid Lagoon. That's in physical terms, of course. Personality wise I am much smaller, more like a mouse looking through its hiding place at all the bendy, confident cats licking their own genitals.

And tonight it happened! The dress and me got our airtime! I had been standing and clapping and crying when a big stick on wheels topped with a big black cuboid was urgently skidded right in front of my face. His paso doble had just ended, and He'd done a really great job, which was unusual as He was usually quite crap. Dancing is not part of His professional remit, to be fair. He's a stand-up comedian, so most of His job involves, well, standing up, but relatively still and on His own. Last week, in particular, He royally mucked up a jive, which are hectic at the best of times, and had to wince His way through the judges' comments, when one of them gave Him a three (that's out of ten, for anyone who has never watched it. It's bad). I say all this to illustrate just how triumphant His paso was this evening. In *Strictly* terms, doing a great job after everyone has written you off is the Holy Grail – you become the underdog the audience roots for, you're Erin Brockovich, or the Jamaican bobsleigh team in *Cool Runnings*.

Incidentally, the paso doble is a Latin dance that depicts a fierce, four-minute fight to the death. The story of each number centres around the male, who takes the role of matador: grounded, controlled and muscular. His eyes burn into the female/bull, who whips up a wild display around him, tearing his arms off her body one moment and begging him 'tame me!' the next. When done well, it's like the sexiest row you've ever had, and reminds me of a quote from Colette Dowling: *Relationships are like a dance, with visible energy racing back and forth between the partners. Some relationships are the slow, dark dance of death.*

So, this car park.

My boyfriend standing opposite me is dressed in black as always. When we started going out five and a half years ago He used to dress in vibrant blues that matched His eyes, because, in His words, 'I'm happy now, so I should probably stop dressing like somebody died.' I can't remember when He went back to wearing black. I can't remember when I stopped noticing His eyes were blue.

His dance partner was wearing black tonight as well, on the telly. A black leather catsuit, with black feline make-up applied by the best in the business. She looked like the type of woman you should be worried your boyfriend was playing the matador to. This isn't really about her, though.

Here the pair of us stand, anyway, in the dark, on the cusp of a nightmare.

'What's going on?' I ask His maybe blue eyes, wondering what I've done.

'Where are you sleeping tonight?' He asks the air over my shoulder.

Something in the gazebo smashes, the cheers waft out and

coil around us. He continues to stare over my shoulder. I'm still staring at His eyes.

'Um, at home?' I say it like it's obvious cos it is, cos I live there. That's where I sleep.

'No you're not.'

'I – I don't . . . What?'

I'm doing that thing where I free-fall standing upright. I try to ground myself by tasting my breath. Marlboro Gold washed down with the champagne I cheerfully glugged when His agent suggested He 'take her over there and tell her'. I slick my tongue around my teeth and try to focus on what is real rather than allowing my unreliable, erratic, overly emotional mind to fly to its default state: 'ways to punish myself for being myself': *Your contour looks like sideburns, like Wolverine, not enough cheekbones, too much thigh, should've gone spinning, should start checking calories, look at the women here, these are proper women, these are what women are meant to be.*

Brutal, obviously, but. It feels good, doing the thing you're best at.

He emits a feral 'UGGGHHH!', interrupting my thoughts just as they're getting going.

And I will never forget this silence. Between His exhausted bellow to the sky and the following sentence, told to His own outline on the wet tarmac.

'The *Sun* have got pictures of me and the dancer kissing.'

A beat. Then I say, 'Oh.'

'And I have to get the fuck out of here before her husband hits me.'

Huh.

Strange.

I feel . . .

I *feel.*

'I'm coming with you,' I say.

7

'No you're fucking not!' He wasn't expecting that. Me, speaking like somebody who had been right. His eyes flick up at mine for the first time.

I step towards Him, and into a spotlight.

'*I am.*'

I Stayed

Because once I was perfect

Brighton, April 2013

Once upon a time, I met a man on the set of a television programme.

It was my first big acting job, and at the read-through He was the only person more visibly nervous than me.

We would cry with laughter, share looks when other people chatted nonsense. He began to save McVitie's Gold Bars from the snack box for me. I began to always know where He was standing in a room. Our trailers were next to each other, and after arduous shoot days He would play Cyndi Lauper's 'Time After Time' loud enough for me to hear, and we'd harmonise badly through the walls.

I had a boyfriend back then – Max – but still my heart would beat faster whenever He and I were told to 'get a room'.

A few weeks later, He invited me and another colleague to the Groucho Club. I'd never been to a private members club before. When I turned up, the other colleague wasn't there. By the third Jägerbomb, I dared to ask Him what I already knew.

'That person was never coming, were they?'

'No.'

'Why?'

'You know why.'

'I don't know!' But I did.

'Yes you do.'

'All right, but I need to hear it.'

'I'M MADLY IN LOVE WITH YOU!' He shouted it.

'Leave it with me,' I said.

I broke up with Max the following morning, got in the car and drove straight to my mum's in Norwich. I had been worried about telling her, she had always liked Max. But she rather cryptically said, 'Once you know for sure you have to break up with someone, you feel so free.'

He's invited me to Brighton for the weekend. I nearly don't go. My grandad died yesterday, very suddenly, of a stroke. I ask Mum if she wants me to stay at home and help her with Nan, who has to be taken to live in a home. But she insists.

The waistcoated-man carrying our cases to the room at the hotel He paid for has no idea we're stealing glances behind him. When the door opens He looks at me for signs of astonishment but I give nothing away. I just stand taking in the roll-top bath, the pinball machine, the biggest bed I've ever seen and a balcony looking out to the sea. I say things like 'yes, this will do' and try not to jump up and down.

The man who carried the cases leaves and we stand silently, trying not to be the first to smile. He sits on the bed in silence. I go and sit down next to Him. He turns to me. I turn to face Him. I've never enjoyed chess as much as this.

'Can you just kiss me please?' I eventually ask Him. 'Otherwise I'll spend all day wondering if and when it's going to happen, a day we could just spend kissi—'

And I stop, because He does.

We kiss, we dance, we drink champagne from the mini-bar. We lean over the balcony in hotel towelling robes and

Ray-Bans, looking out at the sea, at the ice cream castle clouds that Joni Mitchell once promised me. 'All this could be yours!' He exclaims, leaning over the edge with His arms above Him, bubbles fizzing from His glass on to the ground four floors below. We throw back our heads, laughing in disbelief at all of it, and all the seagulls above us seem to join in.

Brighton is like Wonderland, a network of fairy-lit alleys. Spiral staircases that lead up to perfect espresso martinis, more kissing, clouds of oxytocin. He lives so fast that even sitting in a restaurant opposite Him feels like being excitedly pulled by the wrist and flown barefoot through the streets to Patti Smith's 'Because the Night'.

All the rooms He walks into suddenly belong to Him. 'TWO TEQUILAS!' He shouts to no one in particular as we step into the restaurant, and miraculously a waiter brings them. He thinks He's powerful and for that reason He's right.

There's an urgency for life and for mischief and for being famous and being part of this partnership that ain't so professional no more, and it reaches out and strikes me, shakes me. All I can see is *fun*.

'I don't know what any of this is!' I tell Him later, shouting to be heard over Robin Thicke's 'Blurred Lines' that's pounding indoors. We're under a brick arch outside a club, and I'm smoking for the first time ever because He offered me one. 'I know what you're like!' I yell.

'What do you mean?'

'You love putting it about!'

He shakes his head. 'This isn't that.'

'No?'

'No! That's not me! It has been, but I don't want that any more. I've never felt like this.'

'Well, what do you want, then?'

'I want you to be my girlfriend!'

*

13

After the mess of previous relationships, the shame at being kept a secret by literally everyone that has ever shown an interest in me. There's no cloudiness, no grey area. I can feel my organs, my aura, every skin cell activate and I have no doubt whatsoever that this is what being truly alive feels like.

'When I'm with you, I don't feel so fucking *dark*,' He says, and I think, *God, His problems are all so clear, I know exactly what is missing, and exactly how to fix it.*

Plus I get the impression he wouldn't quit till I said yes anyway.

So I say: 'OK. I'll be your girlfriend then.'

And just like that, I belong to Him.

He kisses me. 'This is my girlfriend!' He says to the bouncer.

'You're a lucky man,' the bouncer replies.

We go for midnight fish and chips, the vinegar glitters from the lights strung along the promenade. We walk past closed candy-floss kiosks with giant plastic Mr Whippys stood outside them. We stand on the pebble beach and listen to the sea breathe between Brighton's two piers, one whose lights radiate pizazz all over the night sky, the other nothing but charred skeletal remains.

'I burned that one down with some mates, got arrested.'

I gasp and turn to Him, my sacral chakra spicy all of a sudden. 'Did you?'

'No.' And our laughs are even louder in the night silence.

'You are the most exciting person I've ever met.' I look at Him. 'I can't believe you're in love with me.'

He kisses me. 'You're perfect,' He says. And in that moment there wasn't a death last night, and I didn't just break someone's heart. There's just the inky sea, His blue eyes and His potential, and the rest of my life in front of me.

The next morning, I lie in the hotel bed making lines with my finger on His chest. Drawing a map of where we'll escape together.

We drive back to His flat in West London. I nap on the sofa, and when I wake up, He's been out and bought us both a Wagamamas. We slurp ramen and He tells me He never wants me to leave. He says, 'Marry me', and I laugh, open mouthed, even though there's a gyoza in it and say, 'You're stupid.'

He says, 'Move in with me,' and I look at Him, galvanised by this person who can be bold enough to know exactly what they want, and ask for it. Amazed that what they want is me.

'OK!' I say.

Within three weeks we are living together.

Within three months both our names are on a mortgage agreement for a flat in Shepherd's Bush.

I have been bombed with love, and it's everything I was ever promised.

And even though a little voice somewhere inside me says, 'You aren't compatible.'

And, 'You've just broken up with someone, process it.'

And, 'You're using His power so you don't need to step into your own.'

I shake it off. Because the fact that I shouldn't be doing it is half the fun. It's irresponsible, unsensible, it's the opposite of me, and thank fuck for that. I feel like the door has been swung open to a room I've spent my life with my ear pressed up against. Like I'm part of the fun I've always felt was happening somewhere else, at a house party I wasn't invited to.

I Left

Because enough is enough

Elstree, 6 October 2018, midnight(ish)

I wish I could accurately express the sensation of being papped for the first time. In the dark it's especially chilling. Less than five minutes after the car-park confessional, we are gliding in the back of the Mercedes they provide for the *Strictly* contestants, towards a mass of inert shadows set against the bars that guard Elstree Studios. One or two figures stalk the gate's length, aware it's almost feeding time.

Then BANG.

An instant lack of space from all four sides. Strobe lighting. Screaming, voices slashing through one another to be heard but each one indecipherable. Metallic bangs against the car bonnet as hands and bodies are thrown against it, anything to slow the driver. The carnal faces of complete strangers right by your shoulder. And all at once. All of the above, all at once.

Something that's even harder to convey is that when you're that many people's direct focus, when that much energy is being refracted through a lens at you, magnifying and bending your being, time ceases to be a freeway into the distance. Time becomes lateral, as though it's sitting all around you. As we steadily roll through that tunnel of strobing light, I experience the 'nowness' of my spine pressing back on the leather seat, and the 'nextness' of my face on paper and ink, being paid for by people I don't know.

Oh, Dad, I think as the car drives out through the clamour and into momentum. My dad works in a newsagent's.

I look over at Him. Dumped on the seat like cooked spaghetti on a plate. Thudded up against the car door as far away as possible from where I'm sitting, His blond curls stuffing the space between His coat collar and a fedora I never liked. In fact, I hate that fedora. I had 'suggested' at the point of purchase that fedoras belong in the 1940s, or on *X Factor* hopefuls that didn't make it past bootcamp, or on Justin Timberlake circa 2005 when even he looked like a douchebag. Beneath the fedora and over the coat and in front of the curls are two hands clenched around His face like He's been paused in the midst of pulling it off. Under those hands His face is spray-tanned two shades darker than the rest of Him. I know exactly the shade He gets hosed down with every Friday night before the live show, because thereafter my John Lewis pima cotton pillowcases are skidmarked with it. I've never said anything about this, desperate as I've been to cling on to the last bastion of my desirability and foreseeing the aggro that would inevitably ensue.

'What are you doing?' He asks.

My phone is lighting up my face like I'm about to sing 'Bohemian Rhapsody', beaming out the image of the man sitting next to me passionately embracing the woman I sat in an audience and watched Him do the paso doble with four hours ago.

'You're not googling it, are you?!'

I stare at the screen with the curious pragmatism usually reserved for floorplans on the Rightmove app. He's wearing the striped T-shirt that I've told Him He looks handsome in many times. Nice to know that He was listening, I suppose. I scroll down the article to where there are more pictures. The two of them are running, dancing, throwing their bags on the floor in abandon as they drink each other in. He captures her on His phone, the same phone that had received my miserable pleas asking Him when He was coming home, as they themselves are being unwittingly held captive under the photographer's glare. There's an urgency for life and for mischief and for being famous and for being part of this partnership that ain't so professional no more, and it reaches out and strikes me, shakes me. All I can see is *fun*.

'You're looking at it, aren't you? Why would you do that, are you insane?!'

'Well, clearly not.' As my eyes tear from the screen to meet where His voice is coming from, the weirdest thing happens. Instead of a window with a midnight-lit road behind Him, the sky is a children's-book blue and I can see the sea, shimmering white and silver like a disco ball beneath it. Seagulls swoop around ice-cream castles in the air. He's no longer lurking under his own fedora, but wearing a white towelling robe and Ray-Ban sunglasses in which I can see my own reflection; also be-robed, elated, shaking a half-bottle of pink champagne.

I look down at the grainy picture of the kiss, then up again. The car is back to normal, the sky is dark, the road is just a road, and He is, well, just Him.

'How many times?' I ask it like I'm asking how many eyes are in my head, like I know there's a definite number and that that number isn't one.

'Come off it.' He flings his arms out, indicating the driver. Not one single hair on His head moves but then, they do use a *lot* of hairspray.

'Oh sorry, is this not an appropriate time to be hysterical? Because I'd love to know when is.'

A sigh. He leans back into the seat and looks out at the concrete scribble of the Westway flyover. 'One time.'

'Well, before tonight it was no times, so.'

'I CAN'T BELIEVE THIS IS HAPPENING TO ME!'

I briefly freeze, mouth agape. After a moment, I manage to swallow and continue.

'Come on now, the truth.'

'Fine.' He makes the mistake of hesitating just long enough to let me know a few options are being weighed up. 'One more time.'

I laugh. 'All right, that means a few!'

'Think what you like. I'm done talking.'

And I sit there, suffocating in this enforced silence, wondering whether all love stories go from singing Kings of Leon in the cobbled streets of Berlin, to trying to find the right lid for the Tupperware box, to sitting as far apart in a car as it's possible to be.

Just beyond the loom of the concrete Kraken that is Westfield shopping centre lies Shepherd's Bush Green, an island of sad mucky grass and trees giving living a go. At one end, the unmistakable tang of weed infuses a children's playground full of adults getting off their tits and playing dominoes twenty-four hours a day. Around the whole thing, an aggressive one-way system lined with charity shops, Lebanese bakeries, shifty looking offies, a twenty-four-hour McDonald's and a new luxury hotel that looks like it got lost on the way to Dubai. And just beyond all of it lies Samstat Road.

God, I love Samstat Road. It's the sort of London you'd see in a British romcom, but where someone you're supposed to feel a tiny bit sorry for lives. Which is to say, pretty, quirky Victorian terrace houses that suggest affluence without inviting you in for a six-person 'guinea-fowl-and-cognac' dinner party. Obviously, like so much of London, the price of a flat on this road would make you spit out your sauvignon blanc, which is what actually happened when I once told my Auntie Netti how much our flat had cost.

I could never afford to live here were it not for Him, of course. After tonight, I guess I no longer do.

I'm standing at the kitchen counter when He comes sloping through like the air is gummy and instinctively puts His phone and wallet on the marble worktop, as though it's just another evening after work.

There's silence. Eurgh, excruciating.

'You had that briefing,' I eventually say. 'We sat in that garden,' I point to the French windows in case it wasn't clear which garden, 'with a bottle of Oyster Bay and a chicken madras, and you told me you'd all been called into a big room where the producers said the press would follow you everywhere.'

'I know.'

'Also, not sure if you're aware, but literally every single person in the fucking world carries a camera about in their pocket!' My already quite large Bette Davis eyes expand so they cover my whole face. 'And you thought you'd faff about in the *street*!'

A sigh. 'I know.'

'You thought you were special, didn't you?'

It's more a statement than a question, so I shouldn't be surprised when He doesn't answer. There's the distinct air in the space before me here, in our home, of a person getting something over and done with before they move on.

Something feels solid between my thumb and forefinger, and I realise I've been fingering the necklace He'd bought me for my birthday three days ago. A delicate gold chain on which hangs the letter 'R', embossed with tiny leaves and flowers. I'd been wearing it at *Strictly* – meaning for it to symbolise something, I suppose – and for the first time since before the words 'The *Sun* have got pictures of me and the dancer kissing', I feel like a bona fide mug. I clasp my fist around it, rip it off, and walk two paces closer to Him to the stainless-steel bin that has a massive dent in its side. He shrinks back.

I press my boot down on the pedal.

'Oh, don't!' He says.

I lob it in, where it sits on top of the skin of a banana I'd eaten before travelling to *Strictly* earlier that afternoon. What I'd forgotten about the bin is the lid does that slow and gentle close that's frustratingly measured, and it somewhat distils the drama of the moment. It also puffs the smell of bin around.

'Now what?' I ask once it finally wilts shut.

'I'm going to Brighton. I can't stay here.'

'Back to Mum's?' I don't even try to disguise the condescension.

'*Yep*.'

I look at the soft grey veins of the marble worktop and clock His phone. That palm-sized house of secrets, the screen of which is usually shielded from me at all costs. I think about Him on the train to Brighton, that hour-long journey to reassurance. His agent Vinnie calling him, saying how it'll be tomorrow's chip papers or something dated and trite. Him scrolling through and selecting the people most likely to show Him kindness, to rebuild His self-esteem. I think about Him stepping on to the destination platform and into the possibility of how He can turn this around, with all sorts of ideas about next moves and how there's no such thing as bad publicity.

So I pick up that phone, throw it on the ground, smash my Chelsea-boot heel on it so it cracks into shards, and kick it against the back wall.

Only once it's done do I realise I've done it. Destruction on autopilot. There's a pause when we both look at it, and I stand a little taller, the way you do when you didn't know you had it in you. Then He turns to me.

'Was that mine or yours?'

My brow creases into incredulity and I cannot – I *cannot* – believe that I ever let this cretin near me.

'Yours.' I say it with the inflection normally adopted by mean high-school girls saying 'Duh'.

He does the angriest laugh I've ever seen.

He says, '*Very good*', and it sounds like 'Fuck you'.

He says, 'No, really, *well done*', and it sounds like 'I hate you, you bitch'.

And then He walks and picks up His broken phone, takes His anger and His mess and charges with hot purpose right past my rigid body to the front door, which He walks through then slams so hard it swings back open and stays like it.

I wait.

I wait.

I stop waiting for anything. I just stand. I exhale.

I walk over to the bin and look at the necklace.

I rummage in my coat pocket for my phone, and make a call to my best mate. When she answers and I speak, my voice sounds distant, as though it's happening in another room: 'Bell . . . google Him.' I can't seem to hear her reply. I hang up.

I bring up the dancer's message from my birthday, sent after I'd begged her to send Him home to me:

'I'm sorry! I'm on my way home now. I don't want to cause trouble.'

I think of her hugging me after the show ended tonight. Her saying, 'Wasn't He amazing?!' And me saying, 'Thank you so much, you've worked so hard.' The message I send her now reads: 'You don't want to cause trouble.'

I turn off my phone. I walk into the bedroom as though none of my limbs are joined with skin and are instead balanced on top of one another. Winston, our cat, is sitting on the bed with his ears back and with such tension it's as though he's been tax-idermied. I stop at the doorframe and see something out of the corner of my eye. A four-day-old splash of tomato sauce from a lasagne.

Then I fall to the ground.

I don't know how long I lie there before I feel the two big, soft and firm hands of a bearded giant in a flat cap easing me to my feet. Jim walks me to the bathroom and gets me to point at which creams are mine, which he then gathers into a Tesco bag for life. I ask him to hold the pet carrier, while I scrape out Winston, who's dived under the bed, and smoosh him into it. Jim puts me and the cat in a cab outside. The cab drives to a big house in Crouch End where my mate Bell, Jim's Anglo-French wife, sits me on a sofa and puts a box of Malbec in between the three of us. They ask me shocked questions and listen to my shocked answers.

I Stayed

Because that's how his world works

Pleasance Courtyard, Edinburgh, August 2013

I've never been to the Edinburgh festival before. Castles, secret alleys and Gothic spires, every inch of it covered in banners and posters and bunting promoting clowns and comedians and musicals and the Ladyboys of Bangkok. And those are the bits you can actually see through the hordes of people that have travelled from all over the world, many of them unaware that a Scottish summer is basically their winter. For almost twenty-four hours a day you can buy a pint from a hole in the wall and be hustled into turrets, buses and tents, not knowing whether you're going to laugh, cry or see a hole cut out of a bit of black cloth, then a woman's headless body appear with her tits painted like eyes and her stomach painted like a mouth, which happened the first day I got here. It's overwhelming, really, even the rubbish stuff (and there's a lot) is sort of inspiring. Even when, yesterday, I saw someone pull a Quality Street out of their bum and eat it, somehow within it there was hope, positivity, artistry.

But then everywhere is like that for me nowadays.

'He's brilliant, isn't He?' I tell Theo. It's nearly ten on a Friday night; we've just seen His show, and are standing waiting for Him among the crowds in the cobbled courtyard-cum-pop-up-bar.

'Yes, Mariah, once again, your new boyfriend is fabulous,' Theo says.

'You weren't laughing much, though, I noticed.'

'*Well*, gags about straight white men drinking shots with other straight white men isn't really my sauce. I'm quite surprised it's yours, to be honest.'

Theo's performing at the festival this year too. They're currently dressed in drag as Pocahontas, as they're on in a bit, performing their political musical spectacular.

'Did you know Pocahontas was around ten when she met John Smith?' they'd told me.

'Why do you tell me these things about the stories I love?'

'She was also captured, raped and presented by the British as proof that "savage" women could be tamed. Oh, and they changed her name to . . . ? Rebecca.'

Theo's my oldest friend, who I've known since youth theatre in Norfolk. For anybody that has never done youth theatre, it's a bohemia where all of the not-popular but not-shy virgins from your school met once a week to dress up and belt their inferiority complexes away.

It was only last year that Theo came out as a non-binary person. Theo responds to the pronoun they/them, which I try so, so hard to remember but don't always. They work as a professional drag queen, have a jawline that you could cut your finger on, a 'Tilda Swinton' style bleached quiff made even blonder by the brownness of their skin, and a bible of sex stories ranging from outrageous to hilarious to possibly illegal. But the reason I love them is because they are less 'Thank you for having me', more 'You're welcome that I'm here'.

'Did you know He was going to do that stuff about you?' Theo asks.

'No!' I squeal. 'How cool is that?!'

'And you're OK with it?'

'Why wouldn't I be? I love being shown off. Don't you dare tell me you wouldn't. And He's right, I can't ever pick a Netflix show, and I *am* oppressively cheerful – even you say that to me!'

'Hmmm.'

'To be honest, after Max, it feels lush to be noticed. Rather than wasting my energy competing with a sodding Xbox.'

And before Theo can say anything else, there He is, my star, in His black overcoat, looking famous.

'HIIII!' I throw my arms around Him. I wonder if anyone else in the courtyard was at the gig, and are joining the dots. That I'm the one up there onstage with Him, in His jokes because I'm in His life.

'You all right?' He drops His bag to the floor and kisses me. 'You look nice.'

'You were *incredible*!' My arms are still round His neck.

'Ah, yeah. OK.' He purses his lips together and nods to the ground.

'What?'

'Nothing, Bun.' We call each other Bun now, short for Bunny. 'Just. Crowd were shit.'

'Wingapo, I'm Theo,' says Pocahontas.

'Hey, ah, I wish you'd both been here last night.' His eyes are dull with resignation. 'Better crowd.'

'No!' I say. 'No, they were lapping it up around us!'

'They were,' Theo agrees, and I choose to ignore the way their tone is saying, *And I've no idea why.*

'I'm gonna get a drink, you want one?' He asks us flatly. I've never seen Him like this, no jokes, brightness turned all the way down. My brain feels weary with all the trying I'm doing; this is hardly what I was expecting. Here are the two fizziest people in my life and everything about it feels bland.

Worse is that from the look on Theo's face, I can tell they feel the same. They clear their throat. 'I'm gonna go actually, dears. I'm on in a bit. Nice to meet you,' says Theo.

'You too,' He says.

'You're very lucky,' Theo indicates me, and I roll my eyes.

'I know,' He says.

'She's one fierce queen,' says Theo.

'Well, I'm the bohemian bad boy of comedy!' He says. 'Ask the *Guardian*.' And I laugh.

'My point is, don't you be messing with her now.'

'I'll walk you out,' I say to Theo.

Other male comedians join us in the courtyard as the night wears on. Lumbering through the rabble in their hoodies and waterproofs to where we sit under the big yellow Bulmers umbrella, thirsty for a frosty pint and some good-natured one-upmanship. Some of them seemingly having followed the scent of a bad gig.

'Heard you ab-so-lute-ly bombed!' one of the lads says to Him, loud enough for the group to hear, and the laughter fills all four corners of the courtyard and flies up into the rainclouds.

He deftly throws the insult across the circle, where that person pings it to the person beside them. It's dizzying to keep up with, this human game of pinball, but where the ball is more like a smack round the face. It's breathless, and heady, and brutal, and it's hard to tell whether you're laughing from delight or shock or nervousness but still, you *are* laughing. These courtyard jesters, they rinse one another for their gigs, their reviews, their shirts, their looks, who they went home with last night, and their inability to think of a response quick enough. Beads of sweat drip down the sides of foreheads, and spread under armpits. Whoever gets the biggest laugh is King, and it makes sense, because in this world, loud laughter literally translates into riches.

'How did you meet?' someone eventually asks me.

'On a sitcom.'

'Whose part was biggest?'

'Mine,' I answer truthfully, and He's launched into again.

'Jesus,' I say. 'You lot are fucking horrible!'

My insult prompts howls of delight. Mission accomplished, I'm initiated. I understand what it takes now, and can exhale. When He's still being quiet getting a round in at the bar, I ask if He's OK. He tells me that yeah, they're only joking, it's fine, He can take a joke.

Later at the taxi rank, His agent Vinnie tells me that I'm a good influence on Him, seriously.

'Am I?' I smile proudly and ask Him. He doesn't notice, just looks at His phone despondently.

'No seriously,' says Vinnie. 'He's really mellowed out.'

'Bloody hell, what was He like before?!'

'Oh my God,' He interrupts us. 'OHMYGOD!!!!'

He's had a five-star review. A reviewer who was in earlier tonight just tweeted it. I tell Him, *See!* I bloody told Him He was brilliant! And there He is again, the man I wanted Theo to meet, in full technicolour. Even better, because now He's the bohemian bad boy King of Edinburgh! He tells me and Vinnie there's no way we're going home yet, it's His round. Off we march back to the courtyard, the King and His Queen, to show those clowns who's boss.

I Left

Because it wasn't love

Crouch End, 7 October 2018

I lie on a Scandi-style navy sofa, staring into the dark oblong underneath the armchair opposite where two white circles are staring back.

'Winston,' I rasp, holding out an upturned hand.

The circles blink but don't move, and I wonder whether he'll ever come out and whether I'm a terrible mother on top of everything else.

I sludge myself upright, silently questioning where this wispy duvet came from and why I'm still in this minuscule dress. Over the arm of the sofa are a pair of folded floral pyjamas, and I look at them thinking that Bell is a good person, and that yes that's right, I can't live in my home any more. On the kidney-shaped coffee table is a faded yellow Lucky Strike ashtray nicked from some pub of the past, currently a snake pit of fag ends. A box of Malbec lies empty on its side but my red-lipstick-rimmed glass remains upright, proffering a delicious dreg. Might as well. I tip it upside down over my mouth until every last drop is gone and my neck aches from the strain. It tastes like a 2p from a nightclub floor.

I hobble over to the sliding back doors, which I put my full body behind to open, and step out on to the damp paving slabs of the back garden. The cold travels from my bare feet up my legs as I picture what's going on across the country as the world begins again today. I suppose I will have been dragged into the papers by association. Everyone I know will find out about Him and the dancer, from the news or from social media or from each other. They may be finding out right now, still in bed checking Twitter, or scanning the BBC homepage with mouthfuls of crumpet. As I stand there in my cobweb dress with my arms around myself, I think about those charity adverts with earnest voiceovers. 'Every three seconds, someone in the UK will discover that Rebecca Humphries' boyfriend is actually a dog.'

My family. The friends I haven't spoken to in months. People I don't even know will know. People I respect will pity me.

They will all know about the kiss, and none of what's behind it. Not what it's meant, or done, no nuance, no humanity. Those gaps are there for the filling. Across the country, they will be eating their Weetabix or out for a Sunday-morning run, analysing and shrugging and discussing what they'd have done differently. How do I know this? Because I've done it myself, many times. Ugh, I have positively *revelled* in sweet, sweet judgement: that safe space where we can all be armchair experts in other people's tragedy.

I inhale the chill into my lungs. And it's all because of Strictly Come Dancing. *Strictly Come Dancing.*

I wonder if reporters already know where I am?

I wonder if anyone even cares?

'Good morning.'

'ARGH!'

I jump out next to my own body, then step back in again as I see Bell standing earnestly by the French windows. My brain stops speculating, the slabs are back beneath my feet.

'You look nice!' she says. I catch my reflection in the glass panes right next to her. Huge sad eyes, lank hair.

'I look like the girl from *The Ring*.'

'You're wrong; it's heroin-chic, very 90s Winona Ryder.'

It's hard to know whether Bell has always been the type to do and say the right thing in any given circumstance because I haven't known her that long. Three years or so, and only truly properly over the last one. Owing to a lifelong obsession with the 'coming of age' genre, I've always associated having a best friend with pre-teenage girls eating sundaes in American diners and making bff promises at sleepovers, then many years later when one of them has experienced some kind of hardship (or perhaps has died?) the other will find an old friendship bracelet in a box in the attic and have misty-eyed flashbacks to a simpler time. You don't hear so many stories of acquiring a best mate as an adult, and certainly not as the new wife of one of your pre-existing friends. But in the pub on her wedding day I'd mentioned to Bell that I loved all the flowers, and she'd replied that she and her mum Yvette had cleaned out the twenty-four-hour Tesco near Brent Cross two nights before and stuck them all in the bath like Nigella's Christmas turkey, and that was that. I was in love.

Bell is mysterious, with green eyes, brown bobbed hair, cheekbones and a Renaissance-painting figure – a sophisticated reference I can only make because of her. She's a talented artist, but has a proper job like a sensible person instead of fannying about pretending, which let's face it is what me, Jim and Him all do for a career. She has 'Big Nigella Energy', and will often be found marinating for twenty-four hours, gathering all thirty-seven ingredients for an Ottolenghi salad, and going to Japanese supermarkets to find proper tamari that costs half of what you pay in Sainsbury's.

She is the droll, straight-shooting Louise to my bubble-headed Thelma, and right now she's holding a coffee out for me in a silver enamel mug that I recognise, and that I know on the other side says 'I escaped from Alcatraz'. I don't know what to say, except:

'I drank all your wine.'

'Hardly, we have to practically store it in the toilet cistern we plough through so much of it. Want any?'

'Not yet, thank you, but soon. I'll have this, though,' I say, taking the coffee from her and wrapping both sets of fingers around the warmth. 'I feel very, I dunno. Very silly. I knew, didn't I? When I called you on my birthday I knew.'

'I dunno, Becks. How could you have known, for sure?'

'Well, I *should* have known then, which is why I feel silly.' I take a sip of lovely hot brown water. 'Y'know. If it looks like a duck, swims like a duck and quacks like a duck then it probably is a duck.'

She nods. 'Or a cunt.' I choke with laughter, allowing myself to believe for one glorious second that everything is as simple as that.

'Morning, mate.' Jim appears behind Bell, rubbing vigorously at his eyes. I'm still coughing, so I wave.

'I thought I'd make a deliberately posh breakfast,' Bell announces. 'Eggs Benedict? I can do hollandaise.'

'Please may I have fags instead?' I ask in a small voice.

Jim holds up a finger for me to wait, reaches into his pocket and pulls out a fresh cig box. 'Supplies Deliveroo-d last night.' He pulls the plastic off in one spiral.

'Could you bring my phone?' I ask him. 'I think I can look at it if I'm with you.'

'Yes, for I am a man, and will protect you.' Jim puffs out his chest and speaks in an even deeper voice. 'Now, woman, make me breakfas—' He stops when he sees Bell's face, and is probably right to.

Two minutes later Jim and I are sat on the spindly wrought-iron garden furniture, which is so cold in my little dress the back of my bare thighs will likely be branded by the curly leaf design once I peel them off. My brain is too full of things to register it. My phone lies face down on the table, and the only sounds are the faraway clangs of Bell in the kitchen.

'What's the damage?' Jim asks.

I flip the phone over. 'Two hundredish WhatsApp messages, a hundred iMessages and fifty-eight phone ca— Ooh!' A withheld number is calling me. I decline. 'Fifty-*nine* phone calls. Twenty or so emails that all seem to be from papers. How do they even have my email address?' I shudder. 'Creepy creeps!'

'Anything from . . . ?' He trails off.

I shake my head. 'I did royally wreck his phone, though. And shops don't open till midday on Sunday, do they, so.'

Jim makes a face like 'fair enough', and because I don't know where to start with any of it, we just sit there in the garden, taking deep drags and ignoring the phone between us silently lighting up at regular intervals. Jim has that enviable quality of appearing contented in silences, the ones I have to charge into the vacuum of in order to make them stop. He's a (craft) beer-swilling, broad-chested Grimsby powerhouse that I've known since drama school, rivalled only in comic prowess by his wife. And God, what an actor, a wonderful, sensitive actor, but one whose size and accent means the industry limits him to roles as security guards, 'bread & dripping down the mine' sorts and sinister heavies (incidentally my casting tends to be sex workers, secretaries and – incredibly – betrayed women). In actual fact, though, Jim belongs to my favourite genre of human, which is 'miser with a soft centre'. He looks as though he's been cracked open at the moment, and it occurs to me that he's also starting some kind of grieving process.

'You all right, mate?' I ask.

'It's, uh.' Jim looks like he's been put on pause, staring wide-eyed ahead, fag in mid-air. 'It's mad this, isn't it?'

Jim loved Him too, and He Jim. Their relationship was newer, purer. Jim was mates with the part of Him I had partied with in Brighton in 2013.

My phone lights up on the iron garden table. Three little letters appear at the top, spelling out a name that I never see calling me, ever.

'Right.' I instinctively stub out the cigarette and waft the air around me so it won't smell down the phone.

Jim does a thumbs-up as I slide my finger across the screen.

'Hi, Mum.'

'Helloareyouallright?' It's the same greeting I always get: bright, instinctive.

'Yeahareyou?' It's the same response I always give, cheery, shallow.

'Yesthankyou.'

There's a second when we both recognise we've begun like it's any other Sunday.

'They had the papers out in the hotel at breakfast, so I took them all and chucked them in the bin.'

'That's nice of you.' I choose not to remind her about the internet.

'I just, I cannot believe the dancer hugged us,' she says down the phone in astonishment. 'I thought it then, I said to myself: *What's her game?*'

Mum was at *Strictly* last night as my guest. She was on telly standing next to me as I clapped and cried. She's staying in a hotel around the corner from Samstat Road, we were meant to have breakfast together this morning.

Mum loves *Strictly*. She told all of her colleagues at the Norwich benefits agency who were so excited they made a bingo card to tick off the celebrities she saw up close. She had come in her special sparkly jumper, and told me that as she went to get the bus to the train station her neighbour Viv had been 'da da da'-ing the *Strictly* theme tune and number twelve opposite's Dobermann had gone berserk.

Last night I had suggested that she get a taxi back to the hotel straight after we had left the studio, just as the gazebo lit up for the after party. For the last four weeks I'd felt unwelcome, uncool, and like a nobody. I could handle that, but the idea that my mum could be made to feel the same made my ribcage feel like it was made of chalk that could be crushed if I was bumped into. It prompted me to get that Addison Lee number up faster than you can say, well, 'The *Sun* have got pictures of me and the dancer kissing.' Which is what He'd told me less than five minutes after she'd gone.

'I'm really, really sorry this is your *Strictly* experience, Mum. It's your favourite and now it's going to be all about this.'

'*Nooo*, don't worry about that. When I tell people I'll focus on meeting Darcey Bussell.'

My mum. Never spotted in the wild without a full face on, a different shade of honey blonde every few weeks. I see full well her many attributes. See her land girl, 'Can Do' attitude meshed with her creativity; some of my earliest memories involve her putting up shelves with electric drills and making clear paste out of powder to hang baroque-esque wallpaper on her own. I see her willingness to sacrifice her time and energy and a few quid to take someone that's feeling low to the garden centre for a frothy coffee and a new seedling for the patio.

But despite all of that, our relationship is complex – and when I say complex I mean 'baffling'. I know she's a good person, and that I may also be one, but somehow our two spirits make a funny-tasting cocktail. For example, I mentioned earlier she never calls me, and it's something I will never address with her. As far as we are concerned, the other is always 'fine', because we always say as much. Selfless attempts at not wanting to burden the other with our problems have created distance and, for me at

43

least (because I'll never know about her), an incremental sadness and occasional mild resentment.

We're not big on 'I love you' either.

'Your dad's been on the phone—'

'Please don't tell me about Dad.' My voice cracks with emotion and Jim looks up. 'Please tell him not to ring me. I'll ring him when I'm ready.'

'Fine, that's fine,' Mum says. Phew.

My dad is like a sitcom character from the 70s, one of the ones the studio audience applauds when they walk through the door. Permanently jaunty, often found humming Abba songs to himself as he jog-walks through his sleepy village of Rackheath, preparing for The Great North Run where every year he is outstripped by whoever he's convinced to do it with him. He never minds.

Mum and Dad divorced when I was fifteen. The older I get the more I realise how diametrically opposed they are at their core.

I can't hear about Dad today. Dad is so proud of me, and of Him, that he has told every single customer at that newsagent, every person at the bus stop, the cashiers in the bank, and all his beloved Facebook friends, that his daughter's boyfriend was going to be on *Strictly Come Dancing*. I wonder if he waved and said hello to any of those same people on the way to work today, and whether they knew before he did. I wonder if he opened the shutters and made himself a sugary tea before he saw my boyfriend embracing another woman on the front page of the *Sun on Sunday*. Dad hadn't known Him that well. In fact, in five years Mum and Dad must have seen Him no more than twice a year, much less than I saw His family. Which in fairness wasn't that often either. He didn't much care for family stuff, so I stopped caring too much for it too and I know it hurt mine. I try not to imagine how it must have felt for Dad putting each copy on the shelf, and in their special display case outside by the buckets of £1.99 flowers as villagers walked past. I try not to think about the stack of papers that sit on the counter for people to pick up when they pay, that will be right in front of him all day long as he sits in his swively chair, or about how sentimental and trusting he is, how he would answer the question 'How are you?' honestly, even if it came from complete strangers.

Complete strangers like journalists.

'Mum,' I sit up, and across from me Jim's back straightens instinctively. 'I don't want to blow anything out of proportion here but there is a strong chance that when you get back to Norwich there will be journalists waiting to speak to you.'

'Noooo!' She's trying to give off outrage but I can practically hear her smoothing her hair down the phone. I try to fight the image of some scruffy oik with a notepad sitting at the breakfast bar while Mum fiddles with the Dolce Gusto asking if they'd 'like an expresso?'

'Seriously, Mum, it won't be glam and it may not even be nice, not nice at all.'

'Jake did say there's a flash car parked near the drive.' Jake's my brother.

'I'm sorry if this is patronising, Mum, but this is serious. These people, they are thirsty for anything, and the teeniest tiniest "Please leave us alone at this difficult time" could become a story about how difficult we're finding everything. They could find out where Dad's shop is, you know how he is on Facebook, checking in every time he goes to the fucking carwash.' I wince slightly at saying 'fucking' to my mother, at age thirty-two. But I know I'm right about this. When my friend Stella started a career in journalism she interned for very little money at a very prestigious broadsheet, and was given a choice by her editor: get a comment from the mother of a young man who had recently been stabbed to death or get fired. Stella was so horrified on

45

her way to the woman's door she had to pull her car over on the motorway to be sick, and was kicked in the stomach by a relative once she got there. But she got a quote and later became a war correspondent.

'Just, if they crop up, say "no comment",' I conclude.

'Lovely,' she says, adding, 'I'll tell Jake not to answer the door in his painting overalls.'

'And, Mum?' Even saying 'Mum' in that tone, like I'm bracing her for something, makes me feel like a failure. 'There's something else I have to tell you as well.'

I hesitate. We don't speak about personal things in our family, tending to stick to observations and relaying memories rather than offering opinions or, worse, feelings.

'Our relationship wasn't very good. Mine and His.' I say it like I'm the speaking clock; all fact, no feeling. 'Wasn't nice. For a long time. I didn't tell anybody, it's not just you.'

'Oh.' There's a pause. 'You were crying when He did well at *Strictly* last night, was it because of that, then?'

'No, actually.' Christ, this is excruciating. 'It was happy crying. I was happy because I had thought they were having an affair, they were spending so much extra-curricular time together. And when He did really well and improved loads, it made me think He had been telling the truth, that they had just been practising, just been dancing. I was crying because I was so relieved that I was a psycho, like He said I was.'

'Oh,' says Mum again. 'Oh, right.'

'I wanted to tell you because it means I'm not as sad as you might think about all of this. Actually,' I feel the truth softening me at the corners, 'I'm glad it's over.'

'Well.' I can hear her thinking of what to say. 'That's good then, isn't it?'

'Yeah. Yeah, it is good.'

'Well, there we are,' she says. Then, 'All right, I'll let you go!'

'OK. Speak soon.'

I hang up, and put my phone down.

'Well done, mate,' says Jim.

The phone lights up straight away with a name I've avoided for months now. But I can't wait to answer it. Even the fact they're calling feels like I'm being showered in champagne, like I've won the Grand Prix.

'Oh, it's you,' I say in Joan Collins' *Dynasty* voice.

'I can't believe – I can't BELIEVE – you beat me to a sex scandal.' Theo's voice rings theatrically down the line, car horns arguing in the background. 'I'm in Dalston – got completely obliterated last night, was podium-ing in Adonis till five then kept on it at this after party, what a sad little life, Jane. Anyhoo, I just nipped in an offy for a Lucozade on the way home, and guess whose rotten cheating face I saw, slobbering away on the front pages?'

Theo asks me how I am, then as expected starts on how much they hate Him.

'I know you do,' I say.

'I know you know I do, dear, and I also know that's why you stopped speaking to me.'

'I just thought you knew too much. I was embarrassed. I *am* embarrassed, to be honest.'

'I've been so *angry*.' And they sound it still. 'Before that fucking mangy scarecrow, I could say to you "you're fabulous" and it would have the power to make you go out and conquer the fucking world. And after Him whenever I said "you're fabulous" it was only ever as consolation because your default setting was feeling shit about yourself.'

'Gosh, I *am* sorry you've had such a hard time.' I smile.

'Don't be arch. I'm hanging out of my arse, let me have this.'

I smile harder. 'Carry on.'

'Do you know how long I've felt guilty as hell, thinking

about how I encouraged this relationship at the beginning? I kept thinking my voice must be one of the voices in your head at night saying "he's perfect" or "I'm so happy for you".'

'It wasn't.' I laugh. 'I never remember your voice being nice.'

'Well, praise be. And another thing—'

'Can I just say, I'm living for how much this is now about you.'

'Just one,' and Theo's voice quietens. 'It was so *insidious*, the whole thing. I could see you being chipped away at, stopping wearing sequins, stopping singing at karaoke. And whenever I pointed out little things I could feel them being dismissed as me over-analysing or trying to find fault. Or being a drama queen at Nish's wedding, remember that?'

'Did I say that to you?' My body turns to stone from the toes upwards.

'Doesn't matter.'

'No, it does, Theo. I know exactly how it feels to be called that. I'm so sorry.'

'Don't be sorry, be fierce. Besides, what has *The Sound of Music* always taught us?'

'That you can change horrible men?'

'No,' says Theo. 'The Reverend Mother always says when the Lord closes a door, somewhere he opens a window. So this is me climbing back in, bitch.'

I have kept my friends and family at arm's length for so long. Letting them back in feels like flying. I speak to Oonagh, to Poppy, to my agent Sam, to Jake, to my Auntie Nett ('I never liked Him, Minx,' she lies, which makes my stomach glow), to Paul, to plenty of others. None of them quite know what to say after the initial hello. They're all tone clones; bewildered, commiserative. And the more I'm presented with how sad I should be, the more obvious it is to me that I am not. At all. It's a relief to tell them all how the relationship really was. To

48

see for myself, each time, how the world doesn't end when I speak the truth.

At one point Bell comes out to the garden, to put a blanket over my shoulders and another on my knees, and to squeeze Jim's shoulder.

In the meantime, I've had around thirty emails from different tabloid publications. All the journalists are women, all of them can't begin to understand how I must be feeling at the moment, all of them are there if I ever need somebody to talk to, all of them would be prepared to discuss a fee should that be something I'd be interested in but most importantly, though, all of them send their very best wishes at this difficult time.

By the afternoon, Jim and I have made it back to the living room. I'm back on the sofa I slept on, a glass of maroon liquid in my hand. On the telly the crowning glory of Channel 5's scheduling, *Bargain Loving Brits in the Sun*, plays.

Bell walks in, 'God, I love this programme.'

'Where've you been all day, excuse me?' I prod her.

'Haven't you got better things to think about?' she responds.

'It's happened before, hasn't it, all this *Strictly* affair bollocks?' Jim pipes up, like it's been going round his head all day. He's sitting on the armchair opposite, which now has a tail and bit of fluffy cat bum protruding from underneath. 'I mean, I don't watch it, it being dross and all, but I thought it was a thing that happens a lot?'

'Not while they're still on the show,' says Bell. 'Affairs always happen—'

'All the time,' I agree.

'Yeah, but normally they get kicked off first, *then* leave their wives or husbands or partners or whatever,' Bell tells Jim. 'For a better chance at privacy, I s'pose?'

I lean back into the sofa, acquiring about four chins in the process, and stare for a moment at the screen, where a very tanned elderly woman is getting a Mr Whippy. The cogs in my brain start turning involuntarily. 'OK, so it's the afternoon. I think we can assume the morning pearl-clutching will be done. The story's had time to percolate a bit. This is when people start digging a little deeper, considering *why* it happened. She's a fit, famous dancer for a start; who wouldn't run off with that given half the chance? Good luck to him! Lads around the country are probably labelling him a legend as we speak.

'And I know my character in it, too. I'm the wholesome home bird whose poor testosterone-soaked bloke was unable to resist a siren. I'm the sexless party at the sex party. People will ask, "What's His girlfriend's name again?" They'll speculate – rightly – that our relationship can't have been strong enough. That maybe He wasn't getting any at home. They'd be right about that too, but it wasn't for want of trying. I gave Him a frickin' *massage* when He said His back hurt from practising that bloody waltz posture, I bought *oils*. I lit so many candles the bedroom looked like a Bonnie Tyler music video.' Jim chuckles supportively in the tone of that one kindly audience member watching the new act at a comedy club dying on their arse.

'You're either the Madonna or the Whore in these things. The man is just the man.' I touch my forehead. 'Oh my God. Am I . . . the Princess Diana in this?'

'Yes, definitely,' says Bell.

I tilt my chin down to the left and say huskily, 'Well, the thing is, there were three people in this marriage.'

'Exactly, it suits you.'

'She was a Cancer, though.'

'Yes, well done, you've identified the only difference.'

I sigh. 'Everyone'll call this a curse, you know. As though it was something out of his control, divine intervention. It isn't. "Curse" puts the onus on an abstract concept when it isn't abstract at all. The onus is on them. Their choice. They should call it that: the Strictly Choice,' and I think I might be a genius.

There's a silence. We're all completely spent. Winston's tail flicks around from under the chair.

'The only thing I'm scared of . . . ' I don't even want to say it. 'Is if it *is* divine intervention. What if they're in love, guys? I can deal with an affair. But what if they're in love?'

'So what if they are?' says Jim. 'Fuck 'em, they deserve each other.'

'No. Because it would mean I've . . . that I'm the one who's got love all wrong. So wrong that I'm the one who's wound up on their own. After trying so hard. Everyone always said love takes work . . . ' I pause, and breathe the tears down from my eyes. 'I've worked so hard I've exhausted myself and now I have nothing to show for it.'

'Love can be hard,' says Bell. 'But love shouldn't hurt you, mate.' We all look at the TV, where a man in a bow tie is singing 'Sweet Caroline' at what appears to be a breakfast buffet.

Then Bell says, 'Come on, we want to show you something.'

She takes me through to the stairs in the hallway. I follow her up to the landing, turn left and then up the next staircase to the attic. I've stayed in this attic a couple of times before, in a hastily made-up bed surrounded by cardboard boxes of attic stuff. Stayed in it recently. I hadn't wanted to be a distraction one Friday when He had seemed particularly stressed out about the show the next day, so I'd called Bell and asked if I could stay over. It had become a weekly superstition, that my staying away from home on a Friday was actually good luck. Plus I was afraid that if it had gone badly on live television, on the *biggest show on television*, I would have been blamed for Him having had a bad night's sleep.

Bell holds out the door for me. I walk past her and gasp.

Gone are the boxes, the dust, the faded and generic duvet

cover, the feeling of being crammed into someone's attic. Instead there's a romantic, sloped-ceilinged hideaway. The bed is freshly made with crisp, white sheets, and Winston races past my legs to jump on it and curl into a croissant. A little mahogany bedside table holds a table lamp with a white lampshade and pully chain, and a brown glass apothecary bottle holds gypsophila. There's a bookcase ready for whatever I'd like to fill it with, and a framed picture of Mary Seacole, Bell's favourite from the National Portrait Gallery, to watch me when I do. At the foot of the bed, a chest of drawers with a small flat-screen TV. On the ceiling, a skylight I've never noticed before is creating a tunnel of pale honey-coloured light that shoots across the space, in which tiny flecks of white dust are suspended like the bubbles inside amber. I feel like a reverse Cinderella, one that's gone from riches to rags and somehow wound up richer. Like in *A Little Princess*. A grown-up Sara Crewe!

'This is what you've been doing all day?' I ask Bell, who shoots me a look that says, *Perhaps*.

There's thoughtfulness in absolutely everything. It's in the water for the flowers, in the placement of the remote: perpendicular to the chest of drawers' edge. It's in the way the navy wool blanket is folded over the end of the bed to make it look cosier, and in the freshly washed floorboards beneath my dirty feet. So much thoughtfulness that it seems to seep in through the pores of my skin and not just fill up an empty well, but make it flow over with liquid gold. I'm so grateful but grateful feels too overused to mean what I want it to.

'You can stay here as long as you need,' says Bell. 'You're safe here.'

I turn to her and Jim in the doorway. The thought of living in a home with people that behave as though they enjoy my company is genuinely unfathomable.

'I don't know what to say to you both.'

I think about my mum chucking those papers in the bin, my dad not calling all day long even though I know he's probably desperate to, because I'd asked him not to. All those texts and calls from people I hadn't seen in weeks, months, letting me know that if I need anything – to talk, to cry, to get me some of the nice bread I like – they are there. From people I don't know, tagging me on Twitter, hoping that I'm all right.

What if I *have* gotten love all wrong? What if I've been slaving away, reaching my arm in to prise words and feeling out of the mouth of someone who didn't have it in them, not for me? I've been treating love like a noun, like a trophy I won ages ago and have left to gather dust in a cabinet. But in every single one of those instances today love has been a verb, an action.

And not an action that requires Herculean effort, either. Take up here, now. Love is floating around serenely, like feathers, in this quiet space. The space two floors above the room where last night Jim got up from the sofa and took a taxi to Shepherd's Bush to pick me up from the floor. Love is all around me.

God I wish that wasn't a Wet Wet Wet song; it drains it of all profundity.

I Stayed

Because crazy runs in the family

Our flat, Shepherd's Bush, September 2013

Ever seen a person with Alzheimer's? It can be pretty harrowing. Old-school asylum-level cray, like in horror films with people jabbering to themselves, cowering in corners away from nothing at all, staring into space then flailing with fury. I'd never seen anything like it until Nanny got transferred to a specialist home last week. And when I found out that every woman on my mother's side of the family has died from it, so began my week-long morbid fascination with female hysteria. A hundred and fifty years ago women were sent to live and die in asylums for pretty much anything, meaning that in all likelihood there were ancestors of mine who got committed. For dementia, but also for postnatal depression. Discussing politics. Reading novels, having a wank. Suppressing having a wank, as well. Demanding their rights. It's a wonder women did anything at all. Which, let's face it, was pretty much the point.

I dread to think how early I'd have been admitted to a nuthouse, if I weren't living in the here and now. Madness is running through my veins, and it explains a lot. Like why, at midnight tonight, in my darkened room, I can see the blinds at the window slowly rising all on their own.

Up up up.

I watch them from where I'm lying in bed. Unable to move. As though my organs are made of lead. As though the skin on the back of my body has been sewn into the mattress.

Up up up they silently glide, revealing the black sheen of the window behind them.

I can hear Him through the wall, chatting animatedly on the phone in the living room. He's just back from a gig. His voice was what woke me up, thirty seconds ago. Before the blinds started moving.

They stop by the small window at the top, the one I opened a tiny bit, to get some air in. And then, the fingers slide underneath it. A whole hand, pulling the window outwards, as I lie here in the dark room.

My own hand flies to my phone on the beside table, and I click on His name.

He answers with, 'Sorry, sorry, I'll be quieter.'

'Something is happening,' I whisper. 'Please, you need to get in here, quickly.' I look over to the window. The hand is gone.

His footsteps approach urgently. He opens the door and turns on the light. It sears my eyes.

'What is it?' He asks.

'There's someone outside,' I whisper.

He looks to the window, then back at me. 'No there isn't.'

'There is. They just pulled up the blinds.' There is no air in my lungs. 'I saw it.'

'The blinds were open when I got in ten minutes ago.'

'I don't think . . . ' I hesitate. He seems pretty certain. 'There *is* somebody there, anyway. I saw their hand.'

He looks at the window again. He squints. Then looks at me concernedly, and says with absolute assurance:

'Nobody's there, Bunny. You imagined it.'

'I . . . Oh.' And I think that it makes sense. You know, my mind being sneaky, working against me. Coming to get me.

'OK, well, sorry about that. Carry on your phone call, I'll try and go back to sleep.'

He doesn't say anything, just stands there, staring at the window. Time passes. Then He turns to me.

'OK,' He says. 'You should get up and go in the other room.'

Half an hour later, while the police dust the window frame for fingerprints, He tells one of the officers that He saw the guy's eyes outside the second He turned on the light. The two of them had stared at one another, but He couldn't be sure the guy knew He could see him. So He'd had the idea to tell me He couldn't see anyone, that I was making it up, to give the guy a chance to walk away. Which the guy did.

Amazing.

'You came up with that in an instant, that plan?' We're entwined on the couch, because the bedroom freaks me out tonight. 'So smart. I'd never have thought of doing that, that's not how my mind works.'

He says, 'I can't believe you thought you'd imagined those blinds moving on their own.'

'It must just be on the brain, y'know? Nanny and everything.' I try to breathe in but I choke on nothing instead, and shivers ripple through my body. He hugs me tightly until it stops. Thank God He was there. My hero.

Because everybody makes mistakes

Canary Wharf, early March 2014

The stalk of mint withers in its brown watery grave. Slumped against the side of the glass like it's been scalded to death, which it has. It's what you get, I guess, for ordering a fresh mint tea in a Canary Wharf pub on a weekday afternoon.

I would never have ordered this ordinarily. I actually don't like fresh mint tea, or any kind of tea that my nan would be confused by. But I'd wanted to order something unexpected. I'd wanted Him to hear me speak to a waiter, then snap to attention at the sound of something He'd never heard me say. Something that also silently said, *You don't know all of who I am, either.*' I'm wearing a new pale yellow skirt, vintage, embroidered with daisies. It's too cold for it today. The skin on my face is taut and shiny from the facial I booked in for this morning. Fresh yellow, fresh mint, fresh complexion. I want to look like a fresh start.

This is the first time I've seen Him in almost a week. Last Saturday night He was out with a mate, as He has often been on a Saturday night, which was fine. More than fine, good! I love that He loves His mates. I was at home on the laptop, also fine. Too tired to actually go to bed. I idly typed in 'Fa' to the search bar, and clicked when 'Facebook' came up instantly.

My password was automatically saved, so the laptop took me straight to the main feed. There was an alert that I had received a private message in my inbox from someone called Mia. *Who do I know called Mia?* I clicked on it.

'Sorry I didn't pick up, was at work. Midnight caller' wink face.

I didn't know any Mia, except clearly I must have done, so I scrolled back over the conversation. It was in doing so that something crept over me, as though the underside of my flesh was becoming frostbitten, a sensation I had never before experienced and that began at my heart centre. It was the understanding that:

1. He must have been the last person to log in to Facebook on the laptop (rare, He hardly ever goes on Facebook), and not logged out.

and

2. He has been sending explicit messages to a woman called Mia, for a long time. Mostly Saturday nights, by the looks of it.

They had arranged for her to go to a comedy club in Crouch End after one of His gigs. He had given her the date. I checked the calendar hanging next to the cereal cupboard. It was there, in my handwriting, like the rest of His diary was. 'Gig Crouch End, 7:30.'

At one point she had said to Him, 'But what about your wife?' And He had said: 'Who?'

We had been together for ten months, had bought the flat together and moved in sixish months ago. Our lives had slotted in, we'd started walking side by side and neither of us had needed to slow down to let the other one catch up. The relationship wasn't so different to how it was at first, apart from we now spoke about things like maybe needing a new frying pan because the Teflon's come off that one. He hadn't been acting distant, the texts hadn't slowed, the sex hadn't stopped. We'd done it in the kitchen the week before. I had sat on the counter. I had held on to the handle of the cupboard.

It had been working. All of it had been working.

I called Him. He didn't pick up so I looked her up on Instagram. I found an attractive, slim but curvaceous woman with Elizabeth Taylor eyebrows on a tropical beach wearing a halter-neck bikini. I saw that her best friend is the wife of one of His closest friends, a woman who had asked me last week who my hair colourist was. It was no longer just hurtful. Now it was humiliating.

I called His friend's number, who answered and handed it to Him. I forced my emotion down my throat and asked, 'Who's Mia?'

And He said: 'Who?'

I told Him I'd seen the messages, and that jogged His memory. I told Him I was leaving, that it was over, and hung up the phone. I kicked the side of the stainless-steel bin from John Lewis, leaving a huge dent and my foot throbbing. I packed my pink hand-luggage suitcase, and pulled it in the dark to the soulless hotel just off Shepherd's Bush Green, where the man behind the desk gave me a room key for a room where another man in his underwear jumped up out of bed and screamed at the intruder (me) in panic. The man at the desk then gave me an unoccupied room, which perhaps I should have specified the first time. The next day I went and stayed with Theo.

Now it's six days later. He and I are sitting at an outdoor table for four people on a raised balcony over the Thames. A small silver pot full of sachets sits in the middle. Underneath the table, I am ripping up an empty sachet into tiny segments for something to do with my hands.

Canary Wharf looks like someone has paid billions of pounds to take a perfectly nice riverside village and pour hot liquid aluminium over it. I have no feelings towards this place either way. Nor does He, that's the point. There *is* no feeling in Canary Wharf. It's a plain, grey, blank place of block shapes, devoid of the flow and undulation of things like feelings and art and love. It's made of glass and metal, where big business and hard facts ricochet around. Facts like 'you have ruined something good'. 'It is all your fault'.

Business has been the order of the week. There's a lot of admin when you break up with someone. I am prepared to do all of it. Since last Saturday I have been looking into getting my name taken off the bills, my address off the residents' email thread for the flat. Nobody cheats on me.

Over the last week I have also received countless phone calls and texts begging me to go back. Emails – long emails with so much heart the words press against the screen, emails containing attachments of pictures of things in the house, small inexpensive things he had chosen for me in moments of tenderness. I had managed to look at them blankly in the make-up chair of my new TV job, tell the make-up artist 'Oh, just a stuffed rabbit' when she had asked what I was looking at. Stayed resolute. I am twenty-seven years old. I am talented. I have opportunity, I have time, and I have choices.

But then, you see, His friend called me. I walked around the outside of my trailer in my costume, a mucky pinstripe suit, as this friend told me my ex had been staying at their house, the one he shares with his wife and their two children. He's staying there because He can't bear to be in the home we used to share together. That life-size memory box that I have begun the process of no longer co-owning. His friend told me that my ex is finding it hard to interact with the children, because He's having difficulty being face to face with what He'd always imagined we would have one day.

So I agreed to meet in a neutral place and hear Him out. Because His friend is a decent man, and hearing people out is humane. And maybe I want to see if His friend was exaggerating when he'd told me He was broken.

He isn't, but He's definitely smaller than before. In terms of winning me back, He's not doing a great job. The theme is 'forgive me', that's been said quite often. He's just this second told me that He was drunk when He called Mia. He'd never called her before. It was a one-off, drunken mistake. And He is truly, truly sorry.

I don't tell Him that the phone call isn't the point. I just look at the river that's not doing anything interesting and carry on tearing my paper sugar sachet. I listen to Him say it was all moving too fast, all this relationship stuff, He'd felt trapped, and I don't say I'm pretty sure it was Him who wanted it to go so quickly. I listen to Him pull His aluminium chair back on the concrete. I listen to the patter of His expensively light-weight Nike trainers getting louder as they round the table to be next to me. The loud clatter as He pulls out the chair next to mine. The screech as He shuffles it closer to the side of my body hurts my teeth.

His stare makes me shift uncomfortably. The change in prox-imity has brought on an aching that wasn't there when He was safely two feet away, a table in-between us. But I will be tough. I will allow Him to see closer up what He can no longer have.

'Look at me,' He says.

I take a sip of tea, I make Him wait. It tastes foul. I turn into His eyes, His blue eyes.

He tells me I'm shivering.

'No,' I say, before He can reach for the jacket to put around

64

me. I can't have the smell of Him, the smell of leather and smoke and amber, the smell I'd worked very hard all week to forget, weighing on my shoulders.

He says, 'Give me your hand.' When I don't, He looks as though He knows I want to and reaches under the table, where I drop the tatters of the sugar sachet confetti to the floor.

He clamps my hand between both of His and tells me it was a mistake, Bunny, and I think, *You've already said that.* He says that it's taken this slip-up to realise what He actually wants. He doesn't want to throw our long future away. He says everyone should be allowed to make a mistake.

And somehow putting it in the wider context makes everything clearer. He's right. Everyone *should* be allowed to make a mistake. I put all this pressure on myself to be perfect, and I hate it. Why should I expect perfection from anyone else? What gives me the right to burden Him with my standards?

He's not a criminal. He's a human being, and He got pissed. It might not be because I'm 'less than'. Less than this other woman. Less than what He thought at first. In fact, it might have taught Him a valuable lesson. That I won't stand for anything less than I deserve.

He's begging me to please forgive Him, Bun, please. I've never seen this side of Him. I can't imagine anyone has, except me. I am made of pure status, folded in a delicate yellow skirt. I haven't eaten all day, to be thinner.

Less than a year ago, I had been so in love I wanted to set everything else in my life on fire and start again with just the two of us. What am I going to do – carry on all the break-up admin for the sake of carrying it on? Throw away the points we've ticked off the list, the moving in together, the flat? How will I listen to 'Time After Time' again?

'Remember Berlin?' He's desperate; He's trying to take me to that evening outside the Clärchens Ballhaus, when there were fairy lights criss-crossed above us. Before I had ever said 'I love you', but after we both knew.

Am I really going to be stubborn, like my mother? Will I succumb to my inner voice – the one asking, *How has this become about my capacity to forgive, and not His actions?* – just to *win*?

'All right. I forgive you. I do.'

We both agree we are stronger for it having happened.

I ignore the thought that it was not so much the cheating but rather the concealing, and just get over myself and move on because the important thing is we have overcome a hurdle and when couples overcome hurdles it brings them closer. We can survive things and that is so important because nothing that's easy is worth having, and that's just life!

I order a margarita like I wanted to in the first place. He says, 'Make it two', like a man in a black-and-white film. He tastes of Guinness and tobacco and wraps the smell of leather and smoke and amber around me. Even Canary Wharf looks different now. I see the hazy spring sunshine reflected in the glass buildings, calming down the harsh lines of the city, making everything shimmer. And I think how wonderful it is, how when you choose to start seeing the good in things, you just do. Instantly!

I Left

Because I know the real story

Crouch End, 7 October 2018

'Ah, balls.' Jim is looking at his phone. 'They've made statements. Him and the dancer.'

'WHAT?' I sit up. 'How? He doesn't have a phone!'

'Wherewherewhere?' Bell grabs her iPad.

'BBC News.'

They scan their screens while I scroll through all the messages from unknown numbers I've received. He must have a new phone with a new number! That makes sense.

I scroll. Nothing.

I check my emails just in case. I mean, He hardly ever emails but . . .

Nothing.

Before I can think about what this might mean I see Bell and Jim's brows wrinkling at each other. I give them an impatient hand-scooping gesture, the universal sign for 'get on with it'.

'All right, hers first.' Bell takes a breath. 'Where's she from?'

'Russia.'

'Should I do the accent?'

'No, come on!' But I'm smiling.

'I'm so sorry about any offence or hurt I have caused with

my actions. I wasn't thinking and it was a one-off mistake after some drinks. I love my husband and we are very happy together, this is not a reflection on our relationship.'

I shrug. 'As expected. Careful, bit fembot-y. "I love my husband", etc., nice touch. I mean, I'd love to know what it *is* a reflection of, if it isn't that, but still.' I turn to Jim. 'And His?'

Jim blinks, and sighs the sigh of 'Here we go'.

'"In light of the story in today's newspaper—"'

'Jesus!' I interrupt. 'That's not how He talks! "Newspaper"! When has any of us ever used the word "newspaper" in our lives? PR team in full swing there.'

'Yep. "In light of the story in today's newspaper I would like to offer my sincere apologies for my actions. This is no excuse but it was a one-off drunken mistake which I am truly sorry for."'

Jim stops. I wait for him to carry on, but that's it, the whole thing. No one says anything because I'm not saying anything. Because I can't. I have been punctured, and am leaking out from the inside.

Eventually, I say, 'Jim, that last bit again?'

'"It was a one-off drunken mistake which I am truly sorry for."'

'Bell,' I point to her without looking, 'read the last bit of the dancer's.'

'"I love my husband and we are very happy together, this is not a reflection on our relationship."'

A beat.

'Jim?'

Nothing.

'*Jim.*'

'"It was a one-off drunken mistake which I am truly sorry for."'

Right. I look in front of me at nothing in particular. I very slowly nod my head, though God knows what it is I'm silently concurring with.

'Your phone's going again, mate,' Bell says, and when I see the phone light up with a jumble of numbers I don't recognise, a light goes on inside me too. I snatch the phone up in relief, and answer it ready to swallow up any semblance of contrition, anything at all, as long as it's in His voice.

'I just saw the statement,' I offer the cue straight up.

'Oh 'ello! I assume that's Rebecca, is it?'

I sag. Male voice, but not His. In my brightest tone, I reply, 'Speaking!'

'Rebecca, this is Cockney Bloke at *The Tabloid* paper. How you doing, love, you all right?'

'Yes, thank you!' I say like no one has ever asked me how I am before, and try to bat away the slight kick I'm ashamed to say I always get when a bloke with a London accent calls me 'love'.

'Good good, lavely job. We've just seen the statements—'

'Wow, you lot are fast!' I beam down the phone, to make my voice sound like everything is better than fine, as the words 'A one-off drunken mistake which I am truly sorry for' appear in front of my eyes like an optician has flicked a switch on an eye chart.

'Ha ha, I know, right?' he says, like he's my pal. 'Listen, I just wanted to get your take on the BBC allowing them both to carry on together in the competition?'

I swallow down a blood-curdling scream. 'I actually didn't know until you just told me!' I sound like a Miss World contestant bleating 'WORLD PEACE!' into a microphone.

'Oh, really? Well, I'll give you a little time to have a think in that case. And OK, look, it's too late for tomorrow, darlin –'

I like 'darlin' less than 'love'.

'– but in two days' time, Tuesday, we'll be running both His and the dancer's statements on the front page, and we've spoken to Her husband too just to get his point of view. But it don't seem fair, the three of them having their say and you not. Feels out of order.'

'Yeah. Yeah, I get why it would feel that way.' Jim looks so tense, it's as though he's primed to run out for a crash mat in case I collapse again. But Bell's playing charades. She points at the phone, then does a middle finger.

'Anyway, I was hoping we could grab a comment from you—'

'Sorry, just a sec – can I ask how you got my number?'

Bell does a thumbs-up.

'Oh,' Cockney Bloke from *The Tabloid* says, 'I think it was on your PR's . . . thingy.'

'I don't have a PR.'

'Your agent, I meant your agent.'

'Are you allowed to be calling me?'

He does an unconvincing little laugh. 'All right all right, OK, what I'll do is I'll stick all this in an email and shoot it over. Just get back to me whenever you like, but not too late, obviously, or you'll have missed your chance.'

'Wouldn't want that.'

'And it goes without sayin' that if you were after a fee for this we'd be more than happy to negotiate that with your PR.'

'I don't have a PR. Bye.' I cram my last bit of benevolence into the receiver and hang up. 'They're going to be on the front pages again on Tuesday. Her husband, too, this time. Three out of four. They want to pay me.' Jim nods his head. 'I'm not going to do it, obviously.' Jim shakes his head. 'They pay you so they can own you. If you take the money your words are theirs to switch around, your face is theirs to Photoshop. I feel like my whole life's been a version of that recently.' Behind my eyes, I see images of the flat, that beautiful Smeg fridge-freezer, the golden R necklace, the meals in snazzy restaurants that we ate in loaded silence, looking at our phones. 'I'm a problem people throw money at to get away with what they like.'

'How much money?' asks Jim, and Bell slaps his arm. I try to smile but this time I can't.

I am a thirty-two-year-old woman who lives in an attic with her cat.

Winston gets up, stretches into a bridge until his furry body shakes with delicious effort, then turns himself around so his bum is facing me. I stare at the line in the ceiling where the slopes meet.

I am a thirty-two-year-old invisible woman.

I get Him not calling me. I get not messaging. I fucked up His phone, and behaved all sadistic triumph from the second He told me. But that statement. I know it would have involved a PR team, Vinnie, possibly the BBC. But why didn't He insist on apologising to His girlfriend, the way that the dancer had her husband? Why does it feel like He's used that box on Twitter to not only protest His innocence, but to wash His hands of me?

And as for me, why do I need this? Am I a megalomaniac? Is five years as long a time as I think it is? Is that a long relationship? Does it mean something that we lived together, had a cat? That I stood in The White Company smelling every single candle to pick one His mum would like for her birthday?

I can't tell. I've only been uncrazy for a day; I'm not used to trusting my own answers.

But something I do know is being truly sorry for something can mean many things.

You can be truly sorry for not having considered the hurt your actions would cause.

You can be truly sorry for having been reckless enough to get caught.

And you can also be truly sorry for a one-off drunken mistake

73

because you've learned before that being truly sorry for a one-off drunken mistake gets you off the hook.

And if it's the latter – I swallow, eyes staring straight up at the ceiling, corpse-like – it means that I contributed. Back then, in Canary Wharf. I showed Him that those words in that order work. Now I'm watching Him do the same thing again, this time with the whole country.

I can't put my finger on when exactly but at some point not long after the Mia debacle, the crime went from Him sending explicit messages to me having read them. It became 'What were you doing spying on my Facebook anyway?', which quickly became separate laptops, and passcodes and the importance of privacy. Eventually, the whole thing turned into 'It was only a few messages on Facebook, anyway'. I think back to a fortnight ago, when I'd said I felt as though I shouldn't trust Him, and He'd asked if I'm seriously still paranoid because of some messages He can barely even remember, and when am I going to get over it?

Each thought rushes through me, it's as though I'm gently lifting lids of boxes in my brain that until now have been shut and marked 'Things to forget about'. I think too about the things upset friends have confided in me about their own relationships over the years. And as these thoughts appear, my perspective shifts and I begin to see a new reality. A world where no, it wasn't OK for them to have been called dramatic when they cried. Where it wasn't OK to be called a cunt because there was no milk in the house. Where it wasn't acceptable to be told 'if it wasn't for you, I'd be living in LA by now, no question', or, when they attempted to initiate sex, 'All right, let's get this over with'. Where it's justifiable to be upset that their exciting holiday has been sabotaged by their partner's unexplained sullenness, or when they're given unasked for feedback on their bodies, or haircuts, or clothes and told 'that's just my opinion'. And I see a world where none of us are psychos or lunatics for having felt our partners were hiding things. A world where we are *right*.

I wonder what else I've been right about. I wonder when it all went wrong.

'A one-off drunken mistake,' I say the words slowly, as the smell of Lenor on the sheets underneath me and the honey warmth of the room fades away, 'which I am truly sorry for.'

I Stayed

Because I have a sense of humour

Our flat, Shepherd's Bush, July 2016

He should be done by now. A last-minute preview gig in London normally means He's home by half ten. It's quarter to eleven. Does He want food? Should I wait up?

'Hello?' He answers the phone weirdly, politely, like He's not expecting it to be me. 'Sssh,' I hear Him say, more quietly.

'Hi?' I sit upright on the sofa, suddenly alert. No response. 'It's . . . me?'

There's a suspenseful pause like I'm about to find out whether I won *X Factor*.

'Hello, Rebecca, you are on speaker, and you are also live onstage at the Top Secret Comedy Club!'

Through the phone, the sound of two hundred people laughing.

'Oh, for fuck's sake,' I say.

The audience laughs even louder, and applauds, and as if by magic I'm starring in a studio sitcom.

'Right, I'm a bit busy, what d'you want?' He asks. 'Let me guess: "When are you gonna get home??!!!"' He does that shrill, aggressive voice He does whenever He adopts my persona onstage.

More canned laughter from down the phone. I open my mouth, but my voice is gone. I don't know my lines. The women in these things aren't meant to be funny, are they?

'Hello?' His voice rings through; then, to the audience, 'This is going well.'

They laugh, then they stop. Waiting. I take a deep breath. *Say something, Rebecca.*

'Just, yep, just ... wondering whether you wanted anything to eat? Cos Tesco closes in fifteen minutes.'

No laugh.

'I hate this, by the way,' I ad lib.

Big laugh.

'Yeah, but none of that vegan stuff. She's doing a vegan thing,' He tells them. 'Our fridge isn't a fridge any more, it's an allotment.'

Laugh.

'This is ridiculous,' I say.

'I'M SORRY, I'M SORRY!' His tone switches instantly to exaggerated fear. The crowd's response tells me He's doing physical comedy to accompany it. Cowering away from the phone maybe. 'Sorrysorrymydarling, sosorry.'

The blood simmers under my skin. 'I love that I'm not allowed to go to your gigs, but that this is a thing.'

Silence down the line.

'We've been through this, haven't we? You put me off.'

I want to say, *Is that why, though? Because last week I got a message from my friends Nish and Emily, who were at your gig, saying that you were amazing, so funny, and that I'm 'such a good sport'.* I want to ask what it is He says about me, why I'm no longer allowed to know, why I'm not consulted, why can't He leave me out of it for once, *once* in *four years*?

But we've recorded that episode before. The one where He says that other comics do it and their partners don't mind. That I never used to. That no, *obviously*, that's not what He really thinks of me, He uses that voice for me because that's what comedy *is*, it's taking things to the extreme, trust Him, He knows what funny is, I just don't get it. That He's allowed to make up stuff about annoying things I eat and the OTT polite friends that I have and the infernal blast of my hairdryer in the morning and about who I am or the things I do or say because funny will always triumph over truth.

And you know what, He fills a lot of seats, and those seats make a good point.

Anyway, there's an audience waiting, and I can take a joke, you know; those women who can't laugh at themselves, they're so earnest, so sensitive. So I smile down the phone and say, 'Well, I'm glad I could contribute so positively tonight.'

I hear laughter, and we're back on track.

'Right, got to go. I'm at work, you know.'

'What shall I do, then? What do you actually want?'

'Fish fingers, chips and beans, cheers, see ya.'

The sound cuts as the audience crescendoes. He's hung up.

The flat is all the more silent now all that laughter has gone. I sit there livid, and in dire need of acknowledgement. I hop on to Instagram to post a picture of us taken at London Zoo last year. I wait for some likes but nothing. I'm not the one with the audience.

Jesus Christ, Rebecca, I think. *You're such an attention seeker. Get your coat on, get His dinner, Tesco closes soon.*

I Left

Because I needed to move forwards

I'm at a crossroads here, lying on this mattress in this attic with a cat's furry arse in my face, nothing but a pile of last night's clothes. Knowing I have to watch everyone else stride (dance) forward as though nothing has happened, carry on doing the cha-cha-cha on Saturday-night television, party in the gazebo, walk over the spot in the tarmac where my sanity was presented to me by default. It strikes me that if *I* want to move forward, I will have to throw a part of myself under the bus – the part of me that says I deserve better than this – and watch it get mashed up in the tyres.

'All right,' I say out loud. 'What don't you have? Think. So you don't have a home, yep, not ideal. A job. A regular income, or any security. This is . . . it's quite stressful, actually.'

I exhale. I blink. I don't think I've blinked in about ten minutes.

'I don't have a PR person, like they do, because I can't afford one. I don't have to have a crisis meeting today with the BBC. Ha.' My brow furrows in surprise. 'I don't have any terms and conditions to breach. I don't have the need to save face. I don't have a document in black and white with my signature at the bottom, a document that keeps my free will out of things.'

'And what *have* you got?' I focus. I hold up my hand to my

face. Still there. For years, I had relied on Him to make me visible. Waited for Him to introduce me to people rather than taking the initiative myself. I had waited in the audience at *Strictly* for Him to mention me, so that I would be visible then. And today, even after we had broken up, I had been waiting for Him to release a statement that made me visible too.

'But you *are* visible,' I tell myself. 'You exist. You've got your right mind back, you know that's . . . that's really something.

'You have freedom. You can lie stretched out in bed, like a starfish, and not worry about going over the middle line and kicking anyone in the leg in your sleep. Freedom to ask yourself what you want to do tomorrow, and you don't have to consult with anyone else about whether that's OK.

'You have nothing to lose, it's already been lost.'

I hear a small crackle, like a velociraptor. I look over my shoulder down at Winston, who looks straight back.

'Except yoooou, my most beautiful angelbaby!'

'Crackle.'

It's the noise he makes when he knows it's dinner time. I have a responsibility to this living thing that I have to give fish and water to in order to keep alive. I lean back to stroke him, then pull away sharply when he bites me.

'Crackle.'

What would I do if I denied Winston love and affection for years? I would pick him up and hug him and bury my face in his fur. I would tell him, 'You are *stunning* and you didn't deserve that and I am so sorry, it will never happen again.' Why should it be such a struggle to have that dialogue with myself?

'Cracklecrackle.'

I have to do something.

I Stayed

Because of money

Our flat, Shepherd's Bush, March 2017

I'm getting my finances sorted out, just covering my back, getting my ducks in a row.

In bed. At 2:40 a.m.

It's dark. Orange streaks of streetlight are coming in through the new bedroom shutters, and somewhere down Samstat Road I can hear a fox having a good go on a bin. Or on another fox, hard to tell.

He got home and into bed around midnight. Since then my gaze has been alternating between the ceiling and the skin of His back. A back that has slid even further towards His edge of the bed tonight, like I'm infectious.

We'd had such a good run. Four days without arguing. Of watching the *Game of Thrones* boxset at night with a Deliveroo on our laps, predicting who would snuff it next and applauding whenever tits appeared. Saying things like 'OK sure' and 'I can do that if you'd like', instead of 'Do I have to?' or 'Why can't you do it?' We went to see the live-action *Beauty and the Beast* in the cinema and cheerfully agreed on how crummy it was, and have done piss-takey musical numbers at home with the crockery to 'Be Our Guest' in dodgy French accents.

But then came tonight. He'd received a text on the sofa, I'd instinctively leaned in to see who it was from, and He'd hidden it away. Cue a pass-agg question about what He's hiding, which led to a petty conversation about why His phone screensaver is the QPR player Charlie Austin and not me, which led to a full-blown argument about why there are no pictures of us on His social media. He said I was being controlling, called His friend who runs a comedy night in town, went to do a last-minute appearance, and came home three hours later with a pocket full of cash.

'You're checking out of this,' I'd said as He got into bed.

'No.' He'd done a whole body eye-roll, turning on His side, away from me.

'You are.' I hadn't left it alone.

'I'm here, aren't I?'

'Physically, but a bit of you feels like it's somewhere else. And I don't know what to do about it; I wish you'd tell me.'

A beat.

'Maybe try being less insecure?' He'd said it like a genuine suggestion, like it's all He could think of, at this stage. 'For yourself?'

It's led to another night's worth of making hypothetical future plans as He sleeps open-mouthedly beside me.

OK, Step One: Message someone who has a spare room and will not ask questions (Oonagh?).

Step Two: Learn how to use eBay. eBay my most expensive clothes to make money.

Step Three: Live off rice for a bit.

Step Four: Hopefully get an acting job; if not, probably have to drag myself back to Norwich grey faced, alone and destitute.

I turn onto my side and let my hand stroke the space in-between us. The gap would be big enough to fit two other people, if they were holding each other tightly enough.

The way we—

No point in thinking that.

Because that's not tonight.

I'd begged Him not to go and do the show. 'Stay, let's figure this out!' But He went anyway and when He arrived back there was all this cash and He'd said that I'm not complaining about that, am I? And He's right. I don't have a job at the moment. Not making money is giving me sleepless nights, and the less I sleep the more I forget my lines in auditions (which are scarce anyway), or zone out when I'm being directed, or just look generally exhausted. So He needs to make money, for both of us. And the more money He makes the more sense it makes for Him to pay for everything.

- The takeaways
- The holidays
- The cinema
- The mortgage
- The bills
- The new garden
- The new shutters for the bedroom
- My clothes
- My food
- My whole life

When I first left drama school, I used to steal frozen fruit from the restaurant I waitressed in. I would get one of the sunshine-yellow paper takeaway cups, fill it with berries from the chest freezer, put a lid on it and pretend I was sipping a coffee as I walked out the building. Then I'd have it for my dinner.

How could I possibly go back to that life, after all this?

He makes a *lot* more money than me, and we live on a spectrum that ranges from 'cushty' to 'Elton John Vanity Fair party'. I couldn't cover half the costs even if I wanted to. We go to restaurants I can't afford, stay in hotels that would never even enter my consciousness if I didn't have a high-earning partner. Even this flat, I could never live in a flat like this in London; you should see some of the mouldy opium dens I've had to slog twelve-hour shifts night after night to pay the rent for.

I feel as though everybody knows. I feel like some sort of dowry-less Jane Austen character, winsomely bobbing around at balls and hoping that the elite don't notice her empire-line dress is from the ASOS sale.

I've offered to contribute. He insists I mustn't, that He can easily afford these things and I can't. Which is true.

I'm so appreciative of my generous boyfriend. Money has always made me feel safe.

Only nowadays it doesn't.

Nowadays it makes me feel like I can lay claim to absolutely nothing in my life at all.

And once or twice –

not regularly, by any means –

when maybe things have gotten out of hand –

like I've picked a holiday that's too expensive –

or said yes to one too many things –

He will get a look on His face –

and yell,

'I AM *LEAKING* MONEY!'

I am constantly indebted. I owe Him nice. I owe him pretty. I owe Him agreeable when we're among His colleagues, even when they say twatty things.

Other people would kill for this lifestyle. I know I should be thankful, start taking pleasure in it. Start seeing this for what it is, which is landing on my feet, like Julia Roberts in *Pretty Woman*.

Stop thinking every gesture will come back to haunt me one day.

Stop being so *suspicious*.

Stop feeling like all of this taking on my part will make it easier for Him to eventually discard me, like a greasy paper bag that once contained something sweet and delicious, and watch it blow back down Hollywood Boulevard, dodging crackheads.

I hear a soft rustling at the end of the bed, and I know it's the sound of baby Winston climbing a mound of ASOS packages like Simba on Pride Rock. I slide from under the covers in the dark and go and scoop him up so as not to wake Him. I sit on the carpet with my back against the foot of the bed and a wriggly kitten on my lap.

His foot hangs off the end of the mattress, by my shoulder. I lean my head against it. It's warm. He doesn't even stir.

'It's OK,' I whisper to myself. 'You're OK.'

Because my secret is, for the last few months, I haven't been entirely financially dependent.

Nan died two years ago, so it was a huge surprise to recently receive a few thousand pounds in inheritance out of the blue. It was far more than I expected, because what I'd expected was nothing. She & Grandad had lived a humble existence in a tiny bungalow, with peeling lino on the kitchen floor, brown glass mugs they'd had since the 70s, a gas grill you had to light with a match which would burn the hairs off your forearm if you didn't pull out quick enough. The only thing I'd ever known for her to get brand new was a three-piece suite in 1999, which I helped her pick from DFS. To the outside world they were – and there's really no other way of putting this – *skint*.

I haven't touched her money; it's sitting there in my account. I am determined to keep what's left of her while I process things I've discovered lately about her life. Stuff I learned at her funeral. I put together the pieces in my head when I can't sleep, like one of her Scottish landscape jigsaw puzzles.

Nanny's husband, my grandad, died back in 2013. The night before I went to Brighton to fall in love, as it happens. He had been a very boisterous man, with a raucous sense of humour, and had always had a pound for me to get a Magnum with from the Shell garage down the road. Nanny couldn't have been more different: shy, softly spoken, and . . . well, the word is 'pleasant', which makes me sad even now, that her legacy is as vague as that. I had never seen her have a conversation that went beyond 'Y'alrigh'?' in her Norfolk accent, or 'D'you watch *Emmerdale*?', the latter of which she asked me every time I saw her for over twenty years, despite the answer consistently being 'no'.

Grandad knew Nanny had dementia before anyone. Mum hadn't seen or heard from them for ages. He'd called her in a panic one day when Nanny was looking for her own long-dead mother in the back garden.

But Grandad, my charismatic, ebullient Grandad, didn't want to get her officially diagnosed with dementia before she had signed everything she had over to him in her will, before anyone could legally dispute how sound of mind she was. The problem was, he rarely did anything for himself all those years and so had no idea how to go about the will stuff without Nanny or my mum's help.

So much time went by that a neighbour tipped off social services, who one day out of the blue knocked at the door of their bungalow. He refused to open the door, locked Nanny in the bathroom, and when the police arrived dropped to the floor from a stroke and died the next day. Nanny was taken to a home. She never got officially diagnosed with dementia, she'd deteriorated so quickly without care that by then it was full-blown Alzheimer's.

It wasn't until the funeral that I discovered that she had come from considerable money. That she had met my grandad in the fifties on the farm her father owned, where she was the family's motorcycle-driving daughter and he was the boy who mucked out the stables. I would never have guessed. But the most shocking thing of all to me were the pictures Mum showed me when we were clearing out the bungalow. Photos of my nanny before she met my grandad. As a younger person on holiday by the sea, handing a monkey a banana in a zoo, holding a pina colada with a pineapple wedge sitting cheekily on the side of the glass. Tanned in the sun with a female friend, captured mid-singing, looking ecstatically happy. A woman in her own right, not standing timidly behind a man, being wherever he wanted to be.

And I just looked at that woman in those pictures and thought, *Where oh where did that woman go?*

So look, the point is I have a few thousand pounds that once belonged to her.

But this voice inside me is saying don't use it.

He doesn't even know about the money.

I keep telling the voice, 'I am a liar. I am a thief.'

'Do not spend her money here,' it says back to me. 'It feels wrong.'

I get up from the floor, holding the kitten in one hand. I hold my breath and head carefully out of the bedroom in the dark. Find the expensive cat bed he never sleeps in, dump him in it, then make a beeline for the cupboard under the sink. I rip through it thinking, *Please God, say I haven't taken all the Nytol or codeine or something else with which to roofie myself. Please, I just want to sleep.* Tearing my way through the Benylins and packets with one paracetamol left, trying to ignore the question of whether parts of *me* are disappearing. There are pictures from before I met Him, of me on nights out in Wetherspoons, wearing bin bags with Theo pretending to be witches on Halloween, no money but bags of sassy. Would someone say about me: *Where oh where did that woman go?*

No pills in sight. I close the cupboard door and take a deep breath. I have to stop making escape plans every time there is conflict. If I want to stop feeling like a parasite, I am going to have to start coughing up. If I want to be sexy, I am going to have to stop being something that *needs*.

He quite often points out how his mates' wives cook. I'll do that then. I'll make us dinner and then he'll want to bone me and everything will be reset. And not a stir-fry or something rudimentary, something that requires graft. A salmon en croute! I'll go to Liberty's on my way home from work tomorrow, get one of those Le Creuset dishes I've always wanted for the house too. And I'll buy it myself.

Sure, I pay for this relationship in terms of hard work, effort, self-sacrifice, in not having my life be exactly how I would like it. But it's hardly the same as parting with cash, is it? I have this money stashed away in case I escape, but here, sitting against the cupboard under the kitchen sink, I am deciding not to run away. And if I'm saving money in case He discards me, well, I'm going to have to work harder in order that He doesn't. I choose to stay. I choose to go all in with this.

What's the point, otherwise?

Because I am psychotic

Our flat, Shepherd's Bush, the next day

It hit me this afternoon, as I was picking up the ingredients for the salmon en croute and going over the argument we had this morning about the argument we had last night, that what's been missing is sex. Duh! I've been googling studies and they say the average couple has sex once a week. We are not on track, so no wonder there's so much tension, a lot of energy that could do with a release. Lately my methods of seduction have included:

- being overtly 'sexy'
- wearing new underwear
- wearing lots of eyeliner with messy hair.

None of it's worked, it's all too obvious, too much, cringey for Him. And it's not, y'know, the response I would have chosen, but expressing my complex feelings of rejection is hardly going to get us back on track either. The next strategy was to give Him some space, to let Him come to me, and that didn't really work either because He kept steering clear.

It's not that I have much of an appetite for sex myself,

I should point out. But I've never taken being below average well.

So it's come to this. A fish log for a fuck.

I never cook. I usually consider it pointless as nothing I make will ever come near the flawlessness of a McDonald's Filet-O-Fish. So: tonight is a big deal. Also, do you know how long salmon en croute takes? It's fucking ages! Jim's fiancé Bell gave me the recipe. I'm feeling pretty pleased with myself, though I didn't make the pastry, but I *did* buy an apron, and I'm doing a great job of ignoring my brain insisting this is a charade, that I'm participating in gender-role self-stereotyping, and that the only thing that's missing is Tammy Wynette's 'Stand by Your Man' playing on vinyl.

Anyway, so what if I am enabling gender-role self-stereotyping for one night? Getting laid will save my relationship, and this person is my person to do that with.

I hear the front gate go, and assume the position by the kitchen counter, excited and proud and smug. The front door shuts and I hear Him throw his backpack on the floor and shuffle into the kitchen where I'm standing holding it out for Him in a new blue Le Creuset dish, wearing new blue striped oven gloves. He comes in scrolling on His phone. Keeps scrolling. I'm still standing there. He keeps scrolling.

'Put your phone away, Bun.'

He looks up, sees the dish, and seems confused, which wouldn't be my preferred reaction.

'What's that?' He asks.

'It's a salmon en croute, type of thing!' I am cheerful.

'What's that?' He asks.

'Oh!' That was daft, assuming He would know. 'So it's like a big chunk of salmon, and on top of it you make a kind of spinach-y mushroom-y sauce with a tub of Philadelphia, and then you wrap it all in puff pastry and you cut slices out of it like, I dunno. Like a fish arctic roll?' I smile. 'I'm not really selling it, but . . .'

He laughs. 'That sounds *fucking horrible.*'

And I smash it on the floor.

Le Creuset dishes are famously sturdy. But it smashes.

He looks at the dish, and then up at me completely calmly. I run past Him, down the corridor and into the bedroom, slamming the door in a way that is so hard and sharp there will be no mistaking that I meant to do it. I grab a pillow with my clawed hands and hurl it at the built-in wardrobe, then I grab another and scream into it:

'WHYDON'TYOUWANTME?' My breath makes the pillow burn. 'WHYDON'TYOUWANTME?'

I've broken through into the 'wild woman' part, the one that's usually locked up in a subservient shell for safety reasons. When I smashed that dish on the kitchen floor, I smashed open myself and Medea flew out.

'You are

such

a

CUUUUNT!'

I scream it as loudly and piercingly as I can. I hope people are passing in the street outside, I hope the neighbours upstairs are in and that He knows and comes in here to clamp His hands over my mouth so I can bite them and tear chunks out of His skin and look *there's* my appetite, right there in that savage vision.

I want to open those wardrobe doors and for blood to come cascading out all over me, want to discover dangerous hidden treasures like hotel receipts or used condoms wrapped in a tissue, or feel the lace of another woman's used knickers or find another phone number written on a torn-off lined piece of paper like I *did once, I found one once and fucking hell it had felt so good to watch Him struggle to justify it*. I'm inside the fantasy now, the fantasy I have most days, the one where I am *right* about the images in my head that it pains me every single day to imagine, the one where I am clever and brilliant and not weak or paranoid or broken in the brain.

I am done. I am done. I am done done done done done done done done done done done done done done done done done done done done done done done done done done done done

Done

Done

Done

DONE

DONE.

And then I come to, and my fit is just a memory. I realise I'm standing with the lid of the laundry bin in one hand and a sock in the other, and have been charging around the room picking up smalls like a malfunctioning Stepford Wife.

'What is the matter with you?' I whisper to myself. I'm still wearing an apron. I feel like the worst bits of ten different types of woman. I put the sock in the laundry bin, sit on the bed and think how 'people are starving in Africa' and I just wasted all that food.

Fifteen minutes later I open the bedroom door and slide out in silence. Two friends who have an excellent marriage once told me their secret is never going to bed on an argument. Also I can't get out of the bedroom window because we had bars put on the outside because of burglars.

I am steely and poised, gliding back through the hall the way I had screamed and run in the other direction fifteenish minutes ago. I appreciate my behaviour may have looked, on the surface of things, quite extreme. I'm prepared to accept that was possibly mad-bitch behaviour, but we must address what got me there because it's easy for things smashing on the floor to detract from the actual issue, which is Him. I worked very hard on that dinner, apart from the pastry. I work very hard in general at all of this.

'It was your fault,' I quietly practise along the hall, past the coats. 'Not mine.'

I'm prepared to fight my corner. Prepared for drama. Prepared for almost anything except Him sitting on the floor with a fork and a mouthful of salmon en croute, looking up sheepishly like a naughty little boy. Which is exactly what I find.

We stare at one another in the silence.

'Don't *hover*,' He says finally, lightly.

I try not to laugh. I cross to the dishwasher, pick out a clean fork and sit opposite Him, cross-legged, the carcass of a meal with a broken stoneware spine between us.

A pause.

'Is . . . everythinnng . . . OK?' He's being funny, I'm fighting to keep it together.

'Yes, thank you.' I raise my eyebrows in innocence. 'Are you?'

'Yes,' He says.

'Listen. I know that was demented—'

'Yesitwas,' He interrupts. 'Completely mental.'

'I don't like it when you say that.' My voice tightens, like when I'm inside a lift and the doors don't immediately open.

'You literally just said it!'

'It's different, coming from you.' No, it's less like a lift and more like a cage that He's standing outside of with the key.

'It was a joke,' He says. 'I'm joking.'

'I know, I know.' And I put my hands up in surrender because I can take a joke. We go back to picking the floor with our forks for a second.

'*So* sensitive.' He shakes His head and widens His eyes and puffs out air at the memory of what happened earlier. Seconds after He'd stepped inside His own flat, ready for His dinner.

'I mean, yeah, I know.' I indicate with my hands the mess, us being on the floor, the whole situation as if to say, *I can see it all, I have eyes, I know this is my fault*, and I'm feeling hot again, Christ why do I have to be so *offended* by *everything*?

I flake off a really chunky bit of salmon with my fork and it fans out satisfyingly. 'I just thought, y'know, I was in Waitrose looking at the ready meals and was like, "Do you know what, actually, neither of us ever cooks, so . . . "'

'I cook sometimes,' He interrupts me again.

And look, he does cook, that's true, but there is a subtle difference between 'sometimes' and 'from time to time'. It's definitely not worth saying that out loud. It's also not worth mentioning that when he does cook dinner it's always very good, but the kitchen and every single utensil in it will be reminiscent of Chernobyl, and if I refuse to clean Chernobyl out of principle it will stay like Chernobyl until much later in the week when He decides to do something about it, all the while lecturing me on how I never clean.

It's definitely not worth saying that. So I say, 'That's true, you do cook sometimes. And it's always very good. Sorry.'

I congratulate myself for holding back. Breaking the habit. Because I have said some mean things over the course of our relationship, same as He has. That bit where I called Him a cunt earlier? Happens all the time. From both of us. Casually, angrily, affectionately, in passing. It ceases to carry weight any more. And oh God, there have been many times I have behaved like I did with the salmon. Screaming when the windows were wide open, storming off in shopping centres, crying at parties. Once we were bickering while walking through Leicester Square, and I had wanted to hurt Him so much I said that one of His peers was the best stand-up comedian in the country, better than Him. Taking a hammer to His ego, almost daring Him to threaten me with a break-up so we could make up again. He had walked away and I had followed Him on to the tube and all the way home in complete silence. I'd gone too far, and had to wait almost forty-eight hours before a conversation happened. It was torturous. I can't tell you what it's like lying in bed when silence is that loud, and knowing it's your fault. I am both explosive and fragile, and sometimes I'm so tired of constantly walking on eggshells that have shards of glass hidden among that I just . . . I just make scenes.

'Can we try to be nicer to each other, do you think?' I ask. 'I really want to try that. I hate it when we're not.'

'Yes,' He says.

'It's a good job we go out with one another,' I say. 'Not everybody would be tough enough to put up with our shit.'

'Mmmm,' He agrees.

'We understand each other.' And as I wait for Him to agree with me again I wonder whether Rose West ever said that about Fred, I bet she did.

I look at the salmon en croute. 'Bun.' I pause. 'Do you respect me?'

'Oh leave it out, Bun.'

'Sorry. But like . . . ' God, this is hard. 'Can you actually try not to call me mental any more?' I'm wincing.

'We're eating salmon off the floor because you smashed it over nothing.'

'I know. I know that I *am* mental but I don't like hearing you say it.'

'All right, all right.' He looks annoyed.

'I don't want to make a big deal out of anything but it has a real effect on me, Bunny, it's doing something. There's research that—'

'What?!'

'Letmefinish – research that shows that when you're told that you are something time and time again, you start to believe it of yourself. And I think I am already doing that, and it's fucking with me. So just, help me out, will you?'

'Yep, OK. I mean, I think you're overreacting but fine.'

'Jesus, you can't just say yes without the overreacting part, can you?! If my friends—'

'Could hear the way you talk to me!' He completes my sentence in the same shrill voice He uses when He plays me onstage, when He makes up things I never actually said.

'Yeah, my friends would be shocked.'

'I don't care!' He laughs. 'I don't give a fuck what they think!'

'Well, whatever.'

Change the subject, lighten the mood. I walk over to the Smeg fridge-freezer, a gift from Him, my pride and joy, and stroke it to calm myself down. Then I open it to get the mayonnaise. 'I tried to open the front door with my card earlier on,' I tell Him over my shoulder. 'Tapped the lock like it was the tube.'

When I close the door and look back He's looking out at me from under his brow.

'THAT'S NOT MENTAL!' I can't take this. 'IT'S SCATTY!'

'*All right!*' He stops me before I fully go off. I go back to my place on the floor quietly and unscrew the lid on the jar.

'Your temper.' He shakes His head. 'My God.'

I scoop up mayo with my fork, stab it in pastry, and stuff it in my gob so I won't respond. 'Maybe I don't have a short temper, just a quick reaction to bullshit.' The Elizabeth Taylor quote falls out of my full mouth with flecks of food and I brace myself for a reaction. But He chuckles, reaches for the mayonnaise and shrugs in a way that says, *Fair enough*, and we both eat. He's feeling better. I did that.

'This is delicious,' He says.

104

'Tell me I nailed it.'

'Give over.'

'I want to hear you say it.'

'Well done, you followed a recipe properly, for once.'

'Oh piss off!' I grab a chunk of the food with my bare hands and chuck it at Him, it hits His shoulder and we laugh. I lean forward to brush it off, then sit back again. We look at the floor, at the state of things, then up at each other and we're laughing again, harder this time, leaning into the joy of something so valuable being so unmistakably and irrevocably broken.

He wets His finger to prod pastry flakes off the floor, like a child, and I think, *Poor him*. He licks mayonnaise off his fork and I think, *That poor little boy*. I feel terrible about how much I wanted as a child when, compared to Him, I grew up so privileged. I feel terrible for flaunting it all in His face, which I especially feel whenever I drag Him back to Norwich for a family birthday or a Mother's Day or Easter or something or other. No wonder He never wants to come.

We give one another a great deal of grief, but I won't give up on Him. I'm too strong for that. I am entirely fit for this purpose, the purpose of making up for His past.

It's a good thing to have empathy, isn't it?

'I got us something,' I say. 'Want to see?'

'Do I have to get up?'

'Yes, look.' I hold my hand out to help Him up and we go over to the French doors. It's one of those thrilling seven o'clocks in spring, where the clocks have just gone forward so there's evening light after months of darkness. The promise of not needing a coat, pub patios, those little freedoms.

Our colourful garden is around fifteen feet long, and lined with lavender. Right at the end is a little blue shed, shielded by a tall maple tree meaning nobody can look in at us, it's all our own. A baby fox once got trapped in it for the morning, it was the sweetest thing, watching it smelling all the pretty flowers and trying and failing to climb the fence.

It can be magic out there.

'See?' I point to the tree, on which I earlier nailed a tiny blue house filled with wooden tubes of differing size.

'What is it?'

'It's a bee hotel,' I tell Him.

He gasps. 'Like the play?' He remembered, and now it's magic in here as well.

'Yes!' I've been taking part this week in the early stages of a play about bees. One of the best things about being in a play is you become a sudden expert in all manner of bizarre things. I've wrapped myself up in this one even more than usual because I haven't worked in ages, and now I'm a bee authority.

'Wow!' Bees mean something to Him too. When he was three, He trapped one under a cup in His back garden and forgot about it and went in for His tea. When He came out it had died, and He was distraught. His mum had spoken to Him about how we need to protect the bees because they're kind and they help us, a sweet attempt at sharing a moment with her son that resulted in a thirty-year dosage of Irish Catholic guilt. He now gives to a bee charity. I'd found the hotel at Waitrose earlier when I was getting the salmon stuff.

'Why is it a hotel?'

'They can come and stay in it when they need a sleep after flying around all the flowers before they go home to the hive.' And we look at each other like it's the cutest thing ever.

'All the bees in a hive are girls. Women,' I correct myself.

'Jesus.' He says it like He can't imagine anything worse.

'Yep, they clean the floors, make the wax, fly out to collect the pollen, they do all the drudgery.'

'Good.' He nods solemnly and I push against Him.

'And the men, the drones, don't even live there. They just turn

106

up every so often, fly in, and – get this – all the women will leave whatever it is they're doing and fawn all over them, groom their fur, like, I dunno, like a spa.'

'Yes, good.' He is exaggerating his solemn nodding.

'Oh, shut up. Because, right, these men have one purpose in life.' I'm having loads of fun, watching Him watching the hotel, giving Him the whole 360 bee experience. 'Which is this: when the queen in the hive dies, the princess taking her place will fly out on a maiden voyage, sort of thing. At which point, all the males race to impregnate her, fill her up with semen so she can carry on laying eggs for the next three years or however long she lives.'

'Christ,' He says.

'I know, it's nuts, isn't it? That's their job, it's a drone's only job. Get laid.'

'Sounds great.'

'Yeah, life's good for a drone,' I agree. I look at the hotel, thinking that throughout those three years, every day every woman in a hive will carry on cleaning the floors, making the wax, flying out to collect the pollen, and reproducing. And you know what? It doesn't matter whether they like it or not. It doesn't matter if one of those female bees thinks, *I'd prefer if this wasn't what I had to do*, or, *I'm not cut out for this*. Because it's their job. That is the natural order of things.

I'd read something a week or so ago about how suicidal women are more likely to attempt it in a public space because their loved ones wouldn't be the ones to find them. That consideration for others, despite what they're about to do to themselves. I haven't stopped thinking about it. I thought about it when I stood on the yellow lines of the train platform earlier, the lines you're not supposed to cross. After rehearsals, on my way home. I'd seen the lights of the train, and had stood frozen with my feet on the lines. When you look at the tracks from there, it's a long way down.

Nothing happened. It never does. The train always shoots past my face and shocks me awake. I get on it when the doors open and carry on with my journey. In today's case, it was to Waitrose for ingredients and the bee hotel. There is no need to ever concern Him with it.

'It looks good, that,' He says.

'Oh, I'm glad you think so,' I reply.

Knowing full well that I am a mental person ... it actually *helps* with moments like on the train platform. Or when I feel like walking into busy roads, or violently swerving the wheel of my car on the motorway or whatever it is. It makes sense that I do those things, because my brain is wired wrongly. It's not because I'm sad, or feel more alone than I've ever felt in my life and can't see a way out of it. That's illogical. How can I be alone when I live here, with my boyfriend?

I hear a small miaow, and we both turn to see baby Winston on top of the salmon Le Creuset mountain. 'Winston!' I say. Next to me, He makes a miaow noise, and Winston miaows back at Him like it's a conversation. The pair of us humans gasp and look at each other and smile delightedly at this innocent thing. I really love Him.

'I really love you, Bunny,' I say. And He side-eyes me, the corners of His mouth turning up so I know He's playing. He goes and picks up Winston with one hand, says, 'Come on, that's dangerous,' and brings him over to stand with me.

'I'm sorry about before,' I say. 'I'm so sorry.'

He looks at me. 'It's OK,' He says. He holds up Winston, the most perfect white angel with his big blue marble eyes, for me to kiss on the head, then holds him facing the garden, pointing out things for the kitten to see. The three of us look outside in the golden hour and now I can relax. This is my favourite place – the place where the relationship has been freshly salvaged.

'What's that?' He's pointing at something.

I smile. 'A hydrangea.'

'A hydrangea,' He tells Winston, as though Winston had asked Him, and I laugh, and I wonder if He remembers when we went to see Theo in that play in Stratford at Christmas three years ago, where in the pub afterwards I told Him I'd always wanted to call my daughter Honey and He'd said 'Honey' out loud and smiled and said, 'It's perfect.'

I choose not to ask.

I also choose not to say what happens to the male bees after they race to impregnate the queen.

How when one catches up with her, mounts her and impregnates her, his penis falls off inside her and he falls to the ground dead. Then another one comes along, his penis dislodges the penis of the first one, and the same thing happens. Then another, then another. They keep fucking, and dying, until she's choc full of semen and she flies back to the home where the women are waiting.

There's more.

So the rest of the male bees follow her, and fly back to the landing pad, expecting a heroes' welcome from all the women who've been grooming and just loving on them all this time. But that isn't what happens. Because these men have rendered themselves useless, unfit for purpose. The ones that don't fly away from fear get massacred by the women. All that bloodlust, that rage, in such a small place. And then the hive has a fresh start. The new queen lays more eggs and new drones are born.

And something occurs to me. That it stands to reason that if all the cleaning and the making of wax and the reproducing is the natural order of things, then that female bloodlust and rage in action must be too.

And just for the tiniest, winciest, 'one cell in the honeycomb' second, I look at the man beside me and think, *I fucking hate you*.

Sometimes I am so mad that my madness feels like clarity.

And then He puts his free arm around me, the one that isn't holding our kitten, and it's entirely gone. What was I even thinking about? I don't remember. I just remember all relationships having ups and downs, how nothing worth having comes easily, how sometimes love takes work and sometimes outright drudgery. I go to pick up the giant shards of ceramic and He says to leave it, it's fine.

We have sex that night. I couldn't tell if it was still what I wanted, but I didn't want to be annoyed at myself later for not having utilised the opportunity.

I Left

Because it was emotional abuse

Crouch End, 8 October 2018

In Greek Mythology, Cassandra was a princess of Troy. The sun god, Apollo, promised her the gift of prophecy if she accepted his sexual advances. She agreed at first, but then changed her mind. So Apollo put a curse on her. She could see the future, see impending doom, her family's and her own death. But nobody would ever believe her.

In some versions Cassandra never accepted Apollo's advances, and he cursed her for rejecting him. In some, she was asleep when he tried to have sex with her. In one, Apollo curses her by spitting in her mouth.

In all versions, everyone believed she was either a liar or insane.

We studied the Greeks in year six. Our teacher, Miss Lilith, had the girls act out a 'Primary School appropriate' (i.e. rape / child murdering free) *Trojan Women*. I was cast as Amazon queen and alpha female Hecuba. It was the biggest part, but very shouty and sword-swingy. I knew Joseph Welsh from my class would be watching and I didn't want him to see me as that. So I swapped with Gemma Petty, she played football so I knew she wouldn't mind being Hecuba. And I sensed that I could really impress with Cassandra.

I took the role very seriously. I burst on that stage in my bedsheet toga as full 'swivel-eyed nut job'; eyes crossed, backcombed hair, screeching and spitting as I rang out my proclamations, ensuring no one could mistake my terror, that Troy was about to fall.

The audience wet themselves. They laughed, they pointed, they even applauded. They did impressions in the playground. Joseph Welsh said it was hilarious. I laughed along. It wasn't the reaction I'd have chosen, but I'd stolen the show at least. Many UK theatres will attest that wasn't the last time I left any semblance of nuance in the wings. I got the point across, anyway, that Cassandra was a total loon.

I am sitting at Bell and Jim's kitchen table with my hands hovering over a 'Send' button.

It is just after seven thirty in the evening. Bell is making a pot roast, which she put in the oven two hours ago. Within the last hour I've sat in contemplative silence, and watched her rub a peeled garlic clove around a square glass oven-proof dish and put the clove to one side. She then peeled and sliced four large King Edward potatoes thinly but not too thinly and put them in layers inside it. After that she poured a cup of milk and a cup of double cream into a saucepan with the garlic clove (and another one for luck), then when it was boiled she poured it over the potatoes, then grated gruyere cheese all over the top ('Technically, the traditional recipe doesn't call for it,' she'd let me know, 'but that's just cutting your nose off to spite your face. Add the cheese, stupid'), then salt and pepper. Bell insists dauphinoise is one of her bad dishes she's never happy with because it 'always fucking curdles'. I know why she's doing it, though. Another fancy ploy to get me to eat. It's just gone in the oven and even though it takes an hour the timer's been set for twenty minutes because Bell cooks things with care and patience and doesn't bung them in and hope for the best like I do. Winston is lying by my feet with his legs under him like a hairy puddle.

Myself, I am staring at a laptop screen where Twitter is open. There is a white box on the screen containing an attachment, an attachment that with a click of my finger on the blue 'Send' button beneath it will have an infinite reach. It will go to more places than I will ever go in my entire lifetime. I have the power to send my truth across the world.

And for some reason, as I sit here I'm remembering the myth about Cassandra. How, right or wrong, people tend not to take women seriously. Especially when that woman is me.

There is so much fear in this kitchen.

The timer goes off. Bell comes to look at the potatoes and pull them out of the oven with the gingham oven glove. They are shiny on the top and fizzing with heat at the edges. She prods them with a big spoon, puts them back in, and sets the timer for twenty more minutes.

Earlier today, I politely declined all offers to tell my story in the papers. Theo came over, and I told them I'd written a statement. I then sat Theo, Bell and Jim on the couch, read it aloud, and encouraged interrogation.

'Why are you bothering?' asked Bell.

'I dunno, just feel like I have to,' I told her.

'But Sue, why do you need to say these things now?' asked Theo.

'I dunno, I just want to,' I told them.

'Do you think you should write it again, mate, but sound less angry?' asked Jim.

'I have the right to my anger, actually, Jim,' I indignantly replied, then realised he was absolutely right, sighed and said, 'Sorry, no you're absolutely right.'

I took out the phrases that had made my friends' faces darken as they listened. Got rid of swearing. Took out anything that made me dangerous, any sharp corners. Eliminated the risk of being that kind of woman, a 'woman spurned'. Even though

115

I am one. But I was tactical. If I spoke with an edge, only the edge would be heard.

Once we were all satisfied I took a screenshot of what I had written, and saved it on the laptop as 'statement argh!'. I then sat at the kitchen table, attached it to a blank tweet, and now my hands are shaking as they hover over the 'Send' button on Twitter. Nothing lights a fire under one's arse like being underestimated does, but still. I keep thinking of that play in year six, of the laughter, and the pointing. How I'd taken myself seriously, and they'd laughed and pointed all the same.

My agent seems to think it'll be the case. 'This will cause a storm,' he'd said. I had to talk to more people in the industry, canvass some opinions from women who understood what was at stake. So I reached out to a theatre director I've worked with a few times and have always loved, called Mags. Mags is in her mid-sixties if you ask her, but early seventies if you ask Wikipedia; a former leading actress who happens to be the most 'white wine for lunch at the Ivy, darling' woman I know. I don't say that to denigrate; I would love to be that person. She's also an absolute wrecking ball – she spent most of the late seventies slapping away wandering hands backstage at the RSC, and legend has it once kneed Oliver Reed in the balls.

After she'd read 'Statement argh', she called me and I sat outside on the cold garden furniture again, smoking a fag next to Theo with the phone on speaker.

'Now hear me out, darling,' she said, 'thank God you reached out, because here's the ruddy truth of it.'

She said I'd never come out on top here – she's seen this hundreds of times over the years, and the bloke always gets away with it because that's the world we're living in. It's a sodding shame but there we are. Anyway, she said, I had appeared so beautiful and dignified on the television on Saturday night. So beautiful. So dignified. Theo made a sick face. She said I wouldn't want

116

that to be destroyed, would I, the image the public currently has of me, of being so beautiful/dignified? She said I wouldn't want them saying I was in it for the money, or the fame. She said I don't want to stoop to their level, do I, by getting involved? She said every time a director or employer googles me, I wouldn't want this tacky scandal to come up, would I?

She reminded me of a tabloid scandal a couple of years ago which I vaguely remembered. A 'handsome chappie', as Mags called him, who happened to be a Hollywood movie star, was going out with his Hollywood movie star girlfriend but she was papped kissing her co-star. Mags had waited with bated breath for him to rip into her but instead he stayed com*pletely* silent and rose above it. He came across so dignified, she said, it was beautiful. It didn't affect his career at all in the end. In fact, he's more successful and handsome than ever. Did I want to be a salacious tell-tale or a respected actor? And that's when I stopped being scared and became shocked.

I could never be the same as that person because my options weren't the same as his. I'm a woman, and in Mags' world that meant I could either be dignified, beautiful and silent – or a whinger.

I exhaled smoke over the phone so that it looked like it had caught fire. 'The difference, of course,' I said, 'is that person was a millionaire man.' Theo stood up and made a spaffing gesture, and to be fair I did just win an argument against a lady shark.

'She's just old school,' I told Theo after I'd hung up.

'Look, I'm a queer person, I would die for any actress over sixty,' Theo said, 'But it's fucked up how she can understand how much sexism is going on here, and still encourage you to play into it.'

Still, something about that conversation stuck with me, that threat of losing face, losing dignity and beauty. I'd thought I had nothing to lose, but there's always something. Like those little church mice in the Disney *Robin Hood* film, who dress in rags and are so poor. A scene in it always makes me cry: the one in which they give a big coin they've been saving for a rainy day to the friar for the homeless even though they have nothing else at all. Then the Sheriff of Nottingham comes and casually takes the coin, and then takes them to prison as well.

The timer goes off in the kitchen. Bell comes to look at the potatoes and pull them out of the oven with the gingham glove. They are rusty at the edges and bubbling ferociously. She prods the top with a big spoon, puts them back in, and sets the timer for another twenty minutes.

But after the Mags business, I'd seen Maura. I realised I couldn't leave the house in case a journalist somehow found out I was here, so I asked if I could FaceTime her from the attic.

Maura is my therapist. Back in 2014 I had felt very sad about my career, and about money, and the Facebook messages with Mia, and I wanted not to be. I wasn't doing very well at not feeling permanently gutted, so I took myself off to someone whose job it is to help. Anyway, at first I saw a swanky therapist who wore suits from Calvin Klein and cost £100 an hour, which didn't alleviate my money stresses at all. She was also kind of a bitch, sorry but she was. I then went the other way and saw this shamanic man who would leave huge benign silences that set me on edge, and once I'd had the thought that perhaps those silences were a sexual power thing it wouldn't go away until I did. Then when I had a breakdown during the interval of a Chekhov play I was in, one of the coolest and most together actresses I'd ever worked with said, 'You should see my therapist, she's amazing', so I did.

And Maura *is* amazing. She's an elderly Irish woman who loves a pashmina and has a mischievous smile that suggests she might love the craic as well. She's so amazing that when I sat on the attic bed with the laptop on my knees and casually told

118

her about the kiss in the papers, she shook her head and said:

'Scum.'

She's amazing because when I said earlier today, 'Did you know I was lying about the relationship being fine?' she said, 'Of course I knew, I'm a therapist.'

When I said, 'Do you remember a couple of months ago when you asked me what I liked about Him, and I searched and searched but couldn't answer?' she'd said, 'What do you think?'

'I knew He'd have an affair with His partner,' I said. 'I even told Him so before He started *Strictly*. Is there an argument that this was a self-fulfilling prophecy?'

'No, there isn't,' she said. 'What did He say, out of interest, when you told Him that?'

'Oh, that there was something wrong with me.' Now for the kicker. I took a deep breath, knowing that Maura's answer would inform every memory I ever made from hereon in. 'Doing that, saying stuff like that, that's a thing, isn't it?'

'Yes,' she said.

A while back I heard about this thing – gaslighting. It might have been because of *Love Island*, actually. I'd googled it one night in our bed, when He was asleep, and there was this article on the Stylist site or somewhere like that: '10 signs you're being gaslit.' Some of the stuff I'd never associated with abuse. Abuse feels like an epic, inflammatory word and this stuff, it was so everyday. Like being told I'm making stuff up when I was sure I was right, then being told I 'always' do it. Being love bombed with presents and niceness because He'd felt bad or said something horrible. I'd even thought that one was meant to be a nice thing, and it had *felt* bloody nice. That dopamine – it's like someone's thrown you out of a fifteen-storey window then caught you an inch above the pavement. It's such a rush that, even when the threat of falling inevitably comes back around, you hang in there, if it means getting caught like that again.

There was also stuff on that list that had felt heavier. The not knowing who I was anymore. The mentioning in passing, by Him, that my friends weren't actually my friends. I'd had to stop reading the article there. It had felt as though I was being watched.

It had been months since I thought about that, but for the last few days, the voice inside me had been asking the question, over and over. I asked Maura about it then.

'Is it gaslighting?'

'Yes, it is.'

'Ah, fuck. There's no going back from that.'

Maura's face shone out from the screen in front of me, the pixels creating an aura around her. 'Can you tell me the difference between gaslighting and emotional abuse?' I asked.

'I'll do my best,' she said. 'So gaslighting is calling into question somebody's mental state, making them question themselves. It's a very cruel thing to do, very cruel, because of course when people don't trust their own mental state they often act erratically out of fear that they're insane. And then the perpetrator sees the behaviour and feels justified in calling it out as mental, or psychotic, and the victim feels as though the perpetrator is right. It's a cycle that over time means the perpetrator can begin to essentially write the story of whatever relationship it is, rub out events, do whatever they like. It can happen at work, or between friends, not just romantic partners.'

'Jesus,' I said.

'Emotional abuse, though,' she continued, 'which can also be called psychological abuse, is an umbrella term that gaslighting comes under. But it's more than that; it also includes things like, oh, being insulted, being sworn at, making someone feel intimidated or bullying them, putting them down and isolating them from other people. It's clever, really – if you can call these people clever. There aren't any clear physical signs, like a black eye or an arm in a sling. But signs are there if you look hard enough. Like a person being vacant, or their personality being shaved down. Which is why perpetrators quite often try to isolate them from the people who know them well, saying they're not their real friends or they don't have their best interests at heart or some other crap.

'Feck me,' Maura said. 'Those people are damaged. They're looking for help, but they can't accept it, not really. At their core they don't value themselves enough. It's sad, really. Not excusable but. Not always intentional. Sad.'

I tentatively told Maura I'd written something. That I was thinking of posting it online. She asked me to email it over, and took her time reading it. As I waited nervously for her reply, I considered how I no longer had a life story devoid of abuse. What would I say if I met my younger self? What would I tell her to do differently? Nothing probably. There was no telling me at that age.

'Rebecca.' Maura said my name, so I knew it was serious. 'You have to do this. Because you have a voice.'

I Stayed

Because it's what I've always wanted

The fourteenth of February is a day I've dreaded every year since we all went from just kids, to 'single or taken'. School is a classic V-Day stress dream, red roses and pink envelopes and French kisses once again noted in my life by their absence. Jamie Davis got Kelly Taylor – who looks exactly like Shell Dockley from *Bad Girls* – a box of Guylian chocolate seashells. Her Bunsen burner tap is opposite mine in Physics and I saw her showing Laura Watts. It was a full-size box as well, not the measly one that's only got three shells and a seahorse. It's a level of sophistication and decadence far beyond what I ever imagined Jamie Davis was capable of. Before today I only knew him as the boy who could correctly guess girls' bra sizes.

I am fifteen years old, and me and my Rachelfrom*Friends* haircut are lying on my bed in my mum's semi-detached (formerly my parents' semi-detached). The haircut doesn't suit me. In fact, it only serves to highlight how much I do *not* look like Rachel from *Friends*. On my bedroom wall are posters of Leonardo DiCaprio, Duncan from Blue, Dawson from *Dawson's Creek* ... My Aryan male fantasies have the slightest whiff of 'Hitler Youth' about them. Everything is pink, princess pink, a decision that was slapped all over the walls aged eleven. The pink bookcase is alphabetically crammed with every single copy of the *Sweet Valley High* series, the official *Buffy the Vampire Slayer Watcher's Guide*, and a copy of *Jane Eyre* with the cruellest/sexiest Mr Rochester chapters earmarked. Perched atop it is a small grainy television set, on which a blonde woman called Lolo Ferrari is bouncing her gigantic norks up and down so much her top is riding up over them, as a camp French man wiggles his eyebrows at the camera. This is *Eurotrash,* a real-life sex cartoon for adults that I never know quite what is happening in but that I never miss if I'm at home, which I always am, because it's on on Friday nights. It's almost silent, volume on the lowest bar so no one in the house will hear Lolo's jiggly moans and know that I'm a perv. The glow from the telly is the only light in the room, making the pinks not so princessy, more like what you see on a video in biology of when an endoscope goes down a throat, or up a bum.

Nicola Bailey from my year – year ten – is currently having a Valentine's Day house party. Nicola Bailey is allowed to bleach her hair, and always wears it in a tight ponytail with two strands pulled out at the front, which she gels with VO5 so they are crispy. The popular girls from my year all have crispy strands, most of them carry Jane Norman bags and all of them are going to her party. Along with every single fit boy, and all the boys that aren't fit but are loud. Her parents just *let her have a party*, and not because they're being responsible, not because they're of the opinion that if they're doing it in the house they're not doing it down the rec in the dead of night. Nicola's parents let her have it because they're not boring and weird and they don't hate their daughter and actually want her to have a fun life. Apparently they get booze in for everyone! My mum won't let me get *straighteners*.

Lolo unpeels a banana, and the French man looks to camera. She feeds it to him. The camera cuts to a blond man walking a gimp on a lead.

126

There are three hundred kids in my year at school, Thorpe St Andrew High School. I am not unpopular; I have friends to eat lunch with and a best friend called Katy who's a kooky witch à la Willow from *Buffy* (and who fancies Pacey from *Dawson's Creek*, meaning we're very well matched). But I am in all the top sets and Nicola is in the bottom ones, so we've never crossed paths. Incidentally, I am in the plays and the choir. I have gone in the minibus to other schools for debates and hockey matches. I make people laugh, sometimes even some of the popular girls as we've stood by the long jump pit in PE, which I refuse to jump in as it's pretty much a giant piss and shit tray for cats in the area. But let me tell you, when you add one hard-earned academic record and countless extracurricular school achievements together, it all adds up to me basically having 'virgin' tattooed on my forehead. I have accidentally followed the blueprint of 'good girl' and wound up as Sandy at the sleepover in *Grease*, sitting on the side in my frilly floor-length nightie and getting taken the piss out of by Rizzo. What I wouldn't give to be at that party of Rizzo's right now, drinking Archers and lemonade and maybe doing something glamorous like tossing someone off, or getting taken to hospital to have my stomach pumped the way Paige Harvey did at Nicola's Christmas one.

Something else that happened at Nicola's Christmas party was that Hannah Jenkins got pregnant. She'd just split up with Michael Hunt and wouldn't tell anyone who she did it with in case he properly kicked their head in. She had to miss school one morning to get an abortion. It was no big deal, it was her second one anyway, she'd had one in year nine too. All I took from Hannah's abortion seminar the next day in the changing rooms after tag rugby, which I overheard while trying to flatten my frizzy hair into a tight ponytail, was that Hannah Jenkins had had sex with at least two people, and I hadn't even kissed anyone. Save for some frankly excellent repartee on MSN

Messenger when Greg Osborne thought I was someone else, I haven't even come close.

The French man onscreen comes out dressed as a doctor. He uses a stethoscope on a brunette woman's boobs.

Desirability at Thorpe St Andrew High is very clear. If you are a boy, it's about how good you are at football. If you are a girl, it's how big your tits are. This is unfair to begin with because, of course, being possessed of a natural footballing ability is a plus, but boys can *get* good at football through practice. You cannot practise getting bigger tits. Your fate is sealed from a C cup downwards. Nicola Bailey's tits are udder-like. Jamie Bailey reckons she's a 36DD.

I am a 32B, and that's with a water bra from Debenhams that takes you up a cup.

To add insult to injury, Katy is at Nicola's party! *My* best friend, who got talking to Nicola when they'd both sat out of swimming because of their periods (Nicola didn't actually have her period, she lied because the chlorine makes bleached hair go green). Nicola said Katy should come to the party so she bloody well did! Like it was normal, like it was a simple case of turning up, and not participating in a complete civic overhaul. Katy asked me to go with her, which was so stupid I obviously said no. Not because I'm scared or frigid or whatever, but because I'm clever enough to know what will happen. I will most likely get properly drunk for the first time and I won't be in control of my actions and will do something truly mortifying like singing 'Step in Time' from *Mary Poppins* and it will go around the school that I'm a lightweight and I'll have a stigma attached to me for ever and I won't get a good job or a husband. So I'm staying in my lane, thanks very much.

Poor Katy. I actually feel really sorry for her. She just doesn't get how the world works.

The second-from-last stair creaks just outside my door and I quickly switch channel. I hear Mum opening Jake's door, the one next to mine, and just stand there.

'What are you even *doing*?' I mouth to myself.

I knew a divorce was coming. They didn't tell me she instigated it, but Dad's been doing a lot of crying (and he's the man here!) so I put two and two together. I'm glad he's gone, actually, so I don't have to watch how Mum started speaking to him. Like a trapped cat that had been backed into a corner by an insistent toddler. I literally asked her what he'd done and she'd said 'nothing' but you don't just divorce someone for doing nothing, do you? If he'd had an affair, or had been violent, that would make sense. People don't just *change their minds* in a marriage.

The other day Mum was in the bathroom for an hour so I asked what was wrong with her; she said she was fine. Just like I am: fine. It's like, y'know, whatever. No need to talk it out or anything, to anyone. Katy can't relate, her parents do weird campervanning in the Lake District, they have matching cagoules. Jake's five, he doesn't understand, give him a Sun Lolly and he's happy.

Mum closes Jake's door and I can hear her sigh. Sighing to no one, like she's in a film. She goes back down the stairs and finally I can flick back to Channel 4, where a woman dressed as a schoolgirl is bending over for something on the floor.

Two beeps come from my Nokia 3310. A message from Katy: 'Miss u <3. U shld cum :-)'. Uh, and how exactly would I do that, Katy?! I'll just get a taxi, shall I, being as I'm a millionaire? Even if I had credit I wouldn't text back. Sometimes Katy is absolutely brain dead, to be totally blunt about things. If she gets fingered tonight I swear I'll have to kill myself.

I play a bit of Snake on the phone to calm down. If Rebecca Humphries turned up to Nicola Bailey's party, it would be catastrophic. No one is disappointed by those people, the crispy-hair girls. No one expects better from them. I have too much to tarnish. But oh my God, I want it.

I want to have said yes when I had the chance.

I want to not give a fuck about that essay on Act 2 Scene 2 of *Macbeth* due by Monday.

I want a one-night lobotomy.

The onscreen snake touches its own tail and dies.

I want to pick up a plastic pint glass from the countertop, not know whether it's mine, but let the alcohol scratch down the back of my throat anyway.

How I want to sit on a lap.

Want to do *shots*.

Want to bend over and for everyone to see my THONG.

Want to spray my name in aerosol on the living-room wall then set fire to it with a 50p lighter and watch it go up in flames along with my reputation.

I want to feel my cheeks puff up with chunder as I fling the seat off the toilet bowl.

I want to wear a Wonderbra with two fillets in each cup so my pointless 32As look like they're worth something as I dance to Christina Aguilera's 'Dirrty', the best song in the world.

I want my name to be scratched using a compass on all the high-school toilet doors in Norwich and the surrounding areas, next to a crude drawing of a dick with jizz squirting out.

Most of all I want to be touched in a way that isn't encouraging or congratulatory, that isn't a shake of the hand or a pat on the head. I want to feel my pedestal being ripped out from under me by a year-eleven Jack Ryder lookalike in powder-blue Fred Perry, with bleach-tipped curtains creating crystalline stalactites beneath the rim of his Burberry cap.

I want him to tell me things he's never told anyone before, and when he realises he has, I want him to feel the urge to buy me Guylian chocolate seashells (or Lindt balls if there aren't any).

I want him to look at me and say 'You're beautiful' so that I will hear what that sounds like at least once.

And, even though I hear it hurts like hell the first time, I want to be irresponsible and get knocked up by a boy with no name. Then I would have to get an abortion too, I would have a pill box from a clinic, I would have something to hold in my hands that proved that at some point, somebody had wanted me.

'But you don't like those boys.' That voice again, that stupid voice from inside, the one that doesn't seem to understand those boys are the only choice I have. Besides, no one else thinks they're scary. Or unfunny, or puerile.

'But *you* do,' says that stupid voice again, the voice that's always saying the wrong thing. No one else finds it horrible that those boys have league tables of girls who might give good blowjobs. No one else felt physically sick when they called Hannah a fat slag, or felt sad when loudmouth Adam Bulmer shouted out in history that Kelly Taylor's minge was too hairy, and that he knew cos Jamie Davis had told him. No one else seems to get scared or upset at the fact that if you have sex, you have to be up for discussion.

The French man bobs a small blonde woman up and down on his knee and my vagina is burning in vain. My vagina, what a pointless waste of time. All that thing does is expel expel expel, pours out dark angry gloopy blood that hurts me and gives me diarrhoea and ruins my bedsheets. It yearns so much it physically aches, but the truth is I have never touched it or looked at it. I carry it around with me like it's an embarrassing box I hide under my Diesel jeans and that isn't part of the rest of my body.

The stair creaks again and I change channel quickly. Mum stops outside my door. I hold my breath. *Go away*, I think as hard as I can. *Go away*.

A knock that's barely a knock. Oh God.

'Yep?' I pull the covers up around me, but she doesn't come in.

'Uh ...' She pauses on the other side of the door. 'Areyouallright?'

I swallow. 'Yeahareyou?'

131

'Yesthankyou.'

It hangs there. Nothing.

'All right then, night.' Her footsteps walk to the bathroom, I hear the light switch on. I exhale, and turn the channel back, where the French man is waving at the camera over the *Eurotrash* credits. I flick through the music channels, hoping to come across Pink's 'Just Like a Pill', which even though it's about an overdose and I wouldn't know where to find drugs of any kind, seems to speak directly to me. But the music channels are too grainy so I go back to Channel 4, where on *So Graham Norton* an old woman is fiddling around with a huge dildo in the shape of a tongue and the studio audience is laughing. It makes me want to scream at not finding it funny because I shouldn't be finding this stuff terrifying by now, at fifteen years old, I should not.

The thing I actually want most, you see, more than all the trysts in upstairs rooms in parties with boys who have curtains, is love. Love that is sexy and cool and beautiful and sweet and so profound it's bound to end in tragedy like Britney and Justin but God damn it will be a helluva ride all the same. Love that delivers pink envelopes on February 14th. Love that is everything.

Because love means I will never be alone. Love means I will accept myself. Love means my problems will be over.

I make a vow, here on my chaste pink sheets, beneath the gods of Duncan from Blue, Leonardo DiCaprio and Dawson from *Dawson's Creek*, that one day I will have a boyfriend who loves me, and everything will be better. And when I am in love, I will not let it die. When I have a boyfriend, I will be so thankful to him for saving me from this abject loneliness. When I have a boyfriend, I will do everything I can to make sure he doesn't get away.

But if I want to be in love, I know how this works. I've seen *Grease* about four hundred times. Sandy doesn't get Danny by being Sandy.

To get a Danny, a Sandy has to become a Rizzo.

I Left

Because I make my own decisions

Crouch End, 8 October 2018

The timer goes off again in the kitchen, where my hands are still hovering over the keyboard. The dauphinoise comes out the colour of the brown glass mugs my nan used to have. The kitchen windows go dull with steam, and it's time to sit in the dining room.

No, I can't click 'Send'. I'm too afraid. I will swallow this whole thing down with my potatoes like a good girl. Bell told me last night I'm safe here. If I send this, I put everything in jeopardy.

'Whenever you're ready,' Bell tells me now, holding a big dish full of ruffley greens.

'Yep,' I say as she goes in.

'Red or white, mate?' Jim calls from the dining room.

'Don't mind,' I call back, shutting the laptop, putting my fear to bed.

I get up from my chair, and as I get to the doorway something occurs to me about the myth of Cassandra. That maybe I've missed the point. Maybe it wasn't that she was never believed. Maybe the point is she knew she wouldn't be but chose to speak the truth anyway. Because if she didn't, something worse might happen than being called a liar.

And when that occurs to me, safety doesn't feel so safe any more. Safety feels like yielding. Safety feels like seeing a significant opportunity in my life to assert the person I am, and opting instead to be passive.

And now I'm more fearful than ever. Of, in years to come, looking back on my life and seeing what I *didn't* do.

I turn around, go back to the table, open the laptop and press Send.

Then I go and sit down in the dining room.

'I've sent it,' I say.

'OK,' says Bell, and nobody says anything else.

Not a word.

I hear my phone vibrating from the kitchen, we all do but pretend we don't. I am asked by Jim to please pass the creamy leeks. As I clasp my hands around the navy ceramic bowl, the phone buzzes again.

'Too dramatic,' the vibrations hum. 'Too loud.' 'Too much.'

I Stayed

Because I am too much

The first time I saw a penis there were two of them.

Suburban Norwich, 1992. Roads upon roads of semi-detached houses, some flapping England flags from the upstairs window, all displaying hanging baskets. In each direction, an estate; the Sprowston estate (quite rough), the Dussindale estate (very rough), the Heartsease estate (extremely rough) and the Plumstead estate (terrifying, more written-off cars than houses, slobbery dogs bigger than humans). Picture a more wholesome, more bumpkinny, less culturally diverse *West Side Story*. On Friday evenings, the low wall outside The Frying Machine fish and chip shop by the Heartsease is rammed with pre-teens gorging on Panda Pops and crispy scraps of fried batter from paper bags, the bewildering melody of the Norfolk dialect rising and falling on the air around them. Me, I'd be the five-year-old with big blue cartoon eyes and a thick lisp in the back of her mum's Mini Metro, watching them leapfrog over the concrete bollards, waiting for a battered sausage and singing along to Disney *Sing-Along Songs* tapes as loud as she can.

I've always been loud, in a non-deliberate way, ever since I was two and would stand in Mum's trolley at Tesco holding a baguette like a microphone and being Kylie Minogue. Lots of grown-ups tell me I'm loud, and tell my parents, and tell each other. 'You're a loud one!' 'She's not shy, is she?' 'She's got some confidence, especially for a girl!' That last one is important because being loud is quite boyish, but I don't scream or charge around, and I'm not rough. I love being a girl, I like wearing dresses and things that are pink. I'm loud in a way that's more like putting my hand up to answer questions, speaking in a big voice, and putting out there what it is that I want in a volume that I can be sure will be paid attention to.

St William's Primary School lies right in the middle of all the estates, a sprawling labyrinth that from a bird's-eye view takes the unfortunate shape of a swastika. I'm not allowed beyond the infant corridor; a long hallway with a scuffed parquet floor, coloured classroom displays above lines of coat pegs, and lunchboxes stacked Tetris style (mine is a *Little Mermaid* one). I'm a really good girl. I have never broken a single rule here. But I am the loudest by far of all thirty children in Mrs Mallett's class, the other twenty-nine of whom were sitting in a circle on the classroom carpet yesterday morning, when this story began.

Mrs Mallett had been explaining about jobs, which I hadn't needed to listen to because by five I have everything figured out about the direction my life is headed in. One look at the class sticker chart on the wall will tell you I'll probably be fine for ever – there are so many stars in a row next to my name it almost divides the length of the wall in two. I have never received an 'at least you tried!' star either. When I try, I don't fail, and this is the most important lesson I have learned since starting school.

Mrs Mallett went around the cross-legged circle, each little body clad in the pale blue shirt and grey shorts (boys) or blue and white gingham dress (girls) of the school uniform, asking us what we'd like to be when we grew up. I was half listening, half carefully tapering sections of my hair into a neat point, ready to place them in my mouth to suck on. Zoe Ford had just said she'd like to be a nurse.

'That makes sense, Zoe,' said Mrs Mallett, 'because you're very kind and helpful.'

And that was fair, I had surmised to myself, chomping a strand between my teeth and curling the loose end about my tongue. Zoe is perfectly nice. I mean, nurse seemed a bit 'inside the box', but sure.

'And what about you, Zoe T?' continued Mrs M.

The other Zoe in my class, Zoe Taylor, is always called Zoe T even though Zoe Ford isn't called Zoe F. It was an alphabetical thing, but it'd always occurred to me that if there were two Rebeccas it would be the other one that had the second initial, alphabetical or no.

'A nurse too!' said Zoe T, as I sat with a look of exasperation on my face and a lock of hair in my gob. *Seriously, Zoe T,* I thought. *Have an original thought in your head for once.*

But Mrs Mallett said, 'Well, you're very kind and helpful too,' which is how I knew Mrs Mallett was phoning it in. Zoe T is honestly so blah, and I'm not just saying that because she got given Mary in the Nativity.

'And how about you, Rebecca? What would you like to be when you grow up?'

I stood up. Nobody else had stood up, so twenty-nine little faces turned upward to look at me with guppy mouths. I walked into the middle of the circle, threw my arms into the air as high as Mrs Mallett's eyebrows had raised, and lispily exclaimed:

'A PRINTHETH!'

The crowd went wild. I was being serious, so the instantaneous positivity from twenty-nine others was alarming to say the least. It was the first time it happened to me. Even Mrs Mallett smiled.

The twins couldn't stop laughing till lunchtime.

The twins are Sam and Daniel Watson. They look like the Milkybar Kid standing next to a mirror, but their combined demeanour is less 'Wild West alpha heroism' and more 'Sensitive, softly spoken beta'. Both want to be scientists, Sam a sea scientist, Daniel a dinosaur one. The only way anyone can tell them apart is Sam has a hearing aid, which makes him speak a little louder, but never as loud as me, which suits all three of us. We have been inseparable since I asked them to be my friends on the first day. They were the most dazzling things I'd ever seen. Two bodies, two minds, two beating hearts and *one face*!

Something else important happened earlier at St William's Primary. You see, the whole school swastika building is surrounded by green fields that aren't suitable to be played on until the weather gets better. But in assembly yesterday (following hymn number 5, 'Give Me Oil in My Lamp') our headmaster Mr Scarfe, the scariest man there is, had informed us that at lunchtime the fields would be open and that we would be allowed to scamper about on the grass until summer.

'BUT,' he had added, leaning forward on the lectern, 'you are *forbidden* to go in the bushes. And anybody that does *will* be caught, *and will be punished.*'

This is because the lush green fields themselves are caged in by dangerous, scratchy bushes that are themselves caged in by a six-foot fence. In fact, they aren't really bushes at all but semi-dense woodland that my imagination had for months filled with dark magic and wild animals.

Now, who can say whether it was the sense of empowerment from that first audience hysteria or the excitement at the freedom the fields were sure to bring come lunchtime, but even though I was a good girl with a gold-star record, and even though I was as terrified of punishment as I was of dark magic and wild animals, in that moment of the wild applause a thought had popped into my head:

We're going in those bushes at lunch.

Let me tell you, it is *divinely* easy to break the rules when you are a model pupil and never on the dinner ladies' troublemaking radar. It was the most natural thing in the world, to march up to a set of matching boys, tell them 'Follow me', and merrily lead them to someplace none of us were allowed.

Carefully we crept, over and under and around, beneath triangles of bright blue sky crisscrossed with emerald foliage. Everything else around us was faded and crispy, gnarly roots and fingers of withered branches, all in the sepia tones of a pirate's treasure map. Bits of dry soil gathered in chunks that soundlessly crumbled to nothing when the three of us trod over them. There were a few ancient Frazzles packets here and there, remnants of misbehaviour that had gone before us, and stuck upside down on the jutting limb of a tree was an empty plastic bottle that looked like Vimto but which we couldn't be sure about because the label had gone white from sun fading. Some broken brown glass told us going any further would be perilous, so the three of us stopped on a slight incline, just about able to stand at full height, Daniel a little breathless (asthma). And before I could even register my thoughts, I had cupped my hands around my mouth in secrecy and, though we were totally alone, whispered so fast that my breath had to run to catch up with the words:

'How about we – we – we take our clothes off?' And I smiled a closed-mouth smile of exhilaration and perhaps also fear.

Because you see, I knew being in the woods was naughty. But I knew this would be much, much naughtier.

I hung my blue and white gingham dress, white vest and pink knickers in that order on a too-thin branch that sagged under the weight. I could hear the boys' disbelieving giggles, and saw at my feet a cloud of dirt forming from their clothes being dropped to the ground. I kept my shiny buckle-up pumps from Clarks on, and my white socks trimmed with lace.

And there we all stood, three little white blotches with our arms by our sides. Frozen in the face of brand-new, body-shaped facts. The boys were different from one another. Different from me.

That's when I started breathing from the top bit of my chest, the bit just under my neck. Two of them and one of me. Though no one had ever expressly told me not to ask the twins to get naked, I suddenly was very aware that this had been my idea.

Daniel laughed nervously. Sam did too. Both faces looked at me as if to say, *Is this all right?* And all at once everything that had felt serious felt very silly. I put my hands over my mouth and laughed into my palm in astonishment and glee, and their bodies bent in half from holding their tummies and giggling so hard. The two of them jumped a little in the air (not too high because of the branches). I did the twist like in the Jive Bunny song and thought, *I can do things like this for ever, and there is so much of for ever left!*

'Shall we go back?' I asked once the laughter felt like enough.

'OK!' said Daniel.

'This is a secret for us, isn't it?'

'Yes,' they both said at the same time, and we all laughed again because twins saying things at the same time is funny.

I scrambled to pick the girls' clothes up off the floor, the branch having sagged under their weight, and only narrowly avoided being whipped in the face as the branch shot back up again. My dress was mucky from the dirt on the ground, and I brushed it off as we ran back over roots and under branches and around tree trunks and out of the bushes and back to our classroom and later home to our mummies and daddies.

Now we get to today. This morning, the twins behaved strangely. They didn't sit next to me in the circle, and they didn't wave back from across it. They didn't come and sit with me in milk and biscuit break, and I couldn't find them when I ate my lunch. I was sitting on the field with my legs out in front, picking petals off a daisy and putting them in my pocket to make a perfume with later, when the boys came and stood above me and blocked out the sun. I knew it was Sam who was holding a blue carrier bag that they give you in corner shops, because of the hearing aid.

'Hello,' Sam said.

'Hello,' I said.

'Our mummy said we have to give this back to you because, because we didn't mean to pick them up it was an accident.' He handed me the bag.

'Thank you,' I said. I rustled around the blue plastic. Inside were a pair of pink knickers. My pink knickers. Oh no. I knew from the class on what your mummy and daddy did as a job that their mummy was a policewoman. This is worse than being caught, this is criminality. I'm a felon, I'm like a little girl Burglar Bill. I will probably go to prison. Daniel takes a puff on his inhaler, and I wish I had one too.

'I'm thorry,' I say.

'We don't, we think we don't want to be friends with you any more.' Sam looked sad.

I nod. 'OK.'

'It's because, well ... ' Daniel looked frightened. 'It's just because you are too bossy.'

Something warm happened underneath the skin on my toes. It travelled up through my legs, then up my body and into my cheeks until I was hot all over and it was a miracle the earth hadn't melted underneath me.

'All right then.'

Sam said, 'Sorry.'

My bottom lip trembled. It was so slight, but it caused Sam to wipe his eyes, and sniff. Which made Daniel sniff, and start to cry. And it's then I could see, right before my eyes, how upsetting my bossiness was to other people. How frightening even the slightest movement I made was.

'Don't cry,' I said, shaking my head and sucking my breath in. 'I'm not crying any more, look.' And when I stopped, so did they.

But I wanted to carry on. I wanted to cry for the rest of lunch, sat on the field on my own.

I want to cry now, at my desk, which is why I can't listen to Mrs Mallett talking about sums at the front of the class.

'Rebecca, is everything all right?' Mrs Mallett's voice cuts through the clouds. 'You're not normally this quiet.'

Every little face is turned around to look at my desk. My stupid loudness, drawing attention to me even when it isn't there! I bob my head yes.

Mrs Mallett pauses. 'All right, everyone, put on your art aprons for printing. Rebecca, would you mind coming with me outside? I'd like to have a talk.'

She knows about the knickers. I look at the twins on my way out, who both stand there, thin lipped.

Mrs Mallett closes the door, and the feral noise from art class deadens. She squats so we are face to face. 'Is there anything you'd like to talk about?'

I bite my lip, and look at the pink handprint above my peg, and my pink duffel coat underneath it. There is a bit of blue plastic peeking out of the pocket from where I stuffed the evidence.

'No.'

'Are you sure? It's all right, you can tell me.'

But how can I? How can I tell her that I went into the bushes and ignored the rules because at my core I am nothing but a loudmouth bossy-boots? How can I fall all the way from the heights I've reached, from a sky teeming with gold stars, and not break all the bones in my body?

'You're all right, aren't you?' She reaches and gives my hand a playful waggle.

All the grown-ups were right about me, of course they were, they are grown-ups and I'm only five. I've been too much and upset those nice quiet boys. I have failed for the very first time, and it's almost too big to comprehend. Because I have failed at being what a girl is supposed to be.

Mrs Mallett smiles at me. So I wipe my eyes and my nose with the back of my hand, then I blink, and smile back.

'There we go!'

Hang on. It can't have passed just like that, can it?

'You're a good girl.'

And then I smile for real. It has. No one will ever know. And I smile even wider when it occurs to me that I haven't failed at all, I have succeeded. I've discovered another thing I am good at. I am good at pretending I'm all right when I'm sad.

Back at my desk, as I'm printing with my Maris Piper, I think about what would have happened if I hadn't been so good at pretending. I've been told off for much less than this, so I know it would have been catastrophic. My mummy and daddy would have been called in to the school. I would have been taken to headmaster and scariest-man-there-is Mr Scarfe. Rumours of my threesome with the twins would have spread around that playground like nits, and you can't comb that out with a prescription solution. I might have been thrown out of school, might have been abandoned, might have become an orphan like Oliver and had to walk to London, and I don't know the way. But none of that has to happen. I saved my life by behaving how I *should*, instead of how I wanted to.

I paint a potato self-portrait, and Mrs Mallett chooses it to hang on display.

I begin to get good at saying I am fine when I'm not really.

I make up with the twins too, before the week is out. We hug one playtime, and have our milk and biscuits together again every single day.

And – though it's barely noticeable – I begin to stop singing too loudly in assembly.

I Left

Because I am capable of more

**Crouch End, 8 October 2018,
30 seconds later**

Jim takes the bowl of leeks. From the kitchen, the phone continues to vibrate. I give in and run to it.

'OH MY GOD HAVE U SEEN MUMX.'

Mum doesn't have Twitter. Something is happening.

'Bell?'

She runs in.

'Look at Twitter; I can't, I can't do it.'

She unlocks her phone. She starts to scroll. And as she does her face goes from trepidation to astonishment to euphoria.

'Three thousand likes.'

'What?'

She looks again. 'Three thousand five hundred now.'

'*What?*'

'They're all good,' says Bell. I watch her finger scroll her screen. 'It's all good!'

I open the laptop to the same Twitter page as before. Only my notifications have gone crazy, numbers changing constantly. Papers and journalists are retweeting my statement, quoting sections. Women's Aid have retweeted it. They're saying this is an important moment or something.

'Alexa,' Bell says, while looking directly at me. 'Play "I'm Every Woman" by Chaka Khan.'

Jim runs past us into the living room as the song blasts out, then runs back to the kitchen doorway. 'It's on the news at ten!'

'Nine thousand likes!' says Bell.

I turn my phone over. Message after message. Close friends, non-close friends, people I know, my dentist, Winston's vet has texted me! People I thought would never speak to me again. Everyone is proud of me, everyone is inspired by me. Emails, too. One is from an actor called Spencer who I've only met once and barely know but have always quite fancied. He says my fortitude is beyond compare.

'"And the first ten of the series goes to Rebecca Humphries"!' Bell reads from her phone, then laughs.

I walk out of the kitchen into the living room, slide open the French windows, step on to the cold stone patio and scream at the moon.

Only when all my breath has gone do I realise who would have definitely also seen this, and then I can't breathe anything back in. I find the number of my old upstairs neighbour at Samstat Road. I text her, begging her to check on Him, holding on to Bell's shoulder with the other hand, digging my fingernails in. The neighbour says there are journalists packed outside the house.

'Jim, please text his friends, please get someone round there, get the numbers from my phone.'

Jim does.

My neighbour messages back telling me no one is answering the door of our flat. Fuck, what have I done? My power has unleashed destruction on someone else. I feel so responsible for Him. Him, at home, alone. Him, turning His phone over just like I did and seeing those messages from all the people He knows, but all of them bad. And there's no sound from inside the flat.

This is fear. This is actual fear.

'I never meant for this to happen,' I tell Bell and Jim. 'I just wanted to say my piece. I've ruined His life.'

'He ruined His own life,' Bell tells me. 'And you may have just saved yours.'

What follows is the following:

8/10/18 22:35
Bell, Jim and I sit in the living room on our phones reading Twitter responses out loud to each other as they keep coming through. Bell reads out a thread of tweets from a journalist, entitled 'The ten best things about Rebecca Humphries' statement'. Chaka Khan is still playing: some of her lesser known hits. Jim reads out another Twitter response to my statement that simply says 'Bit dramatic lol' and we all piss ourselves laughing.

8/10/18 23:04
Bell goes to bed. Jim and I continue refreshing and reading new tweets.

8/10/18 23:36
Jim goes to bed and I continue refreshing and reading new tweets.

8/10/18 23:59
I continue refreshing and reading new tweets.

9/10/18 00:57
I go to the attic and continue refreshing and reading new tweets.

9/10/18 01:45
I continue refreshing and reading new tweets.

9/10/18 04:36
I fall asleep.

9/10/18 07:04
I wake up and log on to Twitter. Over fifty thousand likes, countless replies to the statement featuring support and solidarity. Anecdotes of experiences similar to mine. Some celebrity solidarity DMs.

9/10/18 07:42
Aunt Nett texts telling me Piers Morgan has stood up for Him on *Good Morning Britain* but that 'it's OK though Minx, Susanna Reid is on our side'.

9/10/18 07:56
Bell sends a picture from her journey to work. It's of a newsstand near Charing Cross station. My own face stares back at me over and over again. She tells me to zoom in to the *Mirror* because it's the best headline. It says, 'You're Cha-Cha Chucked!'

9/10/18 07:59
Jim brings me a coffee to the attic.

9/10/18 08:12
I scroll through thousands of supportive tweets, many featuring Beyoncé gifs, when one catches my eye. It says: 'If He was that bad, why did you stay eh?!' Theo has replied to it with 'Today's misogynist of the day goes to:' and a gif of applause with the word 'YOU!' in large letters.

9/10/18 09:00
Oonagh sends a YouTube link. It's a clip from Lorraine Kelly's show that morning, the showbiz segment. I see my statement

on a big screen behind Lorraine's sofa, and there's also a picture of me and Him that was taken at a theatre event a few years ago. Lorraine says she has to take her hat off to me. She signs the segment off with 'What a woman', which I repeat softly in her Scottish accent.

9/10/18 09:12
I see I have gained thirty thousand Twitter followers.

9/10/18 09:27
My agent calls to let me know he has been contacted by more or less every interviewing body on television and radio, from *Woman's Hour* to *This Morning*. ITV news want to do an interview special. I am asked if I would like a meeting with a documentary crew who are interested in my presenting a programme about gaslighting. We agree to say no to everything.

9/10/18 09:59
My name is top trending on Twitter. Hashtag Rebecca Humphries. On the 'explore' section of Twitter there is a picture of my face. I always hated that picture.

9/10/18 10:08
I have been emailed by all of the same tabloid papers again. All of them would like to discuss a higher fee than yesterday's should I be interested. A right-wing Sunday magazine has offered five figures (mid range) to do an exclusive feature. I politely decline.

9/10/18 10:13
I have been retweeted by Caitlin Moran, who has also followed me. I direct message her to thank her. She tells me her WhatsApp group were talking about it that morning, and they all send massive solidarity.

9/10/18 10:27

I scroll through hundreds of Twitter replies. Theo has replied to every single negative comment with something hilarious. I find the tweet that says, 'If He was that bad, why did you stay eh?' I stare at it.

9/10/18 11:03

Theo messages saying I'm so famous they literally can't, they just *cannot*. They tell me that on *This Morning* Holly and Phil were joined by Vanessa Feltz and they all talked about me. They had someone on there as the opposition, and when they had argued on His behalf, Phil had said, 'But it was her *birthday*!' Theo isn't sure which is the more iconic, this or *Lorraine*.

9/10/18 11:42

The right-wing Sunday magazine emails back and offers six figures for an exclusive feature. I politely decline.

9/10/18 12:30

Jim brings a cheese and pickle sandwich, takes away the coffee that has gone cold.

9/10/18 13:11

My agent calls to tell me not to worry about Janet Street-Porter and I say I don't know what he means. I google and see that on *Loose Women* she has printed out my statement and has edited it with a large pen because she says it's too long and boring.

9/10/18 13:16

The Sunday magazine contact emails back and says if I'm not interested in the six figures perhaps I would like to do the feature and they would be happy to donate the money to a women's charity, and that they're sure the charity would appreciate it.

9/10/18 13:27

A Hollywood A-lister who got my number from a mutual friend messages to say that they know what I'm going through and are sending love and respect.

9/10/18 13:39

Jim sends a message from downstairs. It's a picture of today's *Times* cartoon. It has the headline 'Strictly Come Brexit' and, in it, there's a caricature of Theresa May storming off from Michael Gove with a speech bubble that says, 'I'm leaving you, and I'm taking the cat!' I text back, 'Wtf is happening.' He replies, 'Mate, I know.'

9/10/18 13:42

I leave the bed for the first time to use the toilet. While there I scroll back through more thousands of supportive tweets. One of them asks whether we were in Disney World Florida in 2014, because she had seen someone who looked like Him shouting at his girlfriend and it was really upsetting. We were.

9/10/18 13:44

I go back to the attic and sit on the bed.

9/10/18 13:50

A teacher at a girls' school has replied to my statement on Twitter letting me know she got rid of her lesson plan this morning and went through my statement with the girls instead, engaging them in discussion in the hope they would begin to consider their own worth.

9/10/18 13:52

I scroll back through thousands upon thousands of supportive tweets to see how many likes 'If He was that bad, why did you stay eh?' has. I read it again and again.

9/10/18 14:38

Theo sends a *Guardian* think piece about my statement. I google my name for the first time and see how many think pieces there are. The *Guardian*, *Grazia*, *Cosmo*, *The Pool*, blogs and local papers. One headline reads: 'Rebecca Humphries – the real winner of *Strictly Come Dancing*'. I get in touch with Marian Keyes, whose work Bell and I have always loved and who has started following me, to thank her for her tweets of support. She is an angel warrior woman, we chat about love and overcoming and those moments when your life goes mad.

9/10/18 15:06

My Auntie Lynne, who is a primary school teacher, texts, 'Minx, one of the young teaching assistants said in the staff room today that she had left her mean boyfriend this morning because of a statement from a woman named Rebecca Humphries. I said, "she's my niece!" and she asked me to tell you thank you (heart emoji).'

9/10/18 15:16

I scroll back through thousands of tweets to read the one that says, 'If he was that bad, why did you stay eh?' And I read it again
  and again
  and again
  and again.

I Stayed

Because I'm a lucky girl

Shepherd's Bush, May 2018

'Fucking hell. I just wanted to have *fun* this year!'

'One Fiorentina?'

The pizza is mine, but I can't say so because I have started to fucking cry again. I try to give the poor waiter a glance that says, *It's OK*, that says, *This is normal for us*. I try to make it less embarrassing for the guy, for myself, for Him, for us all, because that's usually my forte. But I can't today. I can't look up with wet eyes at yet another member of the hospitality industry that has interrupted a low-voiced argument over dinner.

'Actually, no.' I figure if that pizza gets put down in front of me the next step is asking if I'd like any pepper, and sitting weeping in Pizza Express with a giant pepper grinder in my face is the very definition of depressing. So what I do instead is say nothing, pick up my bag, follow the faux-vintage mosaic floor tiles to the front door and leave.

We're supposed to be going to a show later; His agent Vinnie has hooked us up with VIP tickets to a comedy gig down the road at the Hammersmith Apollo. We'd been killing time in Westfield shopping centre before dinner. He'd been sulking because I wouldn't let Him buy me a jumper in Whistles, orange cashmere, but it was stupidly expensive and I hadn't liked it *that* much. In Pizza Express I'd ordered the Fiorentina because I'd said it would make a good Drag name, which wasn't my best material but it'd made Him chuckle. I'd decided to bring up the Edinburgh festival, which is happening in August, three months from now. The show I've written and directed is being performed there, and I'd like to see how it's going at some point. He's due to be performing there for the whole month, staying in a nice flat. 'Can I stay with you for a couple of nights?' I had asked Him. 'There isn't anywhere else, really.' And that was when He'd said that, fucking hell, He just wanted to have fun this year.

I run down the escalators of Westfield. It is hot and loud, too many bodies. I barge past shoppers enjoying themselves, I run across roads without waiting for the green man. I can't see or hear anything because there's a tape playing in my head of my therapy session with Maura earlier this week. She was sat opposite me in that swively leather armchair with an ancient William Morris cushion, asking what it was that I liked about Him.

'What d'you mean?' I'd said.

So she'd smiled and repeated the question.

'What is it that you like about Him?'

I couldn't answer. I had opened my mouth and absolutely nothing had come out. Like a trope.

A horn screams and I spin around to find that I am standing in the middle of a road. A car has swerved to avoid me, almost hitting another. A voice shouts back as it speeds off, 'HAVE YOU GOT A FUCKING DEATH WISH?!'

People on both pavements watch, and I feel sweet relief at behaving like the kind of person I am so tired of insisting I am not.

Because nowadays in these moments it no longer feels as though I've lost my mind.

It feels like I've found it.

I text Him: 'It's over. I'm out. You cannot say things like that to a person. I will not let you paint me as someone boring who hinders your life. Go to the gig, I'm driving to Norwich.'

The flat already feels less mine, when I walk into it. They're already not my belongings any more. Including the fancy bottle of Tanqueray, which I no longer give a shit about saving so I climb straight on to the kitchen counter to reach it, and make a pint of G&T because the only glass that is clean is the emergency Foster's pint glass. No ice or lemon or cucumber, just an unadorned glass of despair that when I was a student we'd call a 'gin & tragic', back when people thought I was fun. I sidestep Winston's arch look that reads, *That's a very big drink*, by taking myself to the bistro set in the garden under the wisteria, bought recently on a trip I'd taken to B&Q so I wouldn't rummage through His kitchen receipt drawer for clues like Jessica fucking Fletcher.

The table is still decorated with fag packets and sticky alcohol reduction from when Bell and Jim were over till two this morning. I sweep a pile of empty IPA tins on the floor and poke around a tobacco packet for the last thirsty pubes in the corners. I call the person with whom I have nothing in common, but in this storm it is the only port I can think of.

'Hello?'

'Hi, Mum.'

'Helloareyouallright?'

'Yyyeahareyou?' I lick the Rizla.

'Yes, thank you.'

'Good.' And when I flick the lighter on, that's when I hear the front door go. 'What are you up to?'

'Just having an Options with the Kardashians on.'

I take a huge gulp of warm alcohol. 'What's that screaming?'

'Oh God, a new woman's moved in across the way, she's got this ruddy Dobermann.'

'Right.' And He's there. Standing in the doorframe, watching me with watery eyes.

'Listen, Mum.' I look right back at Him and take a drag of my anorexic rolly. 'I need to ask you something.'

'I can't hear you, sorry, that ruddy dog.'

He mouths, *No, please, Bun.*

'I'm coming to Norwich, Mum.'

'Sorry, that bloody dog, honestly; you'll have to speak up.'

'Yeah, that's right, it's over.'

He staggers backwards into the house with his hands over His eyes.

'Say again?'

'I'll be there by ten at the latest.'

'Be where?!'

'NORWICH, MUM.'

'Oh, lovely!'

He charges out from inside the house and straight towards me. I recoil in the garden chair, pressing my back against it. He puts a piece of paper on the table and sits across from me.

'Do you want me to leave any dinner for you?' Mum is asking.

'Uh, what are you making?' I'm watching Him point at the piece of paper. I pick it up and read it as Mum says something about fajitas and do I still eat chicken.

Big, frantic letters are written on it. The biro has torn the paper in places. It says,

'I NEED YOU.'

I look at it. Huh?

' . . . could pop to Sainsbury's and get some falafelle?'

I don't look up from the paper. 'It's falafel, Mum. Thank you, that'd be nice.'

'I'll get flafel in, then.' A beat. 'All right, I'll let you go!'

''K, bye.'

I hang up and look straight at Him. A bee flies over from the hotel. He swats her away.

I look at the paper. That's, this is . . . it doesn't make sense.

'Do you even like me?' I ask him.

'Of course I like you.'

'You say it like it's obvious, but you behave like you don't at all.'

'I'm sorry, don't leave, don't.'

'Are you still serious about us?'

'*Yes!*' He says, like it's obvious, then, to the bee, 'Fuck *off.*'

'Then why do you talk to me like that, like a five-star arsehole?'

'I dunno, because I'm a cunt.'

I can tell He's mining his insides for answers. Good. It feels nourishing.

'You're so cruel. Sometimes I feel like you keep me here just to have something following you around—'

'No!'

'Like I'm your dog, shaking in the corner, something that you can take things out on when you feel shit about yourself, can kick about or whate—'

'Don't EVER say that to me.' He looks at me square in the face, His voice leaden. 'I would never – *ever* – hit you.' The air has tightened around us.

'No, that's not what I'm saying.' My brain begins to Spirograph.

'Don't even imply it.'

'No, you're not *listening*!' I say it louder than I'd intended. He nods, and allows the tight air to release. 'What I'm saying is, right, I can take it if you hate me,' I lie, stoically. 'But you have to tell me, you have to set me free.'

'I don't hate you.'

I pick up the torn-off piece of paper from the garden table, and hold up its scribbly big letters. 'What even is this bollocks?'

'It isn't bollocks!' He is slow and firm. 'I don't know what I'd do without you.'

And I feel like maybe I am invincible.

Because you see, at first I was desired. And that part felt really good, that was probably the best bit. But that can't last for ever, how can you desire something once you get it? You can't long for something that you already have, that lives with you, that sleeps in the same bed.

But a damaged person can never stop needing someone to rely on. And look, I may not be able to get an acting job, I may not have seen my family since last year. But with this man, the one whimpering on the other side of the bistro set, I am a necessity. I feel the familiar urge to sprint back across the decades and hug the little boy that was Him and tell Him that everything is going to be OK.

But I'm not finished yet. 'This is a really bad relationship.'

'I know.' He says it as if to say, *You have no idea.*

'Well, I don't want that. I don't want to argue my life away.'

'We won't, we'll work on it. Make it better.'

'It's a grass-roots thing. You have to start respecting me.'

'Yep, understood.' I've never seen Him so compliant.

'Be actively nice to me.'

'Yep.'

'Stop calling me things like mental.'

'OK, then you have to stop nagging me about it.'

'It's only nagging if I have to ask more than once.'

'All right, all right.'

'The more you say these things the smaller I feel, and the weaker my defences get against my own extreme thoughts. Sometimes I catch myself wishing—' I stop. He looks at me. What am I going to say? That I sometimes wish something awful would happen to Him? That it's the only way I imagine my life being better?

I used to think I was a good person. How can I possibly think that any more, now that I carry these thoughts around with me? They're the thoughts of someone who has poison in their veins. Who deserves the bad things that happen to them.

Somewhere in the recesses I hear Maura asking, 'What is it you like about Him?' Well, I may not know the answer to that, Maura, but one thing I know for sure is that someone as awful as I am is lucky to be needed.

He looks at the phone. 'Are you going to call your mum back, then? Come to the gig with me?'

'Yes.'

I watch Him look up to the sky in relief then put His head in His hands and curl into a ball. Like I've rescued Him from His anguish.

Everything is all right, things are different now. Because now I have the power.

I go over and kneel in front of Him. 'It's OK.' I move His hair out of His face. 'I'm here.'

The Apollo is only a ten-minute walk from ours, via the dusty concrete pavements of Hammersmith. On the way I tell Him I'm so glad it all worked out, it shows we're a strong team. He kicks a Diet Coke can and says all right, all right, and I get it because I am going on a bit now.

'The thing that's bad about things like earlier,' I tell Him, 'is that by saying you just want to have fun in response to my being there, that implies you think I'm, like, some fun sponge, and that's what really hurt.'

'You're slouching again; you need to stand straight when you walk.'

I stand straighter. 'But do you see how hurtful that is?'

'What is?'

'When you said you just want to have fun for once, about me coming up to Edinburgh.'

'I never said that.'

'You did, you literally said, "I just want to have fun for once."'

'All right, maybe I did, but I didn't say it like that, not in that tone.'

I'm about to protest when we're interrupted outside the Hammersmith Broadway shopping centre.

'Excuse me, please could you help me I've been on the streets for almost a month now and I get attacked every single night I need sixteen pounds to get in to a hostel and they'll help me get something to eat so if you could spare it I'd be so so grateful thank you.'

It's a well-practised monologue, delivered in one breath. Anyone who lives in London will have been met with a variation on it many times before. But we've stopped, because this time it's a child. Thirteen at most. So small and young it's hard to tell if they are a boy or girl. A high voice, a pale face with a yellow bruise under their eye and crusty redness in one corner of their mouth. They look as though they have spent the last of their feelings a long time ago.

And He, my boyfriend, heads straight to the nearest cashpoint ten yards away without a second thought and takes out a hundred quid for the kid, who snatches it out of His hands and races through the Broadway. When we get to the Apollo we see the kid again, standing with a tall scary-looking man with long unwashed hair. The man is counting my boyfriend's money. The kid is looking straight ahead at nothing.

'And I think I have problems.' I watch the man shove the kid hard in the shoulder, making their arm swing behind them. I watch the man lean his face threateningly close to the kid's, whose expression doesn't change at all.

Last week, the wife of a lovely friend had a last-minute

pregnancy complication. She had to give birth to a baby that had already died inside of her. It was painful; it was like a real birth except there was no joy waiting for her on the other side. Some women experience unimaginable trauma. Some women are raped with machetes. Some women are trans and because of that are burnt alive in their own homes. Some women have stones and bricks thrown at them by people until they die because they got caught carrying a mobile phone.

'I'm so lucky,' I say.

'Yep,' He agrees.

I need to check my fucking privilege. I'm a person who gets VIP tickets to gigs at the Apollo. I have a generous boyfriend who helps children on the street, who provides for me. *That's* what I like about Him, Maura. I like that there are no bruises on my body, or crusty blood in the corner of my mouth. He still makes me laugh, I have nothing to moan about, no reason to cry all the time and make dramas out of pizzas.

I know how it can be with us too. I was there at the beginning in Brighton, when we were the only two people in the universe. I was there in Cambodia at 4 a.m., when we watched the sun rise up in neon pink over Angkor Wat temple. The sky had reflected in the lake, there was pink above our heads and underneath our feet and our faces and bodies lit up in pink too. The birds sang for the morning and a monkey was eating a bag of crisps from a bin. There was romance and reality, there was everything at once.

The stand-up is funny, we laugh loads. We hang out in the green room afterwards while He talks to Vinnie. The McDonald's in Hammersmith is still open on the way home, and we queue up for a Big Mac and a fishy marshmallow. I'm starving, having wasted the Fiorentina. Some people have recognised Him and asked for a selfie.

169

'I think this Edinburgh's going to be really good,' I say when He comes back over and we dig into the hot brown paper bag. 'Good for us, as well.'

'I might not even be doing it.'

'What d'you mean?'

'I've got a meeting on Tuesday.'

'What for?'

'You're gonna love this.' He wiggles His eyebrows and pauses for effect. 'Fucking *Strictly*!' He laughs like He's won the lottery, squeezes His arm around my ribs excitedly, knocking my breath out. The people in the queue who recognised Him laugh, and He laughs a little louder, and jumps me up and down.

The next day I come home to a Whistles bag on the bed with an orange cashmere jumper in it. It's stupidly expensive, and I hadn't wanted it *that* much, but I put it on right away because it means something.

I think I'll stop seeing Maura.

I Left

Because I may just like myself

Crouch End, 9 October 2018

If you carried your heart on the outside of your body, would you be more careful who you let hold it?

I've been reckless with mine in the past. Handed my heart to more than one person I loved, despite knowing they were dangerous. I watched these people I loved hurl it against a wall, or drop it on the floor. One just forgot about my heart altogether, as I walked around with a hollow chest.

Last night, though, when I clicked on that Send button on Twitter, I threw my heart up into the air and thousands of strangers rushed to catch it.

I am sitting on my attic-room bed in another set of Bell's pyjamas, plaid ones with a worn-out waistband, where I have been since I woke up over six hours ago. But I don't exist in the room today. I'm living inside my laptop and with my ear to my phone. In less than twenty-four hours, I have heard from pretty much every single person I know, that I have *met*. Think about how many people you contact daily, weekly, sometimes, never any more. Think about how many actual friends and 'friends' that make up your network on social media, all of the people who you once gave your phone number or email address to, like that time you filled in a form to take that yoga class you never went back to, or when you gave a contact number to that florist for that Mother's Day delivery.

'Hi, Rebecca, you may not remember me but I just wanted to say . . .'

Mum called to say the same journalist who knocked on her door yesterday offering his condolences knocked on the same door this morning and asked, 'How does it feel to be the mother of Rebecca Humphries?!'

Dad phoned from the corner shop, where people are buying papers with pictures of me on the front. In the papers, sentences have flipped. 'His girlfriend Rebecca Humphries . . .' has become 'The actress Rebecca Humphries, girlfriend of Him . . .' I am no longer a supporting character in this narrative. I am the lead, and what is more, I wrote the script.

I'm a hashtag. Have been sent free things to my agent's office, been offered articles, book deals, and more money than I've made in my whole career put together. Enough to buy a flat on the road I just left. Someone on Twitter has made the suggestion that I should pair up with the dancer's husband (who is another of the professional dancers on *Strictly*) and enter next year, and for a good five minutes I indulged my imagination, allowing it to pick out a week-one dance (samba) and song ('I Will Survive'). The samba is notoriously challenging for week one but here, today, I really believe I could take it on.

I've read tweets and think pieces and speculation from psychologists and celebrities. I have googled my name over and over and over again. The only thing I've ever watched on YouTube more than Lorraine discussing my statement is the 'Whenever You're Ready' Cheryl Cole clip. It's all so shocking and funny and unlikely and the thing is, if it was another woman who had done it, I really feel as though I would think, *Good for her*.

Winston is sitting on the end of the bed looking at the wall. 'Baby,' I tell him in amazement, 'you're famous!' He looks back over his shoulder at me, then sets about rigorously licking his own anus.

A girl I always wanted to be in high school called Kelly Taylor got in touch on Facebook to say her boyfriend at the time, Jamie Davis, once saw her sitting on someone else's lap at a party, so spread a rumour that she had an ugly vulva and then told her she was stupid for being upset about it. Another girl called Hannah Meggison also messaged on Facebook to say she had always thought that I was really nice at school, and she had always felt 'stupid and slaggy' around me. My best friend Katy, who I lost touch with after a holiday years ago in Magaluf, texted on the off chance I still had the same number.

And then there are the internet strangers. Thousands and thousands of them. My agent has forwarded emails sent to the agency from women trying to get in touch, telling me they'd read what I'd said and realised they were right to leave their partners all those years ago. They had still thought they were crazy until they'd read what I had to say. One email was from a woman whose ex-husband had messaged her this morning, saying that he sees now that what he had been doing to her six years ago was abusive. He knows he can't make it better but that he's so sorry for the way he treated her back then, and that he is going to get help.

'I hope you don't mind me emailing you . . . ' her message to me had begun.

There are internet strangers who say they saw me on the telly clapping on Saturday night and had thought how lucky He was to have such a supportive girlfriend. Internet strangers who say I deserve better. Internet strangers who think the way I wrote that statement is funnier than anything He's ever said. Ones sharing their own raw experiences under my Twitter statement, ones liking and being encouraging to other strangers, creating new threads, wider networks.

A storm has come, just like my agent said it would, but I was the tempest behind it, whipping up those clouds then letting myself get absolutely soaking wet like one of The Weather Girls in 'It's Raining Men'. It has been the most dynamic electric storm of kindness.

And yet I can't stop thinking: *If He was that bad, why did I stay?*

I get up and shuffle a bit to the full-length mirror on the back of the attic door, holding up the pyjama bottoms by the worn out waistband. Then, for absolutely no reason at all, I decide to let go, let them fall down and just stand there. I pull the pyjama top over my head and drop it on the ground. I step out of the bottoms and skid them to the side. I look in the mirror, at myself.

In general? Too pale. The three-week-old pedicure is chipped, toenails have shiny pink chunks on them. There's a red bump on my shin the size of a caper, I've never known what it is. I can't pull wellies over my calves, they're so chunky. My knees are puffy at the sides for some reason, and my thighs don't so much touch as attempt to merge. Arse has absolutely no hint of solidity, never has done. Hair on vulva regrowing in patches following last week's wax, when it was ripped off entirely (painfully). Small tits, pale nipples. Arms that are either flabby or muscular, never slender. Pits that sweat more than anyone else's, I'm *such* a sweaty cow, and when I have an important meeting will sweat from the crotch most of all. Broad shoulders, short neck. Eye bags that won't go away no matter how much I spend on creams for them. The looming threat of a unibrow. Greasy hair.

It happens simultaneously, this self-critique. One sonic boom of 'BELOW STANDARD'. The fact is that I am not naturally very thin, and if you are not naturally very thin it is near impossible to live in peace. Life throws out reminders, on the telly, in the shops, in the papers, on your phone, on the side of buses.

You are given suggestions, tips, advice, and no one ever asks if it's all right to do any of that, life just assumes you'd prefer to be a different way. Presumes your idea of a beach body isn't just your body at the beach.

There have been select times from the age of seventeen when I have, in this order: deprived it of carbohydrates, fed it only Special K, fed it only Greek yoghurt, fed it ten constipation tablets a day, plunged it in ice baths every morning, forced it to the gym seven days a week, fed it only green juice, sat in a sauna for one hour every day, fed it only a combination of cayenne pepper, maple syrup, lemon juice and water, and put my fingers down its throat after every meal.

I look again at my body and try to be objective. I see . . . the shape of a woman, I guess. I am one of those things. And today, being a woman seems to have mattered more than ever.

'When one of our own is in trouble,' Caitlin Moran had messaged me, 'a tribe of elders will gather in a protective circle.'

When I was tiny I thought all girls turned into boys, at some point. When I got out of the bath aged three, my mum was rubbing me dry with a crispy towel when I looked into her face and announced that I was very excited because my willy was growing. Christ knows where I got that idea but thank fuck I wasn't right. I mean, it's shit obviously at times, being female. It's painful, and a mess, and expensive, and time consuming, even if that time is just spent trying to find tampons or something. But that instinct to nurture. I always thought the idea of being nurturing was so unsexy, so uncool, *mumsy*. But it isn't, it's active, primal and wild. As though you're always ready to burst into flames for someone else.

Women are the most wonderful, powerful things. And now I get to learn about being one without fear of being mocked, or undermined, or of emasculating anybody who lives under the same roof. I get to be a woman, fully.

'You have a nice body,' I say out loud. The woman in the mirror looks like she's been waiting for someone to say those words to her for thirty-odd years. All this critiquing and problem solving. I wonder how much time I'd have had on my hands if I had just chosen to accept myself. I wonder what I could have gotten done, and what, now, I shall.

I can't believe I lived in that flat fighting off a feeling like this. Why the fuck did I stay?

The door opens and I realise I am a grinning naked person and nearly shit myself. I grab the throw off the bed and send Winston flying as Bell appears.

'I'm naked,' I say.

She raises an eyebrow. 'Shall I see you downstairs for spaghetti?'

'Good idea, yes, go away. In a nice way.'

'Enjoy.' And she exits. I put my pyjamas back on and wonder whether it's even worth insisting I wasn't happily masturbating in front of the mirror, whether anyone would believe me anyway.

'His *agent* called?!' Jim is incredulous.

'Oh yeah. He "strongly encouraged me it would be in my own interests to keep quiet".' I try to swallow my puttanesca before I choke with laughter and die. 'But that's not the best bit. The *Strictly* Twitter account has *blocked* me.'

A roar from the crowd.

'I know! Like they're the ones that got dumped!'

We are screaming with heady, awestruck laughter and spilling wine from all the emphasis we're putting into recounting today with our bodies. Bell's been saying 'I just can't believe it' at random intervals, fully meaning it every single time because every single time she's remembered something else about how big what's happened in this house has become.

'I feel like Guernica's horse!' she said at one point, and I had to google it, and lost my shit again.

My nice body is now a clean one wrapped in Bell's fuzzy navy dressing gown, for I have finally showered, and my hair still has wet patches in it. I am drunk and stuffed with an entire frozen garlic baguette, because once it touched my lips I realised that for three whole days I hadn't eaten a single thing. There is a vat of sloppy pasta with huge serving spoons and a thick wedge of parmesan and red wine and red-faced friends. I am famous and have made a difference in people's lives and can't remember ever feeling so in love as I am with being in this moment, and with what I've done.

'Twitter following's gone up by how many?' Jim asks.

'I dunno. A *lot*,' I say. 'I mean, it's like ... *what*?!' And we all laugh because, I mean, it's bonkers; yesterday I was just someone famous's girlfriend.

'I just can't believe it,' says Bell, and we cheer through our spaghetti because she said it again.

'What about Instagram?' she asks.

'I'd forgotten Instagram!' I get my phone out.

'All right, get your bets in,' says Jim. 'I'm going seventy K.'

'That's absurd.' I check, and gasp. 'Twenty-five thousand, fuuuurcking hell!'

'I have forty-nine followers,' says Bell.

I go into my inbox where there's a slew of private messages waiting to be read.

'Hi, you don't know me but ...'

The message starts just like 99 per cent of the others today. But this is different. Because this one says that my ex-boyfriend, the one I took the cat from, tried to kiss them last year at the Edinburgh festival.

'I thought you should know, as this *Strictly* thing probably wasn't a one-off.'

'Everything all right?' asks Bell.

'Yep, no, yeah it is,' I reply.

'More wine, mate?' asks Jim.

'No, yeah, sure,' I say, not really knowing what the question was.

I've received hundreds of messages on Instagram, and around fifteen of them are women who have come forward to tell me about a specific incident. Attempted kisses, invitations to hotel rooms, one-night stands. They're all informative, presented as gifts. They're all encouraging of my life without Him. Some of them insist they didn't know He had a girlfriend, but some of them did know and are genuinely contrite about stuff that happened. They were young, they say. He was charming, they say. I get it. I'd have been the same at their age.

A few of the tour dates and locations they mention I recognise. One of them was about eighteen months ago, when He'd come back after a few days in Manchester. I'd tried to have sex a few times and had been called a nymphomaniac. That's when I changed my birth control as I thought the hormones were making me sex crazed and emotional. I still have the family planning card in my wallet. It had really, really hurt getting that coil fitted.

'Becks?' Bell's voice asks softly, somewhere miles away. I barely hear her, experiencing as I am my very own rejection montage, scene after scene of 'no Buns' and 'leave offs'. Scene after scene of turning His words 'You are mental' on myself, of convincing myself I had a broken brain and that my boyfriend wasn't just a slapdash liar.

Ah. So this is the storm I was warned about.

'What is it, Becks?' I look up and Bell and Jim are both staring at me.

'Nothing,' I say. I straighten up, leaning into the persona I've created, the one where I'm a feminist icon who has a nice body, who likes being a woman, who likes who she is, whose insides aren't crumbling at the dining table.

Why did I stay?

I Left

Because my friends made it possible

Our flat, Shepherd's Bush, 13 October 2018

I am standing stock-still in my old living room watching my ex-boyfriend do the Charleston with the woman He was photographed kissing on my birthday. They are both being very smiley. They are not touching one another and are pretending to make pizzas. They are both wearing red and white stripy T-shirts and trousers.

Around me, a heist is in full swing.

It's Saturday night, exactly one week since the *Strictly* car park, and the only time it would be a hundred per cent guaranteed that he would be out of the house was when he was live on television. Five of us have been on standby from 7 p.m., waiting to see whether He would actually, genuinely be on BBC1 tonight given what's happened over the last week. The second He and the dancer appeared, grinning and waving at the top of those *Strictly* staircases, Bell ordered the taxi and I swung by the BrewDog in Shepherd's Bush where Theo, Poppy and Paul were hustled in by Oonagh. Oonagh always wears black, never eats sugar, and puts one in mind of Pieter Bruegel's painting *Dull Gret*. In the painting, the woman Dull Gret leads an army of women into hell to pillage, to go and rob all of the good stuff. Tonight is that painting. And who am I in it? Well, to

185

the bottom left there's a kind of upside-down bum on legs, but with wide eyes, that seems to be panic eating a bowl of porridge with a spoon stuck in its own arsehole. Doing its own thing as pandemonium ensues. That's me.

The flat smelled of cigarettes when we got inside. All four of my friends had taken their coats off and were wearing sequins underneath, Theo in full drag. Oonagh climbed on the marble worktop in mucky Doc Martens to reach a bottle of champagne. We cracked it open and the five of us have been swigging from it, throwing things into bags, twirling around and slut dropping, grinding on bookcases to the music from the telly and revelling in the absolute naughtiness of it all.

'Does He use this?' Oonagh shouts over to me.

I tear my eyes from the TV screen. She's at the kitchen counter holding up a bottle of extra virgin olive oil. 'Yes, it's delicious, why?'

'I'm just asking, nosy!' she replies.

'I've got my eye on you.' Earlier I caught her with a printed-out PDF entitled 'Queen of Revenge', and a minute ago a packet of prawns fell out of her pocket.

On the telly, He's exaggeratedly wiping sweat from His forehead, from all the effort. I wonder how many people have packed their relationship up while simultaneously watching their ex dancing with (BUT NOT TOUCHING) the woman they've been cheated on with. They were meant to be doing the Viennese waltz tonight; the dancer had told me before it all kicked off. If I were to guess why they're not, I'd say it's because no one has to touch in a Charleston, not really. Or look romantically into one another's eyes.

The judges are giving the pair of them really, really good marks compared to previous weeks. The number comes up on screen for the audience to ring if they want them to dance again. They both point at it in their stripy T-shirts and make their hands into phone shapes, grinning.

'Anyone who calls that number needs to seriously think about their life choices,' says Theo as they slink up to me. '20p from a landline for that.'

'Mmmm.' I take the champagne from them and swig. It hits my tooth. 'Ow.'

'Feeling fab?' they ask.

'Yeah!' I say unconvincingly, looking at how He no longer holds the beautiful dancer at the waist when they stand together. Wondering whether they'll celebrate in the gazebo later. Whether he'll feel freer, without me there.

I turn to face Theo, wobbling slightly. 'I have to tell you something, and you have to try to be understanding,' I say.

'No one tells me what to do.'

'You know the twins?' I ask.

'Naked threesome in the woods twins?'

'Yes. One of them messaged me to say well done for, you know, all of it.'

'That's lovely.'

'It is lovely.' I pause. 'He's gay now. They both are.'

'I see. And you're going to make this about your vulva, I imagine.'

'It's the first thing I thought.' I turn to Theo. 'I thought, *What if when they clapped eyes on my naked body aged four they were like, "Absolutely no way"?*'

'What if they clapped eyes on your naked body and thought, *No woman will ever live up to her so why bother?*'

'No, no, I know being queer isn't a choice, and also know what I'm saying is bollocks, I do. My point is, why did my brain go straight there? Why do I instantly think I'm not good enough? That wouldn't have been something I'd have thought before any of this happened. Has this relationship ruined me?'

'No, we won't let it.'

'I'm making everything about me,' I say. I start to shake, my hands start flailing. 'I feel like such a narcissist.'

'You're not one.' Theo clasps my hands in theirs to steady them. 'Which is a miracle. If I were you, I'd be obsessed with me.' I smile.

Two hours later. The flat is half empty. Only male things remain, it's already a different space.

It's been two hours' worth of me catching Poppy sellotaping the ends of taps and Paul putting parental locks on all the TV channels while we've bagged and boxed up my Zara Home cushions and Whistles jumpsuits and John Lewis God knows what. Paul, Poppy and Theo have taken them off in Addison Lees to Bell and Jim's, where a curry feast is waiting for us.

'Right,' Oonagh throws her hands in the air. 'It's done! You all right?'

'Yeah!' I smile and nod.

'C'mere then, let's get out of this dump.'

'Can I just . . . ? I just wanna say goodbye to the fridge-freezer.'

'Fair. Even I want to say goodbye to your fridge-freezer. But I wouldn't look in the freezer drawer, we may have made an ice cube with the Sky remote in it.'

'Oonagh!'

'*If the damage isn't permanent it's not considered criminal.* See you outside.' And Dull Gret gets the hell out of there.

I walk into the bathroom, to see the floor I once sobbed on until I couldn't breathe when he hadn't come home one evening and I thought about him no longer being in my life.

I go and sit on the sofa where we both sat bolt upright simultaneously the night Madonna's dancer pulled her cape and she fell down those stairs at the Brit Awards. Where I slept when

I first bought a pocket-sized Winston so that he wouldn't be scared in a new house.

I go and stand by the French windows to try to see the bee hotel but it's too dark.

And the strangest thing happens as I turn back. I see myself walk past me, pregnant. I see a baby's cot in the corner. I see the pair of us, me and Him older, in our forties. More settled, more grounded, and I know we've worked at it. We've found a way to communicate, to both take responsibility. We've agreed that all this drama is madness because we love and respect each other.

I see the other version. I see it all.

As I leave I notice the bedroom doorframe: it still has a fleck of red on it. 'Thank God,' I breathe out. 'I didn't make it up.'

My phone lights up in the car when we're by the Westway flyover. It's a Twitter DM from the cool *Strictly* correspondent who's secretly on my side. They've just filmed the Sunday-night results show, as they always do on Saturday nights after the live one goes out.

'He hasn't been voted out,' I read to Oonagh from my phone. 'He's staying in the show.'

A pause.

'Whatever,' she says. 'Margaritas same time, next week?'

I Stayed

Because I had nothing else

Pitlochry, May 2018

I walk so fast to the buffet table I almost plough myself into the three-tiered cake of cheeses. Catch my uneven breath, breathe in, breathe out. Close my eyes and straighten my back, ready to walk back over and rejoin the group. When I turn around, Theo is blocking my way, in full 'bridesmaid blancmange' drag and a huge mauve wig.

'Was that true?' they ask.

'What?' I know what. I turn back around to the table and take a paper plate.

'Back there.' Theo indicates to where He is standing with a group of my male friends, including Nish, the groom. All the ties and top buttons are undone on their suits, each holding a near empty beer bottle. And all of them are keeled over laughing at a story He is animatedly telling. 'That bit about you having to bring his suit to King's Cross at seven this morning because He forgot to come home from a party?'

'Yeah it is, yeah.'

'Right. And you're OK with that, are you? Because He's making a big thing of still being fucked. He just told Nish no offence but He wishes He wasn't here.'

'That was a joke. Nish laughed.' I sniff a hexagonal cracker with green bits on. Rosemary, nice.

'Yeah, and then you walked away.'

I don't say anything.

'Did He at least call you this time? You told me ages ago that was the boundary. If He ignored your messages all night and came home at some rando time the next morning without apologising, that was the line crossed. So did He contact you, or did you wake up alone again?'

I stare down the long table with its sumptuous platters of food. There's a screeching coming from behind me, the voice He uses when He's playing me onstage. Maybe He's telling my friends how I was desperate to scream at Him when I saw Him sitting in dark glasses outside the Leon in King's Cross, and on the four-hour train to Edinburgh, and in the taxi to the hotel in Pitlochry. How once we finally got to our room and got some privacy there was so little time before the ceremony I'd had to have a massive go at him while steaming my dress and wearing a face mask like Michael Myers in *Halloween*.

'Look, He's here, isn't He?' I shake the thought away and grab a fistful of crisps from a bowl. 'He came to my friend's wedding, that's the important thing. Who cares about the circumstances? Everyone at His party thought it was funny when I called Him this morning, I could hear them laughing down the phone. He thinks it's funny, everyone here thinks He's hilarious.'

'They don't.' Theo tosses their mauve locks over their shoulder. 'They're being nice because they're your friends and He's your boyfriend, and it's being presented like one of His routines. But on reflection they'll realise what a fucked-up story it is.'

'Here's a thought – could you maybe try being nice as well? You're undervaluing nice here. I would prefer it to having to defend myself all the time.'

'I *am* being nice. I am being an even better friend because it upsets me to see you being treated like this.'

'Stop being a drama queen, Theo. No one else thinks this is a big deal.'

'What?!' Theo recoils. 'Where have you gone? What is this toxic shit?'

'Sorry, just, whatever.' I try to walk away to be anywhere else, but Theo blocks me.

'Don't walk away.'

I sigh and look at the floor.

'Hey!' They bend their knees so their face is at my height. I throw my head up to the ceiling in exasperation, cross my arms, and stand looking over Theo's shoulder, past all the hair.

'I'm not losing my rag here.'

I nod. I can't look directly at them, it's not an option. I've reinforced toughness around me like a shell lately. Today I've curled my hair, painted my nails, done a face mask, made jokes, given hugs, worn high heels and a huge smile and false eyelashes and fake tan with shimmer and a short pink dress with hearts that He bought me for our first Christmas together. But lately there is nothing I can do about how sad my eyes are. And Theo will be able to tell, straight away.

'I care, you hear me? What if it was *my* boyfriend, undermining me like that?' They point to the group. 'What if *my* boyfriend—' and they list incident after incident, things that over the years I've texted them in moments of quiet despair. Small and everyday things, things that when spoken in Theo's voice make me feel as though my blood is liquid lead, running down the inside of my body and rooting me to where I stand.

'How long have we been friends? Since we were Paris and Nicole living the simple life in East Anglia, and you stank of Glow by J-Lo. I know you. You are fabulous, you deserve to be happy.' They conclude, 'And I don't think you are.'

But behind Theo an attractive, witty blonde girl I know called Poppy has joined His group. She's a bridesmaid, her dress has barely-there straps and is made from whisper thin satin that ripples across the curves of her body. It's not slutty, it's tasteful, and sexy. She looks like a fucking fairy, and is laughing at something He's saying.

'Stop ignoring me.'

'I'm not.' My boyfriend looks at Poppy laughing at Him.

'This, all of this, is a no from me. You would never let me put up with it. Or I hope you wouldn't.'

'I have to go, Theo.' I push past and walk over and stand between my boyfriend and Poppy. I smile, and say 'What are we talking about?' and try to stop my sorrow from overflowing and messing up my eyeliner because I can feel Theo is staring at me from where the cheesecake is.

My friends ask us to do the Photobooth with them, but we don't. Oonagh asks me to sing 'No More Tears/Enough is Enough' with her at the live-band karaoke but I say no. I think about all my friends knowing He doesn't come home at night sometimes, and how I will bring His suit to King's Cross for Him anyway. I think about what Theo said about them realising later it's a fucked-up story, and wonder how many of my so-called friends pity me already. I look around the room thinking about who I've told what to, how careful I've been not to trauma dump on any one person too much. I see the spreadsheet in front of me; Paul knows Venice was difficult but not that Jamaica was, Theo knows Jamaica was but not about the argument at my press night in Stratford, which Oonagh does know about but only because she was there but she doesn't know anything else, or does she? I sit on a toilet of the barn at Nish's wedding reception for twenty minutes, hidden from all these people who know slithers of my relationship. I listen to women share make-up and compliments and chat at the sinks outside the cubicle, terrified of hearing my name come up. Because if all those people shared slithers, they would piece together the whole fuck pie.

I come out eventually. I ignore Theo's presence that night, and squeeze His arm a little tighter. Later, back at the hotel, He asks me what's wrong. I tell Him about Theo sticking their oar in, not letting me leave when I wanted to. He says that sorry, but He can't remember Theo ever having been happy for me, and all I ever seem to do is complain about my friends. He's not even sure they're really my friends at all. And it's sad because when He puts it like that it makes sense.

Theo's text the next morning says, 'I am so worried about you.' I ignore it, and the next one, and the next, for the next few months. And I know it doesn't matter, I know that I have Him to turn to, for everything.

It's still an empty feeling, though, when Theo stops.

I Left

Because I stand for something

Theo is fervently lip-synching to Alanis Morissette's 'You Oughta Know' in Bell and Jim's garden, under fairy lights, relishing the more explicit moments within the lyrics. No one's really watching, but a lack of interest will never hinder Theo's commitment. Oonagh, Paul, Poppy, Bell and I are all cosy under blankets. The air smells of fire and curry spices. On my lap is a plate of brightly coloured splodges, I'm not sure which curry is what any more. In the kitchen is the most takeaway I've ever seen.

'Naan?' Jim is handing around a giant pile of floppy bread on a tray. 'Peshwari, garlic, plain?'

'How many did you get?' I ask, tearing off a slice from the top.

'Twelve.'

'*Why?!*'

'I dunno, mate, I panicked.'

'You – you – you oughta kno-ow!' Theo drops to their knees on the (very wet) grass.

'So, with Tantra—'

'The sex?' I interrupt Oonagh.

'Nah, that's tantric sex,' she says. 'That's what everyone thinks it is, like. Tantra was a counter-culture from sixth-century India. So

201

in Tantra, absolutely everything contains divine feminine power, Goddess energy. And everyone can tap into theirs regardless of gender, but women themselves were worshipped. It made sense to them, because women are the givers of life, their bodies literally make food to nurture it. Plus their orgasms absolutely obliterate men's ones, sexually they can reach far more powerful places.'

'Boom,' says Poppy.

'I know, right, so yeah women are the ones who hold this insane power, so it stands to reason that women are the stronger sex. And that means they could potentially choose to destroy everything too, so they have to be respected.'

'JIM!' Bell shouts over to where he and Paul are dancing to 'Proud Mary'. 'I am very powerful!'

''K!' Jim shouts back.

'So there's more,' says Oonagh. 'There's a theory that for men, on the whole sex is perfunctory. And let's assume when I say this I mean "not all men". But for men, desire is necessary because it's a means to an end; everything is so they can jizz, ejaculating is the high point in sex. And then it's over, like an off switch. For women, orgasm isn't necessarily the high point, because desire can actually unfold *after* we come. Like how many times have you lain there after you've had an orgasm and felt all of these huge feelings?'

Me, Bell, Poppy and Theo all nod, open mouthed. Red-wine teeth and tongues.

'Sex back then, for women in particular, had nothing to do with duty and everything to do with desire. Women were the ones who wanted. Then somewhere along the way, all this power that women were said to have had . . . it became threatening. It damaged some egos. That's when the patriarchy started claiming the power by creating a narrative that sex and pleasure was masculine. Men were the sexual ones, they were the ones that got aroused—'

'"Please take this hard penis as proof", etc.,' says Bell.

Oonagh nods wryly. 'Exactly. And the patriarchy created the narrative that for women, sex was about duty. Which meant part of a woman's duty was having to be desired by men; needing to look attractive, be attentive, to serve, to please, so that they are wanted. Which isn't the same as having wants of your own.'

'I can't believe the things you know,' I say. 'I'm so behind.'

'This is blowing my mind, Oonagh,' says Poppy. 'How did you find out these sexy things?'

'Ah, this exhibition at the British Museum. I went with Lucy.'

Oonagh was straight her whole life. In March she realised she was in love with her best friend Lucy. And Lucy – also straight until then – felt the same.

'And how's lesbian life?' asks Theo.

Oonagh shrugs. 'Really . . . easy.'

Theo has put on 'C'est La Vie' by B*Witched, and all of us are Irish dancing barefoot on the grass.

'Do you want to get married?'

'Oh, aye!' Paul says. 'For sure.'

'Wow. So certain.'

'I'm surprised at myself there, to be honest. I suppose I always hoped for, y'know, a big family. There are four of us kids, aren't there?' I nod, I know Paul's family well. We lived together when we first moved to London, little eighteen-year-old babies starting drama school. 'Yeah, imagined I'd meet someone, maybe find somewhere peaceful up in the Highlands nearer my mum and dad's.'

'Drinking whisky, lobbing some big logs around.'

He smirks. 'Reading Rabbie Burns in our kilts.'

'All the oats you can eat.'

'Aye, just cosying up in the evenings together, appropriating my culture.'

We laugh. Then he says, 'Grace says hi, by the way. In fact, she says that you're, um, a "fierce Queen" aaaand she loves you, that's it.'

'Well, she is the best so it makes sense.'

'That she is, yeah.' We go quiet, look at the chiminea, and bob our heads to Adele's 'Rolling in the Deep'.

Last year Grace broke up with Paul after almost eight years together. With no mess, no anger. They still loved one another, they were just so young when they got together and Grace wanted more experiences, and for him too. Everyone had thought they were made for one another, we were almost as devastated as Paul was, which was very.

He never once blamed her. They're still friends. He's by nature a great bloke, but has done loads of work on himself to ensure he doesn't fuck anyone over. It's meant he's had a terrific amount of casual sex where he was able to leave his sexual partners, as he puts it, 'better off than I found them'. Which when you put it like that seems a really obvious thing to want to do.

Still, despite all the shagging, there's been this very small, very discreet pouch of sadness he's been carrying around with him ever since.

And I think: *What a relief it is to have been betrayed.* I don't think I could handle no one doing anything wrong. I don't think I'm as evolved as Paul.

I don't know Poppy that well. We met four years ago but have never been close friends. She texted me two days ago asking if she could help with the move.

'He broke up with me after Uni,' Poppy's telling me. 'He was like yours. I was always mental, crazy, whatever. Anyway, that was my last relationship.'

Poppy is a bombshell, successful, and that perennially single friend that I'm told everyone has one of. Far from being the threatening sex fairy I had her down for at Nish's wedding, she's actually more of a 'huge jumpers and no make-up' kind of woman, and told me earlier she had been forced into a wispy bridesmaid dress against her will and spent that whole day feeling uncomfortable. I've watched Poppy masterfully dodge the question of why she hasn't been 'snapped up' yet several times, once from her own mum. I'm proud to say I've never questioned her not having had a boyfriend the four years I've known her. I'm ashamed to say I've been glad she isn't me.

'I didn't realise you'd been single that long.'

'Yeah, man.'

'Out of choice?'

She thinks about it. 'Dunno, actually. Tricky question, after something like that. Especially cos he got engaged less than a year after we split up. He's married now, two kids. Still texts me from time to time, whenever he needs a little pick-me-up.'

'You're joking.'

'Nope. He'll be like "You're a superstar", or "Always knew you'd smash it". I almost feel sorry for him. But it's complicated, cos . . . ' She trails off and looks at me like she's said too much.

'It feels really great to hear those things?' I suggest it for her.

'Pathetic, isn't it?' Her hand flies subconsciously to her forehead like she's feeling her own temperature, like it's an ailment: taking satisfaction in feeling craved.

'Nah,' I say.

'I mean, he never crosses the line with what he's saying, there's nothing I could use as evidence against him. But like, why are you texting your ex-girlfriend at eleven p.m. asking what she's up to? Why when she asks how you are do you tell her that "things aren't great"?'

'God, so draining, filling in all these gaps!' I throw my head back in despair. 'AARGGGHHH!'

'We should go on holiday,' Poppy says.

'When?' I ask.

'Whenever!' And my newest good friend pours more wine into my glass. 'We're single, we can go ballistic, do what the heck we like!'

In the garden, the music changes to 'Dancing On My Own' by Robyn. I can hear Theo shouting, 'WHERE IS SHE? THIS IS HER SONG!' from where I stand on my own in the living room, looking inside one of the pick-'n'-mix boxes of stuff at the top of a pile. It's rammed full of candles, expensive candles. Against one side is a picture in a frame. Me and Him on top of an elephant in Bangkok. I'd had food poisoning the day before, and wanted so much to go on the elephant anyway. I'd soiled myself on top of it moments before this picture was taken. In the photo we're both laughing, wildly.

The candles, the picture. The inside of this box looks like a shrine to something dead.

'Are you all right?' Bell's in the doorway, speaking to me quietly.

I look around at all the stuff and try not to think about where I'm going to put it now. All things I pretended I wanted so no one would see I wasn't getting what I needed.

'You know the Dull Gret painting?' I ask her. 'I feel like—'

'The bum on legs?' Bell finishes my thought. 'Spoon in the arsehole?'

'Exactly.'

'Yeah, I see that. The metaphor of it, I mean.'

I reach in for the picture of Him and me on the elephant. 'Everyone's love stories, out there. U-turns and wrong decisions and grey areas and unexpected outcomes. I thought your life was meant to slot into place once you met someone.'

'No you didn't. You're not that naïve,' Bell says.

'No but I am optimistic, and I'd hoped that's what would

happen. I feel cheated, hearing for myself how knackering it is for everyone, how much figuring out it takes. All the layers there are to love. Even this.' I show her the frame. 'I put this picture on Instagram, it got so many likes and nice comments that were like "you look so happy". Let me tell you, on that holiday there was tension, boredom, loads of, I dunno, not particularly enjoying one another. But we were meant to have been in love. And I think we were, is the thing. I don't know what to think, I feel dizzy.'

'Come get some air. You can just sit and be a bum on legs and that's fine, you don't need to have any big revelations tonight.'

'You know what?' I fling the picture back in the box and close the lid, temperature rising. 'Yes I do. If this week has taught me anything, it's that I'm better when I'm not passive.'

'I want to say something.'

I look around at each of my friends, all stopping mid conversation to look at me. Standing by the chiminea, wrapped in blankets like a witchetty grub. Theo turns Aretha down.

'Thank you all so much for tonight. Whatever has happened to us in our lives, I'm so glad it's led to this point here, now, around these majestic flames.' I touch the chiminea. 'Ow.'

Bell rushes me indoors and runs my hand under a cold tap.

'I'll start again,' I say moments later, standing in the same spot as before, a bag of frozen edamame in my burnt hand.

'I want to say: I'm so sorry to all of you. For choosing Him over you. I was scared of the investment I made in my relationship having been for nothing, so I phased most of you out because I knew you were all so clever and right on, and that any concern you had for me would be absolutely founded in something real. I pushed you away, and I'm sure it bothered you that I did that. And ... and here you are. Honestly, of all the people in the world, you are the best ones. And you know what,

I'm glad it all happened this way because I will never forget this evening. This right here, right now, this is what matters. I love you all more than Lizzo loves herself.'

Whoops and cheers.

'There's more,' I continue. 'Because, right, I'm not entirely sure I blame myself for putting Him above everything else. At the flat earlier, I had this thought about ...' I sigh. 'It's *so* embarrassing to say because it's *so* lame and basic. But you know, society has a lot to answer for, OK. Because society's been telling me I was pretty much getting everything right. Following the steps.' I hold my fingers up. 'Fall in love, get a house, get married, have a baby.' I show them four fingers. 'You know, I was halfway, halfway along that conveyor belt, on my way to the supposed simple life.'

'Thank Mary and Joseph the conveyor belt stopped,' says Oonagh. 'Thank the Lord Jesus you didn't get married.'

'Yeah, a lot of people have said that this week. That's hard, though, because, like, I can't help thinking that if we were married, would it have made my sadness more legit? If we were married there are lots of people that would take this more seriously. They would be like, "I'm so sorry this happened to you" rather than, "At least it wasn't worse". I find it hard to believe people on the telly would still say things like: "Oh well, the thing is their relationship can't have been that strong to begin with", if I'd have been His wife, y'know?'

No one says anything.

'Also, maybe if we'd got married or had a kid I would know, know for sure ...' I pause for a second, 'I'd know that He'd really loved me.'

And I don't know how it happens, not sure what divine goddess energy I'm harnessing. But Cyndi Lauper starts over the speakers: 'Time After Time'.

'Still, though, don't get me wrong,' I laugh. 'I'm fucking glad

we didn't have a baby! Because what if I'd had a daughter—'
and then I stop.

'It's OK, Becks,' says Poppy.

I shake my head at her to let her know I'm fine and in the
pause the song, our song, swirls through my head and out again.

'I've thought this week,' I carry on, 'if I'd have had a daughter
with Him, I would have been letting her see that the relationship was good enough, y'know?' My voice is a tone higher than
usual. Bell looks at Jim.

'Or a boy, as well! If we had had a little boy child, and I
stayed and we were a family and that, I would be showing the
boy that it's OK to behave in that way, that a woman will put
up with it?' My words are quivering in my mouth and Cyndi's
voice takes over:

'If you fall I will catch you I'll be waiting . . . '

Theo gets up to turn the music off. *'Don't, it's fine,'* I tell them.
I turn to the group. 'It's good, all of this, because I know no
matter what happens to me from now on, I stand for something.
I don't think I've ever stood for anything before!'

And they all say, 'Yeah, you have!'

'No, please, I know I'm waffling on but it's so tiring, defend-
ing my opinions. Everything I've had to say for such a long time
has been contested or counteracted or just shut down so please,
please just *let me*!'

'No problem, mate,' says Jim, and the rest of them nod.

'Sorry,' I say. 'I was just going to say that I stand for something, for what I'm prepared to accept. And that makes all of
this –' I put my hand on my heart, '– easier.'

I pause. The music continues. I smile and try to ignore my
mouth shaking at the corners. 'I mean, it's not *easy,* but it does
make it easier.'

And that's when I break into pieces.

I can't breathe.

I howl.

I grieve until I have to be carried inside by Paul.

'Why is this happening to me?' I scream.

'I don't know, mate, but we've got you,' says Paul.

'Why didn't he want me?' I throw my arms around Theo's neck.

'Sssh, it's OK, it's OK,' Theo says.

I cry for all the potential that's disappeared. I cry for my broken conveyor belt. I cry for my wedding Pinterest board that no one else knows about. I cry about every boy I've ever loved that has faded out of my life, and I cry that another one is now fading too.

I cry for every kiss on a snowy mews terrace I've ever seen in a Richard Curtis film. I cry for Disney endings. I throw all the closed doors inside me wide open and let the fear of being rubbish at the thing I've longed for since I was a little girl flow through and out of me. I am hysterical.

I heard once that grief is the perseverance of love. I cry because all of this means love is still there, that I can't get rid of it no matter what I now know about the relationship.

When I come to I am lying on the sofa, the same place I slept one week ago after *Strictly*. Each of my friends stroking a different part of my body. Hair, hands, temples, waist. When I want to get up, they help me. We all stand there, our histories having led us to the same moment in a Crouch End living room, hugging in a huddle like penguins. Even Winston rubs against my legs.

'I meant it all, though,' I tell them. 'Even though I cried at the end, it still counts.'

'We get it,' Bell says.

'We're all behind you,' says Theo.

I Stayed

Because the course of true love never did run smooth

I am twenty-three years old and sneaking around backstage in my pants because I am in LOVE.

People think that drama school is all about pretending to be spaghetti, reciting Shakespeare's sonnets as slam poetry, and singing music hall songs that culturally appropriate the traveller community. Well, I am here to tell you that I've done all of those things. But that drama school is *also* about shagging.

Onstage, the rest of my year at LAMDA drama school is about to perform 'Sit Down You're Rocking the Boat' from *Guys and Dolls*. It's the only song I'm not in, my only alone time. I'm taking the opportunity to teeter in a costume of sparkly heels, pants and bra up to the empty boys' dressing room to put a red envelope in the bag of Max, who's in the chorus and is onstage right now singing the baritone line in a pinstripe suit. Max doesn't really go in for Valentine's Day, and nor do I really, I'm not that sort of girl or anything, but I thought it would be fun to go to Scribbler, then Cards Galore, then Paperchase, then back to Scribbler to get the right one for us. Y'know one that's not too overt, or lovey-dovey or off-putting. The sort of card that says 'Lol Valentine's Day, how dumb is this?'; a funny one.

It says 'Nice Buns' on it, with a picture of two little bao buns in a bamboo steamer. We love dim sum. I love saying 'we' where I used to say 'I'.

Max looks just like a young John Gielgud and wears padded gilets like Marty McFly. He's tall, really tall. I once asked to dress up in his jeans and shirt and felt like the prettiest and most pocket sized of all the mice.

Not only that, he's got bags of common sense. I couldn't agree more with his assertions that shagging in fusty backstage corners and never telling anyone is very sexy/steamy behaviour, that it somehow makes us more authentic actors, and that my occasional discomfort at being kept secret is probably because I'm such a show-off. My friend Ben's told me Max has vehemently denied anything has been going on on several occasions. And that hurt, because it's happened before. The first time I ever gave anyone a blowjob it was with a mate of mine, who afterwards said, 'Let's not tell anyone, shall we?' The first guy I had sex with said the same thing. But you know what? I think it's just what men do to make things less intense.

I snoop around the rows of dressing tables, the showbizzy ones with mirrors surrounded by light bulbs, searching through the Kryolan powders and Lucozades for a sign of my man. The boys' dressing room is massive, much bigger than the girls', and the stench of decades of sweaty male bodies is making me squint. Still, it's infinitely preferable to the tang of micro-aggression swirling around the girls' one. Where earlier tonight Lacey had casually held up my tiny costume and called me anorexic, and not one of the eleven other women in the room had said anything. Including me.

The second verse comes through the crumbling brick walls, soundtracking me as I savour the moment, the moment in which Rebecca Humphries finally, finally gets to be a Valentine. I grin at myself in the mirror, standing there in my pants. I am in love, and not only that – Lacey is right, I am thin! It's truly miraculous. Like parts of me have been cut right off, leaving the same woman but smaller.

I've spent the last six months or so living off Americanos, Greek yoghurt and diarrhoea tablets. I don't feel hungry, ever. My appetite is reserved for one thing/person. Who can say whether it's the new body or my new appreciation for my body that has made Max sit up and pay attention, but it has.

And yes, everyone is saying Max is still with his girlfriend Constance, including Lacey who's her best friend. And yes, sometimes Constance's name will light up on his BlackBerry at three in the morning, and he'll be vague about why. But I have a foolproof coping mechanism, which is whenever I find his vagueness frustrating I stop asking questions and believe when he says that Constance is a deluded headcase who can't get over him, and that of course Lacey is out to get me, she hates me anyway because I'm so talented and am in such great shape. I am more than happy to accept this.

As the second chorus starts and my cue gets closer, I recognise Max's black Herschel rucksack, sitting on a chair at the back of the room. It's already unzipped and pulled apart. And at the top, there is another envelope. Ripped along the top. Flagrant.

I hesitate. I know from pub chat that snooping is a psycho's game but my cue is getting closer and closer and I'll get bollocked if I'm late. So fuck it, I pull the card out.

The graphic is serious and sincere and confident and everything my frigid, moronic, 'Carry On Movie' saucy card isn't allowed to be. It must be from Constance. 'Poor, crazy girl,' I tell myself. 'Crazy, crazy girl.' I sigh with relief and go to put it back where I found it and tuck mine down the side. But as I do, there's another envelope. A pink one. I open that too. On the front there is a vintage drawing of a sexy 1940s man and woman smoking cigarettes, and it reads, 'You had me at "Let's go to Maccy D's."' It's witty, sexy, sophisticated. Perfect.

Fuck, they're on the last chorus. I don't have time to read the long message written inside in beautiful handwriting. All I see is 'Love, Vanessa'. Before dropping all three cards on the floor and running to the stage-left wings.

The audience are going berserk, screaming over the band as they whack out the 'Luck be a Lady' reprise and confetti flutters down from the ceiling for the marriage of Miss Adelaide and Nathan. Max positions himself behind me in the curtain call, ready for the lights to go out so he can grab my bridal-gowned arse and sometimes, if he can't resist, kiss my neck.. But tonight, when I sense his hand, I shove it out of the way. He takes hold of my arm and yanks me back towards him.

'You OK?' I hear him whisper in the darkness, under the applause.

'Get off me.'

He clamps tighter around my elbow. 'Why? Tell me, quick.' But once the lights go up for the bow, he lets go like my arm burned the skin off his palm. When it's time for my individual bow, a huge cheer goes up. I wave at the audience, and hear a 'whoop!' from behind me. It's Max, applauding along too, looking proud in that god damned gorgeous gangster suit. I smile back at him and think they're only cards, bits of cardboard. What would Max say about those girls? That one is nuts and the other is irrelevant, probably.

The company heads into the wings, but the audience won't let up. We punch the air and Seb, who's playing Sky Masterson, shouts 'Fuck iiiiiit!' and runs back on beckoning the rest of us. Without hesitation, Max lunges for me, lifts me off my feet and into his arms and rushes back to plonk me centre stage. He takes my hand when we get there, and I let him.

And although there is no card for me
Or chocolate seashells maybe
And either would have been nice even though
idon'tbelieveinvalentinesdayreally
I'm the one whose hand he's holding, and this will do.

Because I'm used to toxic

Bethnal Green Working Men's Club, 31 October 2018

Intro: solo oboe and piano.

The psychologist Elisabeth Kübler-Ross proposed that there are five stages of grief that can be experienced in any order. They are:

- Denial: 'I'm fine.'
- Depression: 'I'm not fine, and never will be.'
- Bargaining: 'If I hadn't been so cold/unlovable/mean, it wouldn't have happened.'
- Acceptance: 'It is, as they say, what it is.'

But by far, my favourite has to be:

- Anger: 'I'm fucking angry.'

This is the first time I've been seen in public for three weeks, since the night I broke down after the Samstat Road clear-out. A few things that have happened since then: a stripper sold a story to the *Sun* about shagging Him when we were together in 2014. I remember finding a message on his phone from an unknown number, and he had told me it was a stripper and swore nothing happened. Another affair from 2016 came out, too. Someone sold a picture to the *Mirror* of him snuggling up with a woman in a pub, an actress. It was taken a week before Christmas, December 2016, on a night I would have been on stage performing in a Chekhov play in which my husband was cheating on me with three different women. A comedy, actually. I cooked his mum and dad Christmas lunch the week after. The woman's friend told the media they had 'clicked' at the Edinburgh festival, when she had seen His show . . . that was about living with me. I visited Him several times during that festival, often I lay in bed waiting for Him to come home. And you know where else I was? I was in Calais sorting through condom donations for refugees, which I'm sorry but is far too virtuous to not signal. Spookiest thing about the affair is that the woman was an actress from a TV series we had watched together recently. I hadn't even known he *knew* her. Reports say he 'lavished her with gifts and flowers'.

Today, it's Halloween. I'm standing onstage in a short black wig, black corset, stockings, green eyeshadow and false lashes, with a microphone in my left hand and a half-drunk bottle of cheap white in my right. I'm trying to forget that I can't quite reach the high note at the end of this song. Light is shining in my eyes. And I'm fucking *raging*.

> 'Maybe this time, I'll be lucky
> Maybe this time he'll stay . . . '

I raise an eyebrow at the audience, and they roar with laughter.

On Monday I was contacted by the comedian Jayde Adams. She asked whether I fancied re-entering the world at the comedy night she runs with another comic, Kiri Pritchard-McLean. The night involves comedians singing songs from musicals with a live band.

'I'm not a comedian,' I'd said.

'I think you'll do all right, love,' Jayde had replied.

And because I am so angry I said, 'Go on then.'

So here I am, having been handed a stage in a low-ceilinged sold-out comedy club, as the surprise last-minute addition to the bill. My first thought was to do Nancy from *Oliver*, having always felt I had a rip-roaring 'Nancy from *Oliver*' energy, until it occurred to me for the first time ever that in glamorising Nancy from *Oliver* I would glamorise a sex worker being killed by her abusive boyfriend, and I started being angry at the musical *Oliver* too.

'As it's a Halloween special,' Jayde had said to the crowd, 'we thought we'd let Liza Minnelli perform an exorcism.' She's wearing a T-shirt that says, 'Woman Power'. Kiri's says, 'Brains are the new tits'. It occurred to me, as I witnessed them nailing their joint warm-up set, that I hadn't seen women doing stand-up since before I met Him.

Now I'm not the world's greatest singer, and there's a high note at the end of this song that feels higher and higher the closer I get to it. But dammit I can sell a number.

'The fact is,' I'd told the audience earlier, 'I would never have done this when I was going out with Him. I'd have been too scared. Because there was a chance that I would be much, much funnier than Him.' And they howled. And I smiled. But I'd wanted to rip my body in half with a scream of fury.

'Maybe this time, for the first time
Love won't hurry away ...'

So yeah, He was finally kicked off *Strictly*. I was surprised how little I cared, in the end. There was a point I believed He never would be. The judges seemed determined to keep Him in, or the show did, or the BBC did, or something. Excellent ratings apparently, highest ever. He and the dancer did a waltz, a sinister one because it was Halloween week, to 'I Put a Spell on You'. The last thing He said on the show was that it had been 'the best experience of His life'.

Rumours abound that He is going to be in the jungle next, in *I'm a Celebrity . . . Get Me Out of Here*. My first thought was that He would never do that. My second thought was, *How would you know what He would do, Rebecca? Everything you thought you knew about Him was a lie.* And I think if I had to pin it down I'd say that's where the anger started.

> 'He will hold me fast
> I'll be home at last'

They're laughing again and I am *incensed* at Him for not seeing me the way they are right now. I'm so angry at Him for being in my thoughts when I'm living my best life. For taking up my space now, by underestimating me then.

I decide on the spot to amend the following section.

'He won't be a loser, any more,

Like the last time and . . . nah, just the last time actually.'

I take a swig from the bottle and wish I could smash it on the floor.

You know what else I'm angry about? That this isn't just about Him. A couple of days ago I spoke with a casting director pal of mine, wanting reassurance that my sector of the industry wouldn't turn its back on me as a result of my being tabloid fodder. He was quick to assure me that nobody in the industry really cared about it all. Too quick.

Last week, right after Bell told me she was pregnant, I auditioned for a part in *The Crucible*. Elizabeth Proctor, another betrayed woman. My first professional audition ever as a single person. The first time in a long time where it was guaranteed no one would say to me, 'You probably won't get it, but do your best' as I was leaving the house. I went in well prepared, excited to be working, hungry for passionate conversation re the play and the role and its themes. I sat down on a plastic chair opposite the production team, and one of the women looked at me, all misplaced compassion, and said:

'Firstly, Rebecca, do you feel you could cope with the demands of the role, given the similarities in your personal life at the moment?'

I baulked a bit, but then said, 'Yeah, course', and did the scenes, and I was good. I haven't heard anything from them since.

When I think about what I should have said to her instead of, 'Yeah, course.'

When I think about how I'd smiled and said, 'No that's fine!' after she'd asked, 'Sorry, was that all right to have asked?'

When I think about how, despite the team clearly believing me to be in a fragile place at the moment, they *still* had not got back to me with the outcome of a job I had scrupulously prepared for. A job that I had hopes for. Work that I need.

'Everybody loves a winner
So nobody loved me ...'

The audience is rapt and I am *so fucking good* at this, I can see it all over their faces. I recount incident after incident where I've sat like a chump and taken everything this industry has thrown at me.

The agent in LA that met me for three minutes, then said the thing with me is that I could never be a leading actress, I'm a classic 'funny best friend' and that's a problem because 'it's fashionable for those to go to Asian women at the moment'.

The director who told me it was in my interests to get either skinnier or fatter if I wanted to get jobs because there's no such thing as normal in this career.

The production that kept scheduling me in to film on the day I had to go to the hospital to have a colposcopy, when your smear comes back as abnormal and they need to look for cancerous cells, and in the end sent an email asking if I could at least come in straight after I'd had it done so they didn't have to switch the days around.

(Incidentally I have to pop out of this to say that it turns out abnormal smears and colposcopies are generally nothing to worry about. It was only after I'd had it I started chatting with mates and discovered four of them had also had it done, and they had gone into it with the same 'Jade Goody died of this in like five minutes' terror.)

All of the incidents where I've been left hanging in the air waiting to hear something, anything, even a 'no thank you', to feel like a human being.

I'm so angry at the industry for not loving me back. Angry at myself for putting in more than I get out, for waiting years for it to change when it never does. I'm angry with my own upbeat compliance in a field that fucks women and old people over, that makes me feel plain looking (if not just plain ugly), makes me feel threatened and envious, will shower me with praise and attention one minute then love-starve me for the next six months, shrinking me and putting me back in my box that's labelled 'Sex workers and secretaries and betrayed women in stories written by men'.

And most of all I'm furious at how devoted I am to it, and how much I don't want to leave it. Because the more my eyes begin to open about harmful relationships, the more I see them everywhere, and the clearer it becomes that the longest running toxic love of my life has actually been my career.

'Lady Peaceful, Lady Happy,
That's what I longed to be!'

Earlier this week I went to see a healer, mainly because it's something I would have wanted to do when He & I were still together but would have been too embarrassed to. I've never dabbled in the mystic before, my main reference being the character of Grandmother Willow in *Pocahontas*. This woman, Emma, was about as far from Grandmother Willow as it's possible to be, which I was relieved about as I used to have nightmares about faces in trees because of that film. Emma was my age, blonde, cool, and hot. She had the most peaceful room of crystals and candles and a framed picture that said 'Dear Fears – Fuck off'. And she knew stuff. Stuff she couldn't possibly have known, that nobody knew, about the relationship and how long I had been unhappy. She also told me that I have a strong voice and an open heart, but that my vagina is like a tangled Black Octopus.

> 'Well all the odds are, they're in my favor,
> Something's bound to begin!'

She delivered that last clanger in a way that suggested it was something I should sort out. I'm thinking it sounds like hard work, I can barely untangle a necklace. Maybe I'll go the other way, just let my minge dry out and become a bitter, repressed, horny spinster like Miss Hannigan in *Annie*, drinking myself to death around orphan girls who hate me.

> 'It's gotta happen!'

I can't have sex again anyway. Every time my hand so much as brushes my upper thigh in the shower, I see Him with other women like I'm in the room watching it. Him with that other actress. I'm so fucking fuming at all of us women for having degraded ourselves by fucking Him and his ego. I'd truly rather the space between my legs were a smooth plastic gusset, like Barbie's. It might as well be. Were it not for a particularly gory, clotty period last week, I would have said it had sealed over completely.

'Happen sometime!'

Bell blurted out that she was pregnant in front of *Mastermind* last night; she couldn't hold it in any longer. I screamed. I'm so genuinely happy for her, and for Jim, and I'm so furious about how when they told me I went into the kitchen and bit down on a wrapped packet of Kingsmill muffins because of how angry it made me about my own life.

'Maybe this time I'll win!'

I was eleven when I started my periods. It happened at my brother's first birthday party. I was wearing a Union Jack dress, a replica of Ginger Spice's from Norwich market. I just remember eating a slice of caterpillar cake downstairs afterwards and thinking, *What does this mean?* I didn't tell a soul for months, hiding used sanitary towels in Jake's nappy bags and stuffing them in my doll's house at the foot of my bed. It looked like there'd been a massacre in a very small mattress factory. When my mum came to my room and asked whether I knew why her Bodyform products were disappearing, it was the most humiliated I have ever felt. Twenty-two years later I'm conscious I know as little now as I did then. Is there an average number of menstruating years? If your periods start early, do they end early? What age on average does the menopause happen, I feel like it could be thirty-five or fifty-five because *no one fucking talks about that either*.

*

Time is sexist. There, I said it. Time discriminates against women. Those five and a half years mean something different to me than they do to Him. That relationship has ripped a chunk of fertility out of my timeline, for ever. And not His.

> 'Cause everybody always loves a winner,
> So nobody loved me . . . '

And the thing is? I don't even know if I want an effing baby. I don't know if I've always just been told I want an effing baby because I have an effing womb. I've only ever been effing asked 'Do you want kids?' in a way that makes it clear the person asking it expects a 'yes', so that's what I've always given them. But now I'm on my own, I don't know if that's true. I don't know if being a mother is something that means something to me at all.

> 'Lady peaceful . . . '

And another thing: what if the reason I'm so unsure about whether I want children or not is because the answer is actually 'no', and I'm too embedded in evolutionary shame to even realise it?

> 'Layyyy-dy happy . . . '

But the kicker is, it's not a decision I can allow to happen organically because sexist old time may run away before I make up my mind. And I hate – HATE – how this has spun me out when all I want is to be able to be happy for my friend who knew she wanted a baby and is getting it.

> 'That's what I *longed* to be!'

226

I hope He wakes up in the night screaming for what He has lost. I hope that getting up in the morning feels like falling off a cliff and into another dark day living without everything He took for granted. I hope He has to be fished out of daydreams about the curve of my lower back.

'Well all the odds are, they're in my favor . . .'

I hope the play I went up for is both cheap and pretentious, and that whenever any of the production team goes up for any job in the future they never hear anything again, so even though they feel deep down their career is dead there's still that constant agonising optimism.

'Something's bound to begin!'

The band is crescendoing, I think. Some sounds are echoing in a recess towards the back of my ears. I've gone partially deaf and completely blind. All I see or hear is white-hot rage.

'It's gotta happen!
Happen sometime!'

This anger, it's viscous and delicious. It feels like an ally guiding me towards an answer. It felt much more dangerous when I allowed it to be contained, and fester into the really destructive thing: resentment. After years of minimising my pain, it feels great to maximise it.

'Maybe this time . . .'

There's silence. The band has stopped. The silhouetted shapes of the audience are still. The only sound is my breath in the microphone. And I realise I've reached the hiatus before the note at the end, the note that's out of my range. I close my eyes and think about being underestimated.

'*MAYBE* this *time I'll win!*'

I hit it effortlessly. Huh. Sometimes anger gets you places.

I am ...

Gaining perspective

Crouch End, 5 November 2018

I missed Him.

Jim had heard from Him that afternoon, He hadn't known whether to tell me. He'd texted Jim to please, come to the pub, He wants to explain Himself.

I went through my Instagram and deleted every picture of the two of us together. The tabloids wrote articles about it within the hour.

Ordinarily Bonfire Night is my favourite night of the year owing to being both cosy and camp. That year I didn't want to go to a display in case someone took a picture of me looking my current state, which is 'sad cold teabag in the kitchen sink', so Bell and Jim brought the fireworks to me at the end of their garden because they're heroes. Jim put on the mother of all displays, truly the firework king. And other than one hectic moment when, as he pelted it from a lit Roman candle, he knocked it at a weird angle and Bell shouted 'JIMGETBACKTHERE' because it was directed right at where she and I were huddled, he really nailed the brief.

I looked up at the sky fizzing with fireworks and missed Him.

I let the rain thin out the squiggly mustard on my hot dog and wished that He was back in my life, but better.

I watched a sparkler burn all the way to my gloveless fingers and remembered that I was well shot of Him, that living in that flat was death, but I still wished more than anything that He was there.

I missed Portobello Road on Sundays, Lush bath bombs and fish fingers, chips and beans. I missed how funny He is. You know, He once went on the TV show *Sunday Brunch*, and Craig David was on it too, and He said to Craig David, 'Hang on, what are you doing here? It's Sunday, shouldn't you be chilling?', which is objectively hilarious.

I even missed that stupid fedora, which is sort of endearing in a naff way.

And just like that, I realised something. They say it takes twenty-one days in a row for something to become habitual. It's been thirty days since *Strictly*, and on every one of them I've recounted the events to someone new, or marched into wherever Bell and Jim were with my new hot take on the situation. In doing so, I've been passively inviting Him into my space. I need to break the habit. Need a change of scene.

'I think I'm gonna visit Seb on his boat in France,' I said to Bell.

'Oh God, not sexy Jacques,' she replied. 'Try not to shag him, will you?'

'Quiet, woman. We're friends, and absolutely nothing about that need change just because we've never been single at the same time before.'

'I can see the romcom now,' she said. '*The Boat and the Black Octopus*.'

Bell and Jim call Seb 'Jacques' after an episode in the first series of *The Simpsons*, when Marge is seduced by a suave, low-voiced Lothario at a bowling alley.

'My mind says stop, Marge,' Bell quoted at me as I skipped off to St Pancras, 'but my heart and hips cry proceed!'

Seb and I were housemates for years during and after drama school. We've known one another since the first week I moved to London and got a job at the Hammersmith Apollo, where we'd sell programmes and pull pints and dare one another to sip from the ullage bucket. We weren't friends then. He thought I had a stick up my arse and I thought he was a Neanderthal. We were very wrong and slightly right about one another.

Word of the scandal had travelled to rural France instantly. He'd messaged saying any time I wanted to get away from the media I should go and join him on the boat, a fixer-upper he had bought down in Carcassonne months ago when he broke up with his girlfriend Nadia and had been travelling on all the way to Paris. I mean, you couldn't get much further from the tabloids, and my old mate being there was a giant bonus.

No contempt was ever so basic, so 'alpha male', as the one held between my ex-boyfriend and Seb. Five years ago, when He & I had just started going out, the two of them 'exchanged words' at my birthday meal. Nine or so of us had sat around with ice-cream sundaes, bearing witness to what was the closest thing we'd seen to one of those chest-thumping silverback wars on an Attenborough documentary. After that, I'd decided the easiest thing to do would be to stop hanging out with Seb. So I did.

He would be gloriously annoyed if He knew what I was up to right now, and it would be easy to ensure He found out. All it would take to be all over the tabloid press would be a simple Instagram story of me next to my ruggedly handsome, six-foot-three, Gillette-advert-type companion.

Should be clear, though, we're just old friends, Seb and I, and this is definitely not a *When Harry Met Sally* situation.

Currently I am on the oak deck of a small Sylvanian-Families-style canal boat that's docked along a deserted French countryside canal. On the bank to my left, a small cobbled path.

On the right, fields and fields and fields of lavender. Edith Piaf is singing 'Non, Je Ne Regrette Rien'. My hair is damp. I am wearing a yellow and white striped towel, having just showered under a lukewarm dribble. It's a nice day for November, and besides, I'd never let a slight chill get in the way of a table of cheese and choux buns, which we bought earlier from the local village.

Seb walks up from below deck, uncorking a red wine. He's soaking wet and his shirt is open. He grins, hands me a glass and pours.

'You know, I could stand to make a lot of money from all this,' he indicates me, the wine, the tableful of treats. 'Sell some pics, spin some hot boat sex yarns.' He pulls playfully at the towel wrapped around me.

'Fuck off!' I clamp it to my tits and he tugs the corner really hard. 'FUCK OFF!'

And my modesty is saved, as behind us on the water comes the unmistakable kerfuffle of a female duck getting gang banged.

'That's me,' I tell Seb. 'And those boy ducks are you.'

He laughs and attacks the brie wedge with a knife. 'Max had journalists knocking on his door, you know.' He rips off a chunk of baguette.

'And he hasn't said anything? I'm surprised. And grateful, too. Max was so livid when I dumped him for Him.'

'Poor old Max. He was never good enough for you really.' Seb shoves the bread and cheese in his mouth in one. 'I called it, if you remember, when he was busy banging you at the same time as Constance and telling everyone you were a liar.'

'I haven't thought about that in years. And everyone believed him,' I rip into a chunk of white paper with a veiny blue wedge inside.

'I hear that. Nadia's been chatting all sorts of shit about things I'm meant to have done, and people are fucking ready to accept all of it.'

'Has she?' I ask, knowing exactly what he's talking about. I've heard all sorts about Seb and Nadia's relationship through the grapevine. Dark things. Contradictory things.

Seb shrugs. 'Whatever, we're not like you and Max were. With you guys it was a masculinity issue I reckon.'

'What, like people were more willing to believe him because he was a man?' I nod and stick a knife in the wedge.

'Nah, I meant I think you were alpha, right, and he was beta. And women who are more masculine, people get intimidated by them.'

I stop spreading cheese on the baguette. 'That's offensive.'

'You do have quite a masc energy, come on. It's not unattractive; Nadia has it too.'

'Oh, I intimidate you, do I?'

'You used to at drama school, you were good and you knew it.'

'I hate this; I always hated having to constantly justify this.' I slam the knife down on the table. 'You know, I worked really hard, and yeah I was talented, but I never threw it in anybody's face.'

'No—'

'Never hurt anyone. I was constantly vilified for being good at things.'

'Don't have a cow, man.'

'Iamhavingacow! Because when a woman behaves like that it's threatening – she's a diva or mental or whatever – but if I was a bloke people would say that behaviour was hot, they'd be like, "Ooooh he's confident, wow, sexy arrogance."'

'How do you know?'

'This is unbelievable, that is *literally* what happened to you!' I'm hitting Mariah Carey notes. 'Except you didn't even have to work hard! We all thought you were so cool and sexy!'

'I bet you did.' He smiles.

'Ugh, I'm gonna get changed.' I get up to leave, taking the baguette nub.

'Humps?'

'What?'

'I'm very turned on by this argument.' His voice is even lower than usual.

'I can't hear you, shush.' And I march indoors, trying not to laugh or let my towel fall down.

Later, I ask him, 'Don't you get lonely?' He's ladling onion soup from a big silver pan into bowls. He made a fire in the grate. There are candles in jars on the windowsill, the table, the steps leading up to outside. He still hasn't put on a new shirt. I, however, am fucking freezing as per so am wearing one of his giant woolly jumpers and joggers. Frankly, I'd imagined this as more a 'Carrie goes to Paris' *Sex and The City* kind of a landscape so only packed foofy skirts.

'This isn't loneliness.' He grates a block of cheese. 'It's solitude.'

'I'd be lonely, I think. Then again, I'd much rather be lonely on my own than lonely in a relationship. At least my brain can make sense of that.'

He puts a bowl down in front of me: a huge island of cheesy bread, oniony gravy bubbling around the edges and running down the sides.

'You ever want to cheat on Him?' he asks.

'Of course.'

'You slaaaag.'

'I never did, though.'

He comes around the table, sits next to me on the banquette. 'Bet you came close.' He smiles.

I smile back. 'This guy called Hugo.'

'I *knew* it! Some sexysexy posho, is it?'

'Yep, a total eyegasm. God, look at me, I've gone silly!'

'Go on then, spill it.' He blows on his soup.

'We were doing this show together. I knew he massively respected *my work*.' I say my work with a regal resonant actor-y voice, hand on my heart, so that I'm less embarrassed about how much I mean it. 'But also he was just so unabashed about how much he liked my company. He was having relationship problems too, with his thin-clavicled shiny-haired girlfriend. So the night before our first performance I asked him if he wanted to go for a drink with me, because I knew he was a drinker, and I thought if I got pissed enough I would have the excuse of being pissed. It's what makes me think that no one does things when they're pissed that they don't secretly think about doing sober.'

'Big time, that's a given.'

'But nah.' I shake my head. 'We didn't do anything. I mean, I think we didn't. I blacked out and woke up in a bed next to Him in my clothes from the night before, covered in red-wine vomit.'

'Classy. How'd you know nothing happened?'

'I apologised to Hugo at the theatre the next morning, he said it was all kosher, nothing went on. He was weird with me, though – cold.' I take a sip of lava-like soup and splutter.

'Do you wish it had?' Seb hands me a dirty tea towel.

'I've thought about this.' I take it, and brush the soup off my front. 'About whether the will-power to not cross a sexy line with a third party is honourable, or an act of self-denial. Was I ever jealous of the other women I thought He was sleeping with, or jealous of Him for having the balls to do whatever He wanted? That's really squeezing the juice out of life, isn't it? I sort of admire it in a way.'

'No you don't.'

'Well, I envy it, then. It's living with passion, spontaneity, eroticism. Not by some puritanical moral code.' I pick up my spoon. 'But I think that night with Hugo was probably enough. Enough to make me feel like,' I hesitate, embarrassed, 'like a *woman*. And not just a part of a flat in Shepherd's Bush.'

I look at Seb. His expression hasn't changed. 'I'm glad you didn't. That's not you.'

'It took a lot of restraint,' I say.

I watch Seb chisel burnt cheese from the edge of his soup bowl and stir it in. He raises the spoon to his mouth and blows.

Try not to shag him, will you? says Bell's voice from somewhere.

Because here in the dark, in the candlelight, I realise that I'm starting to be conscious of the words I'm using. Conscious of not letting Seb notice.

'A lot of restraint,' I repeat, and He looks at me.

Conscious of some kind of charge?

After we've eaten, we take a few little glass jars of candles to the deck and share a roll-up. It's one of those cold sharp nights where your covered bits are cosy but any exposed flesh feels like ice. The night is so still and dark it deadens all sound except the black water lapping against the boat. The moon is full. And the stars ... it's as though they've decided to dome around the two of us as we drink and smoke out here in navy-blue nowhere.

'Here's a theory for you,' I say. 'When it comes to relationships, women are looking for love and not sex, and men are looking for sex and not love.' I hand him back the fag, 'Discuss.'

'Archaic horseshit.'

'Fine, discuss.'

'Because I really loved Nads, dude. I know it's for the best and all that shit. Three years of trying to work it out, yeah, it was right to pull the plug. That's why I was just like, fuck it, I'm gonna get the boat, live the dream I compromised when we were together.'

'Yeah, that's part of why I came here too. Making moving on exciting, you know, doing adventures. Stuff like this, it stops you thinking about what they might be doing without you. Makes you excited for the things *you* can do without *them*.'

I hadn't noticed that Seb was lost somewhere else. 'People take sides, Humps,' he says abruptly, staring ahead at nothing in particular. 'They believe what they want to because of something that happened to them once.' He breathes smoke into the air. 'Y'know, stuff that other people have been through, that has nothing to do with me, can make them think I'm this monster.'

Of course I've considered this. Nadia and I aren't really friends, but we have similarities. Inner fire, seeming fearlessness. It's occurred to me how I'm expecting people to believe me and yet here I am, sitting with Seb and not letting Nadia's story infuse the wine and cheese and French country air.

Life's complicated. We should remember the truth is always subjective, and shouldn't generalise, and to listen to women's stories while understanding there is nuance and that there are two sides. That it's very unlikely anyone is inherently bad – but also that doesn't mean we have to excuse anything. Trying to be fair can spin you out. And it cracks your head open, taking stories with pinches of salt but at the same time hoping your own story will be swallowed down seasoning free.

'All you can do, I guess, is trust in your authenticity,' I tell him. 'You know your own truth.'

'It still hurts,' he says.

I can't help noticing that the more broken Seb seems, the more the candlelight accentuates his jawline.

God, it would be fun to have a project, though.

You know where you are when you're mending a man.

And I do love *When Harry met Sally*.

I look at the moon. 'Bloody hell, it's so clear here,' I say, and throw the wine down my neck. I put the glass down, my hands still shivering.

We're still for a moment. The fire of the fag has burned out. I look at the tufts of grass on the side of the bank. The chunks of dirt. I hear the water moving.

'Do you ever feel like there's something wild about you that you've smoothed over with manners?' I ask him.

I can feel him looking at me. 'Not really.'

I look at his broad chest and briefly think how much wildness there would be to smooth over.

'No,' I say. 'I don't suppose you have.'

His eyes pull mine up from his chest until we're looking at each other. The water on the canal stops moving.

He steps forward until I have to look upwards to stay in his eyes. I can feel my parka brushing against him.

He looks down at me.

He asks quietly, 'Are your hands cold?'

I swallow and say, 'Yes.'

He inches closer until I feel my body press against him.

He reaches down and touches my hands. He rubs his thumbs against my palms, and slides them under the front of his jumper against his warm skin. He guides my wrists around his waist until my arms are wrapped around him, and I am pulling myself in tight.

He runs his fingers through the side of my hair with one hand, and tilts my chin up with the other.

We kiss slowly.

He slides his hand under my jumper and feels the skin of my waist. I move it upwards.

The sex is slow too at first. Careful. When I come it's in waves, it's like sliding into warm water. We lie next to one another afterwards, flushed and astonished. We laugh because we don't know what to say. He is facing me when I wake up, and I worry I have been sleeping open mouthed, or dribbling. In bed his fingers lightly run down my naked spine, and he pulls me into him to keep me warm because after all these years he knows I'm always cold. I feel beholden to Seb for making me feel wanted. We pull the boat into Paris; he never thought we'd make it and I know it's a sign that this was meant to be.

I post a selfie on Instagram: me curled into the nook of Seb's neck with the Eiffel Tower positioned just so in the background.

The headlines will say I've moved on, that wow, my new man is so handsome. He will find out before lunchtime, and He will wonder if I had a thing for Seb all along. On deck, Seb's phone dings and I wonder who it is. I get my Eurostar back to London. I check my phone for messages from Seb constantly. I wonder who he's with when I don't hear from him. I wonder who that message was from and why it made him smile. He calls me later that night and I ask him and he gets annoyed that I'm even asking. I ask him when he's coming back to London and he says he doesn't know, and I'm pissed off with him for not being everything I want, especially given all I've been through. I begin to resent Seb, and him me . . .

'Are your hands cold?' Seb asks.

'Nah, they're fine,' I say, and put them in my pockets.

Two broken halves don't make a whole. I smile at my mate, who I appreciate is attractive but who I've never fancied, who has never fancied me either.

'*Je t'aime*, mate,' I say genuinely.

'*Je t'aime*, dude.' He grins at me. The water splashes against the boat.

Something occurs to me on the Eurostar home, staring in the window at my translucent reflection set against the whirring fields. That if I was told a story of a single woman alone with a rugged, outdoorsy Mr Bear Grylls Poldark Darcy, who fixes things and cooks hearty meals and doesn't feel the cold, I would want her to have sex with him. Even if I knew she was fragile, and some of the things I'd been told about Him were borderline toxic. Even if I'd been told time and time again the relationship between them was platonic, I would still have willed for a spark of something 'more'. I am hardwired to want more when what there is is enough.

*

Back in Crouch End, I float through the door with a suitcase full of sweaty leftover cheese and a heart as light as anything. I have a new romantic memory to rival any of the others, of opening the door to the deck in my pyjamas to find Seb pointing at the Eiffel Tower. Of cruising along the Seine into Paris with him, my old friend, sipping stove-made coffee, listening to Nile Rodgers' *Desert Island Discs* and watching the city of love getting closer and closer. And not only that – I can finally feel the space in front of me for new and unexpected love stories.

I find Bell covered in flour at the kitchen table with her little French mum Yvette, forming a gyoza production line.

'How's the octopus?' Belle asks. 'Still tangled?'

'We didn't shag, if that's what you're asking.'

'You *are* crazy!' says Yvette. 'He is magnifique!'

More aware

Great Marlborough Street, November 2018

For some it's their teenage bedroom. Their mum's kitchen table. Something about stepping into their childhood surroundings that connects them with their right to peace and quiet.

For me, the place where nothing bad could possibly happen is Liberty's Beauty Hall. Which is exactly where Bell and I met one Friday evening after she finished work, to spritz and smear and create colour palettes on the backs of our hands.

In the last few weeks, I have teetered about the house in full face like Little Edie from *Grey Gardens*. I've still been trowelling on the products. I love doing it, love how they make me feel, and it feels important that my outer self be an extension of this new-found confidence I have buzzing inside, irrespective of who sees it. Apparently, Neanderthals used to crush up pyrite and gemstones and wear it as highlighter, so there you are: the desire to look hot is primitive.

I love everything about Liberty's Beauty Hall: the bottle-green tiling and the golden plaques on each concessions stand, the staff lacquered to within an inch of their lives, how it lightly smells of talc, the phials and tubes that look richer than you are, all printed on the reverse with over-effusive nonsense. 'Unrivalled', sixty different brands will claim, 'Used by the great mystics, sages and healers of the ancient world', says another, which is a bold claim since Liberty only opened in 1875. One set of under-eye patches claims to 'tap into your creative muse'.

'They're just testing us to see if we read it,' said Bell, shaking her head and splooging more £36 hand cream tester past her wrists and up her arms.

Sometimes, when I worry third-wave feminism is yet another myth the patriarchy has created to make us feel better about pandering to the male gaze, I think about Jane Fonda approaching Dolly Parton to star in *9 to 5*. Dolly agreed to it when Jane explained she knew Republican women of the US South, arguably the ones most oppressed, would go to see it for Dolly, and connect with its feminist message.

Beauty has force.

Anyway, I was having my face painted on a stool at the Nars counter when my agent called.

'OK, don't freak out but something's royally ballsed up everything.'

He told me a person had come forward saying that I stole somebody's boyfriend, Max, while I was at LAMDA. They've sold the story to a newspaper. He doesn't know who it is.

He said the good news was the papers need at least one other person to back it up. The bad news is they'll be offering people fat wodges of cash for it.

I ran straight out the door in half a face of slap and on to Great Marlborough Street for air, Bell right behind me. I told her to smile and laugh in case we were papped, then explained.

'HAHAHAHA!' she bleated in my face with saucer eyes. 'What a cunt! What will you do?'

And I decided that nowhere is sacred, so I might as well go to Norwich.

*

Some people relish the opportunity to visit their home town. I see Norwich more as a task to tick off. This has to do with two things. The first is that it used to take over three hours to drive there from Shepherd's Bush and every three-hour drive in a 1998 Toyota Yaris feels like a gamble.

The second is more complicated, has to do with guilt, and is really hard to get across without sounding like an ungrateful little shit.

There were approximately zero violent incidents in my childhood, thank God, because I know how hard that can twist a person's insides up. I was blessed in many ways: Beanie Babies to grant me future wealth (they haven't, you need to have kept the tag on apparently); family buffets with egg mayonnaise vol-au-vents and creamy loaves of Viennetta; and mantelpieces rammed with Kinder Egg and McDonald's Happy Meal figurines. Carveries, Argos catalogues, Next sales. But, much like the *Little Mermaid* – who cares? No big deal. I wanted more.

When I finally minced off to live in London, and found the 'more' that I craved, I assumed that without me, the city of Norwich would oxidise. Not so. In fact, the city centre itself started getting cooler and more popular the second I left, which is the opposite of what you want your ex to do. And everyone my age that lived there got busy living without me, fucking busy – getting married and having kids. That was when I more or less left them to it. Over the years I let the hundred-or-so miles between me and my family become a gulf, and in some ways that was made easier by the fact He wasn't big on visiting. It's a gulf that's present every time I see them, is always unspoken, and makes me feel like a gaping sphincter.

And now, to make matters worse, I am back here in my mum's kitchen, fully infantalised, drinking Ribena from a carton and watching a woman wrestle a Dobermann across the cul-de-sac.

'It's not even hers!' says Mum, peering through the blinds next to me. 'It's her partner's!'

'I thought they didn't live together?'

'They don't.'

'Well, why's she got this—'

'Her name's Debbie.'

'All right, why's Debbie got this whacking great dog, then?'

'Well, obviously he wants her to take care of it.'

'Yep. But she must have agreed to it.'

'Well, she's such a lovely person Debbie is, honestly.'

I sip at my straw and watch Debbie on the other side of the double glazing, gripping the collar as the animal strains against it. She leans her bodyweight backwards to be as far from its jaws as possible. Her T-shirt reads 'Keep Calm and Drink Gin'.

'No, but what I mean is, why did she say yes if she clearly didn't want to?' I continue.

'I should think he probably badgered her, don't you?'

'Still, she always has the word "no", Mum.'

'I bet it eats like a bloody horse,' Mum tuts. 'And he parks this great big Harley-Davidson right in the middle of the cul-de-sac as well, so Jake can't get his van out.'

The dog yanks Debbie forward on to her bare knees. Imagine falling in love then months later winding up wrangling their Dobermann, and if not their Dobermann then their admin, or their washing, or their anger. There is an epidemic of women in this country who will put up with any old shit, from any old shit. Irresponsible shits. Lazy shits, thick shits. Cruel shits.

My pocket vibrates. Seb. 'Re: the papers, it wasn't Max. I probed. He's just had a kid, he cba with the hassle.'

I reply, 'Didn't think so. Not his vibe to get involved.'

'Me & Paul are on it. We don't know who they are. But we will find them. And we will kill them. PS say hi to ur mum 😉.'

'Seb says hi,' I tell her.

'Oh, does he?!' She couldn't be happier if I'd told her Tom Selleck had joined the local Slimming World.

'Dad's here, I can hear the Fiesta.'

'Is it Merchants of Spice you're going to?'

'Yeah,' I say, putting my hood up. The public restaurant wasn't my idea, but it's only Norwich, no one will care. 'What will you get up to?'

'Nothing,' she says instantly.

'You can watch *Strictly*, Mum,' I say. 'It's OK.'

'Well, I do like Stacey Dooley, is the thing.'

'Me too, she's lush.'

The bell rings. From outside, I can hear Dad idly falsetto-ing Sheena Easton's 'For Your Eyes Only'.

'So who's going tonight, then?' Mum asks as I pull on my coat.

'Oh, no one really,' I say, running out the door, 'just the two of us and Jake!'

Around the table are Dad and Mel, Jake and his girlfriend Ellie, Auntie Netti and Uncle Dale, Auntie Lynne and Uncle Graham, Uncle Ady and his girlfriend Colette, and cousins Harry, Bill, Sam and Eleanor, who have come without their partners but who most certainly have them.

As much as I like Liberty's, I also hold a deep fondness for cheap curry houses so I'm actually very (Maldon) salt of the earth (must confess to stealing that joke from the actor Harry Trevaldwyn). I'm talking about the BYOB restaurants with metal baskets of poppadoms and a chutney carousel, LED pictures of waterfalls, that always bring an After Eight with your bill and that, at the very back of the menu, have a 'chips and omelette' section.

I lied to Mum about who was going to dinner. She was close with my aunts before the divorce seventeen years ago. It was the first divorce anyone had experienced unless you count soaps.

I say that I'm the only person in my family to have been part of a tabloid scandal, but when you live in a small town that's riddled with gossip culture, your business might as well be front-page news.

bell hooks writes in her book *All About Love* that 'One reason women have traditionally gossiped more than men is because gossip has been a social interaction wherein women have felt comfortable stating what they really think and feel'. I have never found this to be more true than in small cities or towns, particularly working-class ones, where the glass ceiling of the patriarchy looms lower, and the cheaper the magazine, the more violent and salacious it is. Rings of shame and wobbly beach shots and speculating on why women can't keep a man down. I say that as a woman who used to be *gleefully obsessed* with chatting shite about other people: who they were banging and what they were wearing and how his wife found out or whatever. Now I hate it, how it perpetuates the stereotype of women knowing fuck all except how to be a horrible friend. Still, I think of my relationship to gossip as a bit like when those headlines came out in *Woman's Own* about Vanessa Feltz drinking custard again. I dislike what it does to me and I know I'll regret it later, but my God, I don't half crave its sweet taste sometimes.

'Excuse me, ma'am, what would you like please?'

'Oh, hi, sorry, I haven't even looked buuuut, yeah, I'll have a tarka dal, onion bhaji, a chapatti and – Netti, you want to share garlic rice?'

'Aaaah, lovely.'

'And a garlic rice to share, please.'

'Aaah,' Auntie Lynne says. 'That sounds lovely, Lovely.'

'Lovely' is the word of the evening. It's even been said by the countless strangers who have come up to the table and let me know they're rooting for me. Should have known I'd be even more visible here. Everyone feels so, so sorry for me. When I arrived my Aunties Lynne and Nett (both with big 'Christine Baranski in *Mamma Mia*' energy) agreed that I'd 'lost loads of weight' in such a sorrowful way. I was chuffed, obviously. Less thrilling has been the adorable but misjudged attempts at making me feel everything is going to be OK.

'You'll meet the right bloke in the end, Lovely.'

'Plenty more fish in the sea!'

And the harrowing moment when someone spoke about their twenty-eight-year-old colleague's new baby, and the table went silent.

I've been desperate to say I've recently concluded that I am excellent on my own.

But I haven't. I've said 'thanks, guys', because I know they are being, well, lovely, and saying those things because it's what they would want to hear if they were me. Because we are in Norwich, where I am the only person at the table – and perhaps the entire restaurant – who is single. Because they may not believe me anyway, and because if another table overheard there's a chance I'd be burned at the stake.

A fleet of waiters glide over with piled-up trolleys. My aunts repeat the orders louder for the table. Everyone passes bhajis and tears naans and spoons out one another's bhunas in what has over the years become a choreographed piece worthy of Pina Bausch: frantic and vibrant, with a stable foundation you never realise is there until someone trips over. Some of these couples have been married for over thirty years. As I watch them rib one another, hold samosas for the other to bite and still speak kindly to their spouse after all those years, something Alain de Botton once said occurs to me, something I've never understood before. How love is a skill, not a feeling. I think how we're taught a lot in our culture about how to find love, but hardly anything on how to sustain it. The answer to that was here, all along, and I never noticed.

I should come back more often.

Jake motions to me from across the table, pointing at his phone. I check mine. A text. 'Coach + horses with me + lads later? Be well mint (Wacky face emoji, ten beer emojis).'

I grin at him and type back, 'Yes please, thankyoooooou'.

Might as well do a cheeky check of Instagram. Fifty likes for my picture of Beyoncé with the baseball bat in 'Lemonade', not bad. A couple of comments. One from a stranger, 'You, woman, are a hero.' Another is from two minutes ago. It looks more hectic on the screen, as though someone wrote it while drunk.

'Hw bout when u stole my best freind Constance's boyfrend tho????!!! You aint no feminist hunni, jus a cheater urself.'

I read it again. And again.

Lacey. It's fucking Lacey.

I stand up. Netti stops scooping half the garlic rice on to my plate and looks up at me.

'What's up, Lovely?'

I look around the restaurant and everyone seems to look back at me just standing there, and all I can see are stories with headlines like: 'Korma Blimey! Humphries Has Hot and Spicy Breakdown!' I feel trapped, desperate not to make a scene but conscious that this person, Lacey, is unleashed and God knows what she'll do next.

I walk slowly without saying anything and sit on a bollard outside of the curry house. I message Seb and Paul and everyone else from my year at drama school asking if anyone has Lacey's number. I check her comment again to see if anyone has liked it. Three people. Oh God, if any of them are journalists I'm dead. I delete it. Seb sends Lacey's number. I call her, she doesn't answer. I call her five more times. I text her.

'Please pick up, Lacey, please. We need to sort this.'

I call her again, nothing. I leave a voice note.

'Lacey, please. This is bigger than you think. Please, you can hate me but this could ruin my life, y'know, I'm trying really hard to step away from it all and not be in the papers any more now I've said my bit. Please let me talk to you.' *My job as well*, I think as I pace relentlessly up and down by the bollards at the front entrance. The pressure of having a public-facing career means I've always tried hard to be nice to people, to work hard, to keep my head below the parapet. Who would hire me at the Royal Shakespeare Company if I'm all over those tabloids in my dad's shop, branded a liar? Who would hire me anywhere if I'm all over internet sidebars above words like 'hypocrite'?

She's not responding. I go back to the table with my head down.

'Are y'all right, Lovely?' asks Lynne.

'Y—' I start. Then. 'No, not really.'

They all drop their forks and lean in. I have to whisper to them everything that's happened because I don't want anyone thinking I'm upset about not being engaged or pregnant by thirty-two. Dad takes me home.

The next morning I sit in my teenage bedroom under a poster of Leonardo DiCaprio. In the background of a phone call, I hear a child ask for a yoghurt.

'I don't know whether Lacey spoke with them or not.' I'd forgotten how posh she was, which considering she's called Constance was an oversight. 'But I gave Paul my number because there are some things I'd like to say.'

'Right, yep, that's fine,' I nod.

It was clear Lacey was never going to pick up last night, but then Paul came through with someone even better/scarier. So here I am, listening to a voice I haven't heard in over eight years.

I'm afraid. I haven't known Constance for ages, I don't know what has happened to her since, what effect her experiences have had on her tolerance levels. I don't know what kind of day she's having today, how she slept, whether she's already stressed this morning from picking up toys and wiping mouths. I am aware she has the power to fuck me up with a phone call, an email, a social media post even. My public reputation hangs on this conversation.

'I hear everything you're saying,' I say. 'I'm sorry. I've always felt absolutely terrible about how it all happened. I know that sounds really vague, I can hear it myself, but it's genuine. I felt so bad at the time.'

'If you felt that bad why didn't you ever speak to me? Wait there.' I hear her say in a softer voice, 'Arlo, sssh, you've already had a Frube.'

'To be honest, Constance, I didn't speak to you because I was really ashamed.'

'Oh please. You didn't care about me.' Ugh, she's right. 'You're right,' I say. 'But, thing is, he said you were crazy.'

'I thought you knew it was wrong to dismiss women as crazy?'

'Yeah, *now* I do. But only since it happened to—' I can't even finish the sentence, it sounds so selfish. 'Because of what happened in my instance,' I say, like I'm making a complaint to HR.

'You knew that I wasn't crazy. You just wanted your own way.'

'HOW ARE WE STILL ARGUING ABOUT MAX, CONSTANCE?!' I can't deal with it any more. 'There was nothing so great about him! He was kind of a loser, he called his mum "Mummoes" without irony!'

'This isn't about Max; this is about all this sisterhood business.'

'What?'

'You're supposed to be this big feminist,' she tells me. 'Where's your solidarity?'

I grip the side of the bed with my free hand; I think that I could tear a chunk out of the mattress. I want so much to tell her all the horrible things Max would say about her to me. That she was a spoiled brat, that private schooling didn't stop her being thick, that their sex was limp, that she was obsessed with him. I know that, in all likelihood, none of it was true. But I can't say those things to her. The thing is, Max wasn't calculated, he was just set on 'easy mode' all those years ago. The patriarchy practically prints out a 'How to Cover your Back' guide for men that age, and it ensured he said stuff that was so out of order even my relaying it years later would be devastating. It would make him a mere flying monkey, and me the big green witch.

'Look,' I say slowly. 'It's easier to hate me, I get it. I don't want to force you into questioning your past choice of boyfriend. Believe me, it's shit, it unravels everything. I'm doing it at the moment, but the stakes are lower because I have nothing to lose – no home, no kids, no family like you. So hate me, it's fine. I am the easier villain of this piece.'

'How selfless.'

'But I'm here to tell you that I've learned some things recently. And the most important one is that women against women is the patriarchy's trap.'

'Please don't accuse me of being against women, just because I'm calling you out.' She's being annoyingly impressive.

'You're happy, aren't you?! You had your big beautiful wedding, I saw it all over Facebook, all those tasteful jars of peonies and bridesmaids wearing slightly different dresses in the same colour! You've got kids, Constance! So has Max!' And I feel stupid the second it comes out of my mouth. Comparing the inside of my life with the outside of someone else's, assuming she has everything she wanted the way everyone used to assume it of me.

The truth is, I was a coward during the Max thing. I had thought having a partner the most important thing in the world. When I was growing up, most people were part of a pair, and the ones that weren't were at best an anomaly, at worst criticised like in those countless magazines I would devour. Not only that, I was that pre-conditioned to be half of someone else, I never even noticed the full extent of how bad that situation was. I'd wanted to be loved by Max, by anyone, so much that I had convinced myself other people's feelings didn't count. Including my own.

Mum pokes her head round the door. 'D'you want a cup of tea?'

'Yeah, OK.'

'Who are you talking to?'

'No one, I'll be down in a sec.'

I made the conversation up – of course I made it up. I've been sitting in my room all morning, having it out with a memory, going round in circles.

In actual fact Constance doesn't want to speak to me. She messaged Paul saying that she's spoken to Lacey who won't bother me anymore. But that as far as she's concerned, what Lacey said was true. Sometimes you just don't get the redemption arc you've been craving. All I could do was tell Paul to thank her.

I have my cup of tea downstairs and ask Mum how *Strictly* was. I ask if she'd like to go to the Norfolk Broads with me because I've never gone. She says no because she's got *The Good Wife* on Sky Plus and I think how little we have in common.

It's grey outside. I take my sheepskin coat and drive. On the way I go past St William's Primary School; I can't believe how small it is.

Behind the University of East Anglia there is an Art Gallery I never knew was there, called the Sainsbury's Centre. I go in and there are Francis Bacons and Picassos and Hockneys and other stuff I am baffled to discover. I go to the gift shop and get a magnet for Bell, because she likes art.

And because I've nothing much else to do, I walk out the back of the building towards the Broads. I go over a wooden bridge, and notice how the breeze makes the surface of the river shudder with delight. And because there's nothing much else to notice, I see a heron with a hunchback striding through water, on stilts! Tiny minnows skating on the surface, coots with their milky-white beaks. I used to go on school trips to places like this and be bored shitless. I had thought Norwich totally unbeautiful.

And because I'm open to noticing it, I notice the tree in front of me. It occurs to me how it's constantly expanding into something new. How it will only create pink blossom next spring by shedding the bits that are no longer helping. How it will stay resolute against the odds, the parasites, the storms, to become its very own thing.

And my heart seems to swell in my chest and my bones feel lighter and I think that, if all this mess amounted to one afternoon when I stood still and noticed how the force of beauty is absolutely everywhere, maybe it was worth something.

Codependent

Amsterdam, 2 December 2018

Three years ago to the day, I arranged a thirtieth birthday surprise for Him. I woke Him up first thing in the morning and told Him, 'Get in the car.' I drove us to the airport, got us on a plane to Amsterdam, and got a taxi to a *Rosie and Jim* style houseboat, one that had a Breville espresso machine (*salivates*), where twenty minutes later two of His best friends turned up with their girlfriends. It pissed it down all weekend, one of the couples had an argument and someone got attacked by a swan. That last one was actually pretty funny.

Exactly three years later, I'm back. Theo had the idea to reclaim Amsterdam for a cheap weekend so that my lasting memory of that date and that place will be of us getting wasted, being petty, drinking fondue like it's water and flirting with strangers.

'I don't wanna flirt with strangers,' I'd said.

'Not you, me. You can froth around in an alley somewhere.'

'What if someone recogni—'

'No one cares about you there, Princess, sorry to break it to you. Everyone's either off their tits or getting laid. 'And PS if you even mention He Who Must Not Be Named, you're getting thrown in the canal.'

'As if.' Amsterdam is a fairytale place, but what I like most about it is how it owns its split personality. How for all the twinkly-lit canals, cobbled bridges and 'Ding ding!'s of fresh blond people on basketed bicycles, there are these little pockets of bleak. For the last couple of days, Theo and I have taken seedy refuge in smoke- and neon-filled coffee shops, where we've watched groups of teenage girls deciding which one of them will be brave enough to order from the weed menu (and been truly made up for them when they got served).

We've gone back and forth past a seemingly endless queue of cheery tourists, and on asking discovered they're all there to see the house where Anne Frank was captured by the Nazis. Or, perhaps to see Justin Bieber's entry in the museum's guest book, where in an *incomprehensible* flourish of narcissism he wrote that 'hopefully [Anne Frank] would have been a Belieber'.

Down an alley between an ice-cream and doughnut shop, there are near-naked women of all sizes sitting in windows like mannequins and with similar levels of enthusiasm. Watching with flat expressions as Stag Dos in candy-coloured polo shirts cover their nervousness with shit banter and try to poke one another in the testicles.

'I can't tell who's got it worse,' I say, 'store-front sex workers—'

'That's a judgement for a start, they might enjoy their jobs,' Theo interrupts me. 'Their body their choice. Carry on.'

'Or the lads who don't want to be here but will get rinsed if they don't get involved.'

'Ugh, I have zero time for fragile masculinity. Those men are the same sort who would shout "poof" at me at school, then get me to wank them off behind the art block.'

'That didn't happen.'

'Tim Leyton, year twelve. Told me after he'd spaffed in my hand if I told anyone he'd beat the shit out of me. Happened a few times. He's married with two kids now, works at Santander.'

One of the lads enters the brothel, fanfared by cheers and cries of 'LADSLADSLADS!'

'Sex addiction,' I say. 'Discuss.'

'Don't believe in it.'

'I thought you were meant to be the open-minded one.'

'Well if you'll listen, I'll explain. My theory is that at least with alcoholism and drug addiction, the packets you dispose of don't have feelings. I've never heard "sex addict" being used unless it's justification for repeatedly hurting other people. The way I see it, we're all young, dumb and would love to be full of cum. But there's a way to have as much sex as you like without making anyone cry.'

'Michael Douglas was a sex addict, you know.'

'Michael Douglas said eating Catherine Zeta-Jones' pussy gave him throat cancer.'

I've always wanted to own a leopard-print suit, but I never got one in the past as I thought my ex wouldn't like it. Hence why I bought one as a late birthday present to myself, and why I'm wearing one now, in Amsterdam, on His birthday.

We're in our fifteen-quid-a-night cell-like Airbnb, that would be otherwise devoid of personality or charm had Theo not pointed out it's quite like Whoopi Goldberg's room at the convent in *Sister Act*, and now we love it. Theo's bought no less than three make-up bags and is fully dragging me up to, yes, the *Sister Act* soundtrack for our big night out. We've taken mushrooms we bought from a shop from the happiest, highest, most moustached salesperson I've ever seen. Well, Theo bought them, I stood nervously in the corner awaiting the sound of sirens. I've never taken mushrooms before but I'm very much hoping to have some kind of *Mary Poppins* fantasy where I dance around with cartoon penguins or perhaps win the Grand National on a carousel horse (though to be clear, I am against non-cartoon Grand Nationals).

'From what I gather,' I tell Theo, who has glittered a Bowie lightning bolt across their face, 'in London at least, Tinder is mostly hook-ups because you can just put pictures up and don't have to answer any questions—'

'Pretty much. It's not quite as direct as Grindr, but the gays tend not to fuck about.'

'Raya is for celebrities and people with loads of social media followers but you can sort of buy your way on it, Poppy got a friend to get her membership and she only gets requests from greasy boys with yachts. 'Hinge is for people with certainty, of which I am definitely not. There's an option to say if you want kids. Probably good for people thinking long term, which is naat mee.'

'Close your eyes and mouth,' Theo says. I do and from the smell of it they spray hairspray all over my face to set it. 'Good for you. Don't bother for a bit, figure sex out, see what you've been missing. Feeld is good, you don't have to put your real name or a photo but you put all of your sexual kinks on it – like threesomes, anal, domination, watersports, whatever. Then people request to match with you based on that and you can decide whether to show them who you are. It's good, it removes weird conversations down the line.'

'Or sexual dissatisfaction.'

'Quite.'

'I went with Bumble in the end; when people match, the woman makes the first move. Which terrifies me, but I appreciate the sentiment.'

'Lemme see your profile.'

I unlock my phone. 'You can't judge.'

'Of course I can.' Theo practically snatches the phone from my hands. 'Oh Fraulein Maria, this is good!'

'Yeah?'

'Yes! Your pictures look like you; essential. You're honest

about not wanting anything long term. It's funny but not neurotic, which let's be honest I was bracing myself for. Plus you don't give everything about you away, you're better in real life than on the app. Brava!'

'Theo! That's, like, the nicest thing you've ever said to me!'

'Must be the drugs kicking in.'

'I don't feel them yet.'

'I'm starting to come up, stuff's gloopy at the edges. The fridge is melting. So how've you been getting on?'

'Well, here's the thing. I am cleaning. Up. I'm as surprised as you are.'

'I'm not surprised at all.'

'I can't believe this many people think I'm hot.'

'*Get some confidence*, you're a famous bad bitch now! Show me.'

I open the app and hold the phone between us. A photo of a blond man in a wetsuit with a surfboard appears onscreen. *Stefan, 35, 0.4 miles away.*

'Fit, right?'

'You'd hate surfing, you hate the sea.'

'Not when it's warm. Anyway, watch.' I swipe right, and the words, 'It's a match!' appear. 'See?!'

'Gorge-y!'

Another photo appears, this time of a man in a boat holding a large fish. *Dom, 29, 1.2 miles away.*

'A lot of them have pictures with big fish for some reason.' I swipe right. Another photo, this time of a smiling person in a crop top with henna-red hair. 'OK, there we are,' I say, closing the app.

'Whatwasthat?!' Theo asks.

'Nothing, just whatever.'

'A woman, dear, it was a woman!'

'Was it?'

'Uh, yes it was, you know it bloody was, give me that!' They wrestle the phone from my hands and reopen the app. '*Ella, 30, 0.9 miles away!*'

'This is a bigger conversation that's not necessarily for now.'

Theo points a manicured finger in my face and chants, 'BI NOW, GAY LATER! BI NOW GAY LATER!'

'YOU ARE SHAMING ME!'

'I'm swiping right!' And they do.

'*THEO!*' I'm laughing. 'Give me—'

I stop dead. Because the photo that has appeared in Ella's place has made both of us stop dead and my blood run cold.

Him, 33, 0.3 miles away.

We scream. And scream. And scream. I scream, 'IS THIS REAL OR AM I HIGH?' at Theo, and Theo screams, 'HIS ACCOUNT'S BEEN VERIFIED, IT'S REAL.'

It's the closest I've been to Him since the night He stormed out of the flat.

'WHAT DO I DO, THEO?!'

'TAKE A SCREENSHOT!'

I do.

'WHAT NOW, THEO? HELP ME.'

'JUST *DO NOT* SWIPE RIGHT.'

'I CAN'T TELL WHICH IS RIGHT OR LEFT.'

'IT'S THAT WAY.'

'THIS WAY?'

And I swipe right.

'**AAAAAGGGGHHHHHHHHHHHHHHHHHHHHHHHHHHH**'

That's when the trip begins.

The walls start closing in until our tiny little room feels like it's pushing against my sides.

'I've ruined your holiday,' I say over and over again as the flat melts into the black leather seats of the car at Elstree Studios. 'You shouldn't have come with me, Theo, I'm no fun, I'm no fun,' as the carpeted floor underneath me becomes the tiles of the Pizza Express in Westfield.

The sequins from Theo's jumpsuit dig into my hands as I cling to them and beg them to not make me go outside.

Theo puts me to bed instead. I lie in it and above me see the ceiling of Samstat Road.

'Breathe,' they say. 'He doesn't know you're here. He can't get to you.'

I look into their eyes and quietly say, 'I feel like Anne Fr—'

'You mustn't compare yourself to Anne Frank, baby girl.'

Theo sits on the edge of the bed, strokes my hair, and slowly becomes a cartoon as I begin to feel very sloppy. I'm still wearing my leopard-print suit. I ask them to give me my rose quartz, and to sing 'Feed the Birds' from *Mary Poppins* to me, and they do. I smile, hold my crystal, and cry a little bit.

The next day I check my pictures and there it is, the screenshot. Concrete proof of our proximity. One of His photos is of Him with the dancer.

'It doesn't work, does it?' I ask Theo over cold chewy morning pizza. 'Running away, the holidays, the booze, the drugs.' I'm still wearing the leopard-print suit. Theo shakes their head. 'Wherever you go there you are.'

Theo looks dire; they stayed up taking more mushrooms on their own and watching *Drag Race* till 3 a.m. Their red glitter Bowie lightning bolt is now spread across their face, like a fabulous rash. 'Here's something. Have you ever thought you might be an addict?'

I choke. 'Sorry?'

'I mean a codependent.'

'That's not addiction, that's tragic.'

'Wrong, it's an addiction. It's people who use the idea of love as a kind of substance, they have a proper group for it, Sex and Love Addicts Anonymous. I think it might apply to you.'

'You don't believe in sex addiction. Michael Douglas, remember?'

'Love addiction is different, it doesn't leave a trail of hurt people, but it eats up the addict. It can bugger up a person, they renounce everything in their life that doesn't involve their partner, become obsessive, try to control everything—'

'That's the neediest thing I've ever heard.'

Theo raises an eyebrow. 'You systematically tore out your best bits to save a relationship that was already dead. Worth looking into, maybe?'

'This is just what I need. More problems that require more therapy I can't afford.' I can feel prickling in my hands. 'I really don't want to have to move back to Norwich.'

'Where'd that come from?'

'I've had no auditions. The whole industry knows what's happened to me, and everyone has gone silent. I've been ghosted by my own job. My agent says there's nothing at the moment for a woman of my age and type. And I'm like, literally why? Isn't art supposed to hold a mirror up to life? Where do women like me disappear to in art? Also, can't we just take one of the countless male parts and make it female? It's only theatre! It's a play, for God's sake, it's ultimately just dicking around in silly outfits!'

'Agreed, it's just Drag that favours straight men. Speaking of Drag, Fela's moving to Brooklyn next month, he got a residency at a club.'

'Wow!'

'Meaning his room in Shoreditch is free, in the flat down the hall from me. I'm basically there always because mine is so fucking rodenty. You'd be living with this fit pansexual couple, Luca and Kyan.'

I look at them. 'Uh . . .'

'You gonna overthink it and get back to me, or just save yourself the neurosis and say yes?'

'I can't afford it.'

'Babe, everybody we know manages to pay their rent. You gonna stay scabbing off Bell and Jim when the baby comes, watching old *Stars in Their Eyes* repeats in their front room?'

'You loved that evening too, Olivia Newton John wowed us all.'

'Come and live in Shoreditch like you've always wanted to. You'll make some money of your own, and you won't do it by taking help or handouts or selling stories to any rags.'

'I'm not good with money, Theo. Even having this conversation makes me feel like I'm fighting my way out of a duvet cover. I've been spending and spending my savings from my nan's inheritance and not looking at my bank balance because when I think about it I just—' My eyes are welling up. 'I see myself back in my teenage bedroom, living off Aldi own-brand replicas of proper things, thinking I used to be an actress.'

'Ho-K, I know we don't like using this word but your imagination is *insane*. You will clearly never stop playing out the consequences of stuff in your head. So I'm going to suggest you start to play out the consequences past the difficult part. Instead of being like, "My money will run out", be like, "My money will run out, and then I will make some again".'

'Yep.' I'm shaking. 'Can I get back to them, about the flat?'

'Sure. But just know you'll be all right, you're not proud, you'll get a job in a bar or something to pay rent. Fuck what other people think about you, that's none of your business. You keep livelaughloving. Look at me. If I gave a single shit about other people's opinions, if I played it safe instead of living my truth, would I be sitting here in a sequin two piece? No. I'd still be very, very sad . . . ' They pause. 'And I'd probably be dead by now, let's face it.'

I nod. Then I pull my chair round next to them and hug them while we're still sitting down.

'God is good, Becks,' Theo says over my shoulder. 'She sees us trying.'

I am ...

Back in the game

The Spaniards Inn, Hampstead Heath, 20 December 2018

Back in the attic, on the bed, laptop open, cat sprawled on his back across the keys for admiration, I googled codependency. It turns out codependent people:

- Allow other people's moods to control their own emotions
- Think and feel responsible for other people
- Feel bored, empty, worthless if they don't have a crisis in their lives, a problem to solve or someone to help
- Feel angry when their help isn't effective
- Find it easier to feel and express anger about injustices done to others, rather than ones done to themselves
- Overcommit themselves
- Find themselves saying yes when they mean no, doing things they don't want to be doing, doing more than their fair share of work, doing things that others are capable of doing themselves
- Have sex when they'd rather be held, nurtured and loved

I was thinking about how I relate to every single one of these things. And what's more, I realised that they are all things that have, as a woman, been *expected* of me to some extent. How I've watched the generation before me be praised for playing the role of this kind of 'selfless' woman.

How women have been conditioned for codependency.

Conditioned to become love addicts.

Just as I was gathering up the pieces from my blown mind, starting to consider how I could kick the habit and get sober, a text came through from this guy I knew once, the man of my dreams, called Hugo.

'Been following your triumph for some time. Not in a creepy way. Maybe a bit. Hope your OK – just had break up myself so get it. Keep up the awesome xxx'

Before I knew what was happening, I ignored the improper use of 'your' and did something I've never done to a man before, which is text:

'Drink next week?'

The cool-dude sunglasses emoji came back within seconds.

London is Christmassy. Outside, there is light icing-sugar snow. At the heavy wooden door of The Spaniards Inn on Hampstead Heath, there's a wreath made with dried slices of orange. Nat King Cole's Christmas song is playing. There is an actual open fire, and a vat of mulled wine on the bar. Earlier, when I arrived, Hugo was already sitting at one of the low-lit carved wooden booths. When he saw me he jumped up and bowled over like the world's sexiest Labrador in a vintage flannel shirt. Like a Disney Prince had come out of the telly to sweep me up in his arms, like I'd used to dream about happening.

'You smell incredible,' he'd said into my neck with his posh-boy voice.

'It's very expensive,' I'd whispered back.

He'd laughed.

'Time is a healer' everyone keeps parroting. Give your career time, your heart time, yourself time. Well, it's been two whole months and all I can feel is time slipping through my fingers. I want to cover up my gaping problem with a blond Band-Aid, one who has movie-star looks. A Band-Aid that, earlier this year when we'd both had partners but still got smashed together, had made me feel like a fantasy and not a reality.

'Fuck patience,' I'd said to Bell, as we'd stood in front of the mirror figuring out how low the buttons on my shirt could go to stay the right side of suggestive. 'I haven't spent two hours getting ready to be patient. I haven't shaved the octopus out of patience.'

'Good for you,' she'd said, unbuttoning me even lower, almost fully revealing the new hot-pink bra underneath. 'I hope you get objectified the shit out of.'

I've not been on a date in over five years. I mean, neither of us has actually called it a 'date'. But two newly single people with a weeny bit of history having a drink in a London pub on a Friday night at Christmas?

I got a bus here because I figured if someone followed me with a camera, I'd be thrilled. The man sitting in front of me was watching porn on his phone with AirPods in. Anal. Everything has gotten very *graphic* since I last went on a date, if that's what tonight is.

But the good news is that if this is a date it's the only one I ever need to go on ever again because this man – I shit you not – is *perfect*.

Perfect like 'spends his spare time volunteering at a kitchen that makes hot food for refugees'.

Perfect like 'when I told him about being Sara Crewe in the attic, he showed me that the last thing he listened to on Spotify was the soundtrack to *A Little Princess*'.

I show him my rose quartz and he pulls out an identical one from his bag, strikes them together to make them flash, looks directly at me and says, 'They spark', and it's probably the best thing I've seen since I first saw Patrick Swayze's pectorals in *Dirty Dancing* circa 1998.

He's been enthusiastic about every new piece of information I've offered. I wish I could tell you the relief at the man opposite me doing that. Making me feel as though I am something that's exciting to learn about. Making me feel confident and the best version of myself. Rather than some ancient *Woman's Hour* feature on domesticity that's on in the background.

We drink mulled wines, whiskies, gins and pints, and speak about our therapists, our respective upbringings, his thin-clavicled shiny-haired ex-girlfriend and my own ex-perience.

'That bloke,' he points a triple-cooked chip at me, 'is toxic as hell, and I always knew.'

'No you didn't.'

'No I didn't, never met him. But I know it now.'

'Well, toxic takes two to tango, in some ways.'

He makes a face and I say, 'Seriously. Cos, it's societal stuff too, isn't it? With men. I read this thing by Dorothy Dinnerstein, that says apparently when a little boy learns that their mother, who is the most powerful person in his life, really has no power within a patriarchy, he gets confused and it causes rage. And there's nothing anyone can do about that, so long as the patriarchy exists. So yeah, that's where that instinct for dominance over women can come from.'

'Wow, that's interesting.' He rolls his chip around the mayonnaise ramekin. 'But to be fair, not all of us are arseholes on making that discovery, are we?' He takes a bite. 'I think that sometimes the patriarchy can be a cunning decoy for bad guys. To take away from individual responsibility. "It wasn't me, it was my patriarchal oppression", y'know?'

'OhmyGod, that makes so much sense.' I tilt my head to one side and sweep my hair in front of my shoulder.

'I think it's evolutionary.' He leans in. 'So you look at Clinton – yes I've had a drink, I'm getting Clinton out—'

'Slippery Bill.'

'Slippery Bill, love that! So he was this massive big dog right, with an unfathomable amount of power. And when he spunked it – quite literally – spunked his promise to uphold his so-called "values", and spunked his commitment to his wife and child, his first response was: "The thing she said happened? And all those other accusations from all those other women as well? They never happened."'

'Yeah, and obviously that didn't work, did it, because Lewinsky is a legend who stood up to the barefaced lie of it.'

'My theory, right, is that, because it was such a far-reaching scandal, it did something to men across the world. They got the message: "Lying doesn't work any more." So other tactics started getting deployed in order to carry on behaving like dicks. Convincing women that they're crazy, for example. But now that's starting to be seen for what it is.' He smiles. 'No small thanks to the person opposite.'

It's very hot in here. He takes a sip of pint.

'So, right, the *next* evolutionary step, now that "she's crazy" is less reliable, seems to be to wade in on the patriarchy conversation and be like, "Hey, babe, you know how the patriarchy fucks women over in every which way possible? Men too! Poor men!" And so we're back to square one, of women throwing their arms around men and saying, "There there, you poor thing." It's another method of oppression: the boys who cry victimhood. I'm not saying that men aren't victims of the patriarchy, my point is that all of us could dick-swing our privilege about and take advantage if we wanted to. But not all of us want to.'

'Uh huh.' I swallow, thinking being taken advantage of wouldn't feel so terrible right about now. 'So what are you saying, that some guys are good, some are just . . . bad?'

'Ah, I dunno what I'm saying really, I'm kind of pissed.' He softens and smiles. 'I'm just enjoying the saying of it.'

'So am I. Did you know as well there's a theory that the reason women go after bad boys—' I stop. 'Actually, the term "bad boys" gives me acid reflux. Calling grown men "boys" when they act cruelly or disrespectfully is enabling.'

'Yeah, we should call them what they are, which is bad adults.'

I laugh. 'Anyway, the reason women go after bad adults is because they can have the things that we really want that society and "the laws of femininity" tell us we can't. Things like career success and money, but also confidence, power, status, ambition, ruthlessness. And all of them simultaneously.'

He wrinkles his nose in surprise. 'Are those the things you want?'

And I pause for a second and think, *Yes, they are*. Of course they are. I want to be a success. I want to walk into a room with 'Madonna in the "Music" video' energy; newer, powerfuller, every inch the woman I am meant to be. I want the audacity of Sisqo, who sang 'Thong Song' *at his own wedding*. I want to be so confident in my convictions that I will stand up for them no matter who disagrees. I want money and a nice house and a great career, and I think it's really unfair that I have to waste my time and energy blurring my edges in order to get these things that I want, because if I behave like a man would I may intimidate someone, or rub them up the wrong way, or put them off.

But I don't say that. I smile and I fiddle with a lock of hair and say, 'Oh, I dunno, I'm just chatting shit and having a nice time.'

He dips a full-figured chip in the pot of mayonnaise. 'You know what the excellent thing is, for us good guys?' he asks.

'How all these meatheads are too afraid of being emasculated to realise that strong, smart women are the sexiest ones.'

My new knickers are on fire.

What a relief.

I do not just fancy bad men. I fancy good men, too. I have not been programmed wrong.

Now, how to make this good man behave like more of an arsehole?

'So, you gonna tell me why you stopped talking to me, then?' I ask him in the smoking area under the brazen orange light of an outdoor heater, as snow swirls around the both of us.

'Ah, my girlfriend thought there was something going on so I promised her I wouldn't speak to you again.'

'Weellll, you didn't have to stonewall me entirely,' I say.

'Weellll, I didn't want to but she was pretty paranoid about it,' he says playfully, and leans in very close to my face.

'So it was her fault, then?' I raise my eyebrows, mimicking his tone.

'No.' His face drops, and he pulls away. 'No, that's not what I meant.'

Oh fuck, I've fucked it. I smile. 'No no, I'm just kidding!' Even though, am I? That's a red flag, isn't it, slagging off your ex?

But he rolls his eyes and smiles. Thank God, he still likes me. I think.

I continue, 'What I'm saying is – I mean, like, we just went out for a few drinks, this was always a very honourable, upstanding—'

'Upstanding?!'

'Yes, I'll stop being Hugh Grant. What I'm saying, Hugo, is nothing ever happened that night. I mean, I don't actually remember, to be honest, I was so pissed. I feel shy about it, actually.'

'No, no, don't! It didn't.' The orange light of the heater goes out.

'Good! But that's what I'm saying, I wasn't going to cheat on Him, you weren't going to cheat on her, she didn't have anything to worry about.' *Apart from our clear connection and my raging horn for you*, I think, as I push the button again.

He's nodding seriously as the light comes up. 'Oh no, absolutely not.' He brings his mulled wine mug up to his mouth and blows on it.

'I mean . . .' He pauses and looks at me. 'No, definitely not.'

'What?'

'No no, you're right. No danger at all with the two of us.'

And he smiles his matinee idol megawatt smile, and I smile too, and then we laugh and I think this is definitely a date, I think.

'Excuse me?' A woman in a scarf and a baker boy hat exactly like Keira Knightley's in *Love Actually* is next to us.

'Hi?'

'I just wanted to say, you're so cool, and I'm so glad you kept your cat, and seriously, keep being yourself because you're so inspiring.'

'Oh Christ. Thank you so much for saying that.'

'You're in my prayers.'

'Oh right! That's lovely. Sorry about the Christ.'

'And PS,' she indicates Hugo, 'you've got yourself a serious upgrade.'

'Oh no, no no no, we're friends just friends,' I laugh loudly. The woman wishes us Merry Christmas and goes back inside. Hugo is gazing at me.

'What?'

'Wow.'

'?'

'Do you get that a lot, then?'

'Uh.' I can't tell what the right answer is. 'Truthfully? Yes. The prayer thing is new. That's not me being up myself or anything, by the way, I don't think I'm, like, I don't know, *important*, it's just people are so nice to me.'

'Huh.' He's looking at me in a way only beautiful men can. Knowing they can stay silent as long as they like and no one will lose interest.

Did I give the wrong response? I tuck my hair behind my ear and think of something to say to stop being looked at. 'Another drink?'

He snaps back to life. 'Yeah! And some shots. We should celebrate.'

'Celebrate what?' I ask as we approach the door. The wreath has pinecones painted gold within it.

'You!' He indicates the wreath. 'Christmas!' He holds the door open, and as I walk past I catch him flashing his eyes down at my spicy pink bra. 'Our *friendship*.'

I had told Him about my close call with Hugo one evening over dinner about a month after it happened. We were staying in a very stylish hotel in the New Forest. I remember looking at the Jerusalem artichoke with edible flowers on my plate. I was wearing a black satin slip dress and lipstick the same colour as the Merlot I used to clear my throat before I said it. I felt telling Him was the right thing to do. Plus I had wanted so much to remind Him I was fanciable. I had wanted for Him to boil over. Wanted Him to demand to know who this man I had feelings for was. But instead He'd barely looked up from his steak.

'Uh. Thanks for telling me, I guess?'

I took another sip of red wine and felt sure that if anyone in the restaurant looked over, they would see it trickle down my oesophagus and through my digestive tract.

Just totally transparent.

*

'The prollem with me, Becks, is—'

'Yeah, I'd love to know akshully please.'

'Shhh, cos thissimportant. The prollem with me is,' he sits back against the booth, framed by the myriad empty glasses covering every inch of the table, 'I'm juss too romantic.'

'Shut *uuuup*!'

'I meanit.' He shrugs. 'I wanna be in love like in films. Wanna big wedding wiv *allmafriends*!' He's being very loud, the young waiting staff are laughing and so am I. 'I want kids and dogs and a big house and to growold with someone an tell them they're beautiful every single day! Annn I blieve in that, I blieve in love like that!'

'So do I.'

'WE BLIEVE, HUMPHRIES!'

The bell dings and he marches over to the bar very fast.

'Two mulled wines and two tequilas!' I hear him proclaiming. 'An' one for yourself, good sir!'

'No, Hugo, please, no more!' I protest from the booth.

He laughs. 'Ignore her, she's drunk,' he tells the barman. 'An' one for yourself, good sir!'

The man at the bar is chuffed and I think wow, all these people in this pub must think that I am really something, to be here alone on a Christmas night with the most handsome generous refugee-feeding Disney Prince in the world. They all must think I'm a really cool, hot, fun, worthwhile person for someone like that to like me.

If he does like me. Surely something would have happened by now? But I don't know, it's been ages, I don't know how it all works.

In the taxi he says, 'I'm going to Calais for New Year to help out. I think you should come.'

'OK!' I say to both of him. Fuck, I really am battered.

'I juss think you're so—' He stops.

'So . . . ?'

'Nah.' He smiles and looks straight ahead.

'What?'

'No, nothing.'

'What am I so?!'

He looks at me. 'So clever.'

'Oh,' I say.

'What?' he asks.

'Nothing,' I say.

'What?!' he asks again.

'*Nothing!*'

He laughs and runs his fingers through his hair.

Clever. Oh, right.

He claps his hands and says, 'Here we go, then!' Because we've arrived by Leicester Square.

We get out of the Uber.

And it all happens so quickly.

We go to the doors of the casino by the tube station.

The bouncer stops us and asks how much we've had to drink, but Hugo gets us in.

We take money out from an ATM machine inside. Hugo knows where the bar is. The casino has a deep red carpet and green islands dotted everywhere. It's very busy. We order Moscow Mules and they come in the same nondescript tumblers they have in the Norwich working men's club.

The barman swaps some cash for casino chips in black and red. Hugo takes them.

He leads me to a spinning roulette table. I try to talk and laugh but Hugo is very quiet and focused.

He puts chips down.

I stand next to him like a Bond Girl. Lean my body against him.

He wins more chips.

He puts more of them down. He wins even more.

I squeal, 'Oh my God!'

He says, 'Time to move on.'

We go to a different table where a person deals cards very quickly.

Hugo says, 'Hit me.'

He wins more chips.

I say, 'You're Rain Man!'

He says, 'Time to leave.'

'But you're winning!'

He says, 'Sometimes you have to know when to stop.'

I ask how much money he won. He doesn't count the chips and says three hundred pounds. I gasp and ask what we're going to do now. He looks down at me and says with absolute serious-ness: 'We're going to karaoke.'

And I thank God I wasn't patient.

He takes my hand and guides me out of the doors into crowded Soho.

It's just after midnight.

Everyone who wanted an early night has gone home.

There are neon lights and taxi headlights and a group sings 'Last Christmas' at the top of their voices on the way to their next good time. Strangers sing along with it and dance in the street to make their own friends laugh. The bits of snow that haven't turned to grey sludge is gathered in clumps by the edge of the pavement. People wear woolly hats and kiss in doorways holding their coats around each other, and my hand is being held by a man who makes food for homeless people.

And I think this has to be the most fun night of my life.

And I wonder if he thinks so too.

We bambi down a set of icy steps to a karaoke bar in Soho. 'A booth!' says Hugo to the person behind the counter.

'I'm afraid we only have a booth for six people.'

'Perfect.' Hugo puts down the cash. 'And a bottle of champagne!'

I squeeze his shoulder in excitement and he turns and puts his arms around my waist and lifts me up.

'Wow,' he says as he puts me down. 'You're very *slender*, aren't you?' He has one hand on each of my hips and oh my God, talk about saying all the right things. I like my own body more than ever in an instant, and I like even more how it's Hugo that's turned it on.

A member of staff in a company polo shirt shows us down a dark corridor into a dark room with leather banquettes around the walls, and a big screen on one of them but I'm not sure which one because I'm spinning.

I look at the person showing me how to use the microphones but I can't focus. Hugo lines a song up as another member of staff comes in with an ice bucket, the neon orange of a Veuve Clicquot bottle neck protruding from it.

The members of staff leave, Hugo says 'To fun' and we down our glasses.

He presses play, and I laugh because the words 'The Circle of Life' appear on screen.

We belt the opening strain right into one another's faces, and then both drop our microphones and begin ferociously making out.

For such a nice guy he tastes like a bad one.

Alcohol and the smell of musk, the feel of stubble under my palms.

I've forgotten how good it feels to kiss someone for the first time.

To have permission to touch their body.

The euphoria that they are kissing and touching you back.

We do this for the entire hour. He lies back on the banquette and I straddle him. He pulls away from me from time to time and looks at me intensely, like he can't believe how sexy I am, like he wants to take all of me in, then kisses me harder.

I feel like prey, in a good way.

He is on top of me when the member of staff comes to tell us our hour is up. The skin on my back is stuck to the leather seat.

When we climb the karaoke stairs it's snowing. I put my arms inside his coat when we kiss. The Christmas lights are above us, giant white snowflakes. No one else is around.

'We can't go t'mine,' I slur.

'Or mine,' he says. 'I'm a lodger.'

'Hotel?' I suggest.

'You know a good one?'

'Fuck yeah!'

Now I'm the one leading the way through the alleys of deserted snowy Soho, stopping every so often to put my free hand on his warm chest and look up at him and wait for him to bend down and kiss me, which he always does, on occasion putting his hand inside my blouse.

'I love this,' he murmurs, his thumb rubbing along the lace of my bra.

'Oh, you noticed, did you?'

'Are you kidding?' he says. 'Fuck.' And he squeezes my boob and now I know I've got him, I turn around and keep leading him on.

'Wait,' he says. 'Have you got a condom?'

'Oh shit,' I say. I let go of his hand and unzip my shoulder bag to rifle through. 'No, I don't. I, uh, wasn't expecting this, to be fair.'

I look up and smile.

At nothing.

'Hugo?'

I turn around. I'm in the middle of the road. Alleys lead in every direction. To one side of me are the lights and sporadic traffic of Shaftesbury Avenue. I see a red-haired woman staring back at me at the end of the road, on a poster for the musical *Company*.

'Hugo?!' I am smiling dazedly. 'Hello?'

But I am on my own.

I get out my phone. I call him.

Nothing.

I feel like prey. In a bad way.

I open WhatsApp, conscious of being suddenly so, so drunk.

'Wht the duck?'

I walk towards Shaftesbury Avenue. It's hard because the streets are cobbled, and slushy. I don't want to have my phone out when I am on my own but God, what if he's been abducted?

'Are yo OK?'

No reply.

'Its cool jus where r you? I'm on 5%.'

He appears online. Thank God. He's typing!

'All good, getting food.'

I stare at it. Huh?

'Where?'

'Burger King.'

I call him, and this time he picks up. He tells me he's walking down Shaftesbury and I tell him to meet me at *Company* and please be there because my phone is about to die. When I get there he has a Burger King bag and is smiling.

'Where the fuck did you go?'

'Sorry, I was hungry.'

'But it was so quick. One minute you were asking if I had . . .'

I can't even say condoms. I feel afraid. What if I'm wrong?

So instead I say, 'You left me.'

'Sorry.'

'Are we still gonna do the hotel thing?'

'Sure, let's go.'

We walk together along Shaftesbury Avenue. We're almost at Piccadilly Circus when he stands on the side of the pavement. What's he doing?

'No, s'thissway,' I call out as he crosses the road.

'Yep,' he calls back without looking at me.

'Wha're you doing?' I ask him.

He turns around so he's walking away from me backwards. 'What are *you* doing?'

'No, wha'reyou actually doing?' I ask.

'Nothing!' he shouts back, taking a huge chunk out of his burger as he steps on the opposite pavement.

A double-decker bus passes him, and somehow he is gone. Like in Harry Potter. Magic.

And I am very conscious of being very cold, very drunk, and very alone in the middle of Piccadilly in the middle of the night.

The next morning I wake up in my new underwear. Bell tells me I called her and she got me an Uber from outside Fortnum's, which for some reason was the only place I knew how to get to when I was as pissed as I was. I ask her why these mad things always happen to me, and she says a great story is almost as good as a pissed shag anyway.

I get a text from Hugo. He says sorry, that he's not over his ex. I ask him why he didn't just say that to me last night, that I would have understood. He says he doesn't know. I ask why he went on a date with me, then, and he says he never said it was a date. I feel confused and too embarrassed to say it was him who asked about the condoms. He asks if we can be friends. I feel like a sad lonely bin bag. I think that we do get on so well. We laugh, there is never an awkward silence with the two of us. We've always felt comfortable opening up to one another and have really listened to what the other is saying. I've always liked when someone cool wants me in their life. Without thinking, I type the words 'of course' with my thumb.

But I hesitate. Because I've been thinking a lot recently about who I've allowed into my life.

There are two types of people – radiators and drains. Ones that make you warm and energised, and ones that leave you feeling empty. They're not easy to identify. Most people present as a radiator, but then they'll do or say something that leaves you sitting on the bed after you've seen them, feeling weird, or confused, or embarrassed, or stuck about what to do.

I have loads of friends who make me laugh, and who I can talk to, and who can provide unforgettable nights out for all the *right* reasons. Plus I've just got a lot of my time back, and I'm not going to waste it educating a faux woke bro.

So I delete 'of course', and replace it with, 'My friends wouldn't have left me like that last night.' He says he's sorry, please, that he's a good guy. I ask what they would say in the refugee kitchen.

And I can't help thinking if I'm too fragile to ask about whether something is a date or not, I'm not ready to date.

And that no matter if they present themselves as good or bad, all men are exactly the same.

I Stayed

Because they love him

Our flat, Shepherd's Bush, June 2018

In the summer of 2018, I learned there was such a thing as true chemistry. Dates in low-lit restaurants, £3.99 disposable barbecues, watching the World Cup on a giant telly with tinnies and pizzas.

We'd dated other couples before, but sparks just never flew.

I've known Jim for years, but we only became proper mates after we both got cast in a play together where I was a sex worker his character visited. Last year he'd married Bell in Islington town hall. Everyone had gone to the pub down the road for a pint or six and danced to Louis Prima's 'Buona Sera'. The bride, groom, me & Him had been the last ones standing, had to be shooed out by the landlord, and have been fanatical about one another ever since.

Tonight we're in our back garden, patio doors open, the yellowy glow from indoors spilling out and mingling with the summer sunset. The TV indoors got angled to where we're sitting at around five for *The Chase*, and over the last four hours the patio table has accumulated a plethora of corner-shop munch: nachos, guacamole, bottles of Yellow Tail Malbec and tobacco packets.

I've heard this story loads of times, but Jim and Bell haven't, and I'm hanging off their hanging off His every word.

'So there's this stand-up in the nineties, who shall remain

289

nameless, right, but everyone in the industry knows who he is. He's massive. And he's on the road cheating on his wife *constantly*.'

'Another upstanding member of the comedy community.' Jim nods sarcastically.

He laughs. 'Wait. So he gets a tip-off right, from his agent. One of the women have sold their story, and the papers are running with it the next day. Front-page news. Naturally, he cacks himself but is like, all right, got to do the right thing and tell my wife.'

'What an interesting definition of the right thing,' says Bell.

'So he does, and she's fuming, of course she is. Kicks him out then and there, "you're never seeing the kids again", all of it. He's sitting in this Premier Inn all night long, edge of the bed, you know, like this fucking middle-aged waste of space. Hang on ...' He's fighting to contain the story, to get to the good stuff without laughing. 'He's thinking as of tomorrow morning, that's it, life, career, over.'

'Then what?' Jim leans in.

'Next morning, papers out. Diana dead. He's not even in it.' And He throws back His head, howling, and we're laughing too. It's hard to tell whether it's because of the story, or how much He loves it, or both, but the fact is when all four of us laugh at the same time it's like a Westlife key change, it raises you up.

'Oh my God.' He wipes away tears. 'No danger of that on *Strictly*, they hauled us into a room and warned us all journos are gonna follow us everywhere. We won't be able to get a coffee without getting papped!'

'Fucking hell,' says Jim. 'Horrible.'

'It's nuts!' He says, His laughter belying His excitement.

I sit up straight. 'What time is it?'

'Twenty past nine.'

'Oh shit!' I fish the remote from under the dip lids and switch to ITV.

'Not *Love Island*!' Bell groans.

'Yes *Love Island*!' He and I answer unanimously.

'Nonsense,' says Jim.

'Noooooo!' We say as one.

'It's fucked-up and we love it,' I say. 'Watching these little blonde sticks mess up and make up and mismanage love and give each other hand jobs in sweatshop-made swimwear. There's this girl on it, right, Rosie, who got dumped for another girl by this guy, and all the other blokes were like calling him a "god" for it but then Rosie confronted him and when she started getting upset he just sat there smirking.'

'It's great telly,' He agrees.

'Right, that sounds awful so I'm going to respectfully change the subject,' Bell says. 'My annual leave's coming up; I think we should all go on holiday.'

'When?' I ask.

'Next month,' she says, indicating the male side of the detritus table. 'And let's face it, they'll probably be non-committal about things so really it's you and me, come on.'

'You should go, Bun.' He smiles at me and my mouth goes as dry as the nacho shards.

'Yeah, it'll be great!' Jim says, and Bell nods and I wonder how she doesn't feel like she's being pawned off.

'VIPs-only party when they're away?' Jim asks Him.

He laughs. 'This guy!' He puts a hand on Jim's broad shoulder like He can't believe Jim exists and shakes His head at me. 'Where's he *been*?'

'What?' Jim smirks.

'All her other friends, they're all,' He screws up His face, '*actors*.'

'Well, this is awkward,' Bell says and unsheathes a new Yellow Tail from a blue and white plastic bag.

'Yeah, mate, I'm sorry to tell you that I'm also an actor,' Jim says solemnly, even though he knows He knows that.

'No you're not.' He shakes His head vehemently. 'Not like that. Actors aren't normal, they're either models or mental. You should have seen this wedding we went to, whose was it?'

'Nish's?' I ask.

'Oh, I know Nish.' Jim nods.

'Then you know what I'm talking about. All of them prowling around, looking ripped and talking about Shakespeare. They're not proper people, there's no grounding, they wouldn't enjoy this.' He indicates the sorry state of the garden table. 'But this guy,' He points exaggeratedly at Jim, 'he's not an actor. He's a *legend*.'

We all laugh. I can see He's made Jim feel special, which has made Bell feel delighted, which has made Him feel magnanimous, which has made me feel relaxed in their company the way I no longer do with anybody else. It doesn't matter that I don't have Theo, or Oonagh, or anyone. I know for sure they see something in Him, something that I'd once seen, and it's a sweet relief to watch them fall in love with it.

These people are good people. If they love Him, then what the hell is my problem?

I am ...

Open

Clapton, 31 December 2018

'I think you're super hot.' Every one of her fingers has a ring on it, they glint in the dark. The eye tattoo on the side of her hand beneath her little finger gazes at me as she brings a roll-up to her mouth.

'Oh!' I laugh and peel off my fake moustache.

'I mean, why mess around?' She blows out smoke and passes the fag along to me. 'Wait – you're queer, right?'

Inside, Oonagh and Lucy's New Year's Eve 'Icons' party is happening. Earlier this evening was the talent show portion. A fake stage was set up in the front room, with a five-quid glitter curtain. Theo kicked off the night dressed as Thatcher, making her Section 28 speech, after which came a drag Spice Girls group, a drag Cilla Black, and two men dressed as Russian lesbians Tatu, performing 'All the Things She Said' underneath a watering can. I forced Bell and emotionally manipulated Jim into dressing up as Brian May and Roger Taylor and performing a lip-sync of 'I Want to Break Free' with me. Bell's wig is truly enormous. I was Freddie Mercury, in pink turtleneck and leather skirt like in the video, lugging a hoover around. It was a pretty impassioned bid for freedom, people I'd never met before actually cried and I refuse to put that down to the amount of pills I've seen going around.

Currently, by the sounds of things indoors, we've moved on to the second part of the evening where everyone is off their face enough to think they can hit the high notes of 'There Must Be an Angel' by Eurythmics. Rainbow balloons and glitter from the countless confetti cannons have spilled out from the front door and down the concrete steps along with me and Lucy's friend from work, Pearl.

'Sorry,' she says. 'Did I just make a big assumption?'

Pearl is originally from Arizona. I've met her before, we went axe throwing for Oonagh's birthday. She's about to qualify as a teenage counsellor. She has big brown eyes like a cartoon deer, and dark hair pulled back into a low ponytail, which I'm jealous of her being able to pull off because when I wear a low ponytail, I look like one of the Founding Fathers. She is wearing a long black dress and leather jacket because she forgot it was fancy dress. She's chill about it.

And about making her feelings very clear.

'No. I mean, yeah it *was* an assumption,' I say, fiddling with the furry moustache in my lap. 'But also, no one's ever asked me that before. And I want to answer honestly.'

'Hey, we got time.'

I take the roll-up from her hands and inhale. 'I've never thought much about it before. I've historically only ever been with men and so I've not questioned that narrative about myself. But there must have been little glitches in the matrix, moments of complexity. Because when I think back over the people I've fancied, there are girls' faces. And I definitely want to learn to embrace that.'

'Bisexuality?' Pearl says it like it's easy, like it's obvious. But I squirm.

'See even that word, "bisexual". Where I grew up, "bisexual" was viewed as a sort of lame cousin of "gay". Like the middle of a Venn diagram, between straight and gay but not its own circle.'

'So be a lesbian, then,' she says and sways so that her body nudges mine. OK, now this – *this* – is flirting. 'If you want a clear circle.'

'But I'm pretty into dick, you see, is the problem.'

'Yeah, that is a problem.' The corners of her mouth curl up. 'I'd suggest you try being OK with who you are, which is a bisexual person, and try to stop being so disparaging about it because really you're only disparaging yourself?'

'Do you think I'm an arsehole?'

'Nah, I hear ya.' She blows out and smiles. 'I like it when cool people evolve into queer. And you're right, people totally write bisexual off as sex tourism.'

'Yes! It makes me feel like I'm a teenager trying to be cute and slutty, getting off with my friend at a foam party to impress boys.'

'That happened a lot, I'm guessing.'

'It did, yeah. They used to hand out bottles of prosecco if two girls pashed. I once did it with my mate Katy in Magaluf and got an allergic reaction to the foam, like there was this raised red map of the world all over my face and body. Had to stay in the shade all holiday while she went and shagged one of the reps.'

Pearl laughs. She has a really husky, dorky laugh. It's different, talking sexuality with another woman. I'm not trying to be more feminine, like I might do if I was with a man who fancied me. It's a relief. Being vulnerable is fucking difficult, but when you're with someone who appreciates how much it takes it's like admitting weakness actually reinforces you. It feels like we're solidifying one another, like we're both silently saying, *I know what it's like. I'm proud of you.*

Now that I'm thinking about it, there's definitely been women I've fancied in the past. Geri Halliwell in the 'Say You'll Be There' video. Spinelli from Disney's *Recess*. Christina Ricci in *Casper*.

'I wonder if I never considered it because where I grew up everything felt binary,' I continue. 'You know, every single story, film, book I enjoyed as a child ended with a kiss between a woman and a man, or a big wedding. Jesus, my favourite game was Dream Phone, where you had this big pink phone and the aim of the game was to call boys' numbers and find out which one had a crush on you. You know, us millennials ... I swear we were the last generation to be fed stuff that was so overtly patriarchal. It's meant that here I am, stuck somewhere between understanding full well pop culture conditioned me to want a big white wedding and a handsome prince, but still *really* wanting it!'

'Well, I saw those movies too, and that's the last thing I want. I never had Dream Phone, though, which sounds as fucked up as it does fun.'

'It was really fun, actually; it was a great game.'

She laughs her husky laugh. 'I guess I was lucky in some ways. I just knew that I wasn't into the guys in those romance stories; I always imagined I was them kissing the girls. Ariel, man. Hot as hell. And Nala from *The Lion King.*'

'Nala was a lion, Pearl.'

'She was hot, watch it again.'

I think about female bodies (not a lion's obviously, a human's). Maybe I've never thought I'm sexually attracted to women because I've never fetishised them. Maybe that's because most images with tits or vulvas are targeted at men, and a male gaze?

'A lot of it's probably down to the fact I can't take pleasure in pictures of naked women,' I say. I rearrange my sponge jugs, which have fallen to my waist. 'That's why I don't like porn, because I can't look at the woman without wondering what she's thinking, what got her there, whether she's enjoying it. I can't enjoy naked images of women because I can't see them as one-dimensional, I see myself in them! And I care!'

Two girls in their early twenties open an upstairs window

from the house opposite to smoke. From the sounds of it their party is even heavier than ours. One of the girls wears huge fake glasses that say '2019'. They wave at us, and we wave back, and the four of us smile with the shared understanding that Londoners never usually reach out to one another.

'What about female-made porn?' Pearl asks me. 'It's good; real bodies, good sex, feels more intimate and you don't hate yourself when you come watching it.'

'I don't really watch porn. Of any kind.'

'What do you masturbate to?'

'I don't . . . ' I can't believe I'm admitting this, ' . . . really do that.'

'*Gurl*. If you can't get yourself off, how do you know what you really want?'

'I dunno if I do?'

'If you don't know what you want, how do you tell the people you sleep with?'

'I sort of let them do what they like.'

'Do they ask *you* for things *they* want?'

'Yes, what's your point?'

'Sis, you need to get busy finding out what works for your body, and learning how to use your damn words. Because let me tell you something – up until now, any orgasm a man has ever given you has been a coincidence. And ain't nobody got time to wait around for the next coincidence to happen.'

'I've looked at sex toy websites but there's so many weird shapes and sizes and colours, I feel like someone's pointed to a heap of pipes and told me to build a car.'

'Yeah, it's a lot.'

'Happy New Year!' the girls opposite shout over at us as they stub out their fags on the outside wall.

'You too! Have fun!' I shout back.

'Hey, ever heard of pussy gazing?' Pearl asks me as they slide their window closed and the sounds of their party deaden.

'Am I a virgin again? This conversation is making me feel like it.' I sigh. 'No, I haven't heard of pussy gazing, what is it?'

'Exactly what it sounds like. Candles, dreamcatchers, dried flowers, super Instagrammy. You sit in a circle on cushions with other women who look like they wish they hadn't signed up; everyone has a hand mirror in front of them. Then when the leader tells you to, you all face the outside of the circle so you have privacy, take your panties off, take the mirror and just follow what she tells you to do. It's just looking, and it's not sexual or anything. It's actually kind of scary. But spiritual as hell; people cry, you know. When my group were done, one woman told us she'd never seen herself like that before. That she always thought it would be ugly, but that it wasn't at all, that she felt more whole than before. It was pretty beautiful.'

'It makes you think how unfair it is that guys get to just look down and see all their sex organs right there. Unless they're very fat, of course.'

She does the husky laugh again. 'Right. Most guys, they can see what happens when they get aroused right there in front of them. No wonder they feel so entitled to it, most of them. We don't get to see what our body does when we open up to desire, the juiciness and the swelling and the unfolding. It struck me, when all these women were sitting in this circle in the candle-light, how few women throughout history will have seen their own sexual organs. How, throughout history, far more men will have seen vulvas than women. The imbalance made me emotional, actually. I feel as though we all have a responsibil-ity, to them.'

'Hey, y'know, maybe we don't get to see what's happening down there, but that's an opportunity to lean into feeling. The female experience is a lot more sensory, and I think that's more profound.'

'Girl, I barely know you, but from what I've seen of you

tonight I gotta say you have the relentless positivity of a YouTube yoga instructor.'

I smile. 'I know, sorry.'

'I'd like to kiss you,' she says. 'Would that be all right?'

I swallow, 'Yeah, OK.'

Theo once asked me whether a woman had ever gone down on me, and I said no, and they said that I haven't truly experienced it, then. They said only someone of your assigned gender truly knows their way around. That it's mind altering, and that everyone should experience it.

It runs through my mind as I kiss Pearl, whose kiss back is so soft I instantly feel stronger than I am. I feel more dangerous and can see why it turns straight men on. She touches my neck with her hands, the rings on her fingers are cold.

But it doesn't feel right, and not because I'm heterosexual. But because even though I like her company, I'm not sure I really fancy her. Theo/Thatcher staggers outside and tells us it's nearly midnight. They stand in the doorway as Pearl says she has to pee and will meet me indoors. As I hoick up my tights I spy Theo eyeballing me.

'What are you looking at? This isn't a store front.' I whack my moustache back on. 'And before you start, I don't feel the need to define my sexual preferences tonight, or any night.'

'Well, look at Sue,' comes the response. 'Peeling off her label!'

It's a new year, I'm ready, and I'm not rushing. I'm stepping out, unencumbered, into a world that has never been more open for women, never held as much opportunity. Maybe I'll watch some feminist porn. Maybe I'll get good at self-pleasure, and not in a 'spa day' way, although I might have a few of those as well. Maybe tomorrow I'll look into one of those ooh-la-la East London workshops where you can hand paint a ceramic dildo and try to ignore the horrific thought I just had, which is to paint Winston on one.

301

Someone starts the countdown to the New Year. There is so much noise. I hug Bell, and we're both hugged by Jim. Instead of 'Auld Lang Syne', Oonagh starts a chorus of 'Believe' by Cher, and kisses Lucy. Around the room, Prince, Tina Turner, Ruth Bader Ginsburg (whom, I'm afraid, I'd initially thought was Judge Judy) belt along at the top of their voices.

Theo shouts in my ear, 'I made a resolution!'

'What's that?' I shout back.

'I'm going sober!' Theo shouts. 'I've got a problem!'

'Do Kyan and Luca still have that room?' I shout back. 'If I'm near you, I can help!'

'YES!' And they pull me over to where Tatu are standing (still wet), announce that I want to move in with them, and both of them scream at the disco lights on the ceiling.

Maybe I'll dye my hair pink like a My Little Pony and become the mythical Goddess of Shoreditch.

Maybe I'll book dinner at the Ritz and go on my own in a Wonder Woman outfit just to see what they do.

Maybe I'll write. Maybe I'll run. Maybe I'll dance every single day.

Maybe I'll do ayahuasca in Costa Rica and puke my way to a new beginning.

Maybe I don't need to, maybe I've already begun.

Maybe I'm a phoenix.

Maybe I can do anything, now I'm through all this.

It all feels very promising, this thing called life.

I Stayed

Because I am no fun

Denmark, August 2018

A naked bronze woman sits on a rock in Copenhagen.

'. . . she rises up to the surface and sees a birthday party being held on a ship for this handsome prince. She instantly falls in love vith him, OK, this human man, but hides in the shadows so he doesn't see hur fur vot she is.'

It's mine and Bell's third afternoon here and we are on a boat tour along with around twenty or so others. Different nationalities, different fashions, different types of hat. All here to see the same woman.

The boat has stopped still about twenty yards from the shoreline. This is where the bronze woman is sitting, on top of a pile of rocks no taller than a dining table. She looks over one shoulder and into the sea.

She's smaller than you'd think someone so famous would be. I expected her to be bigger than me, like when I met Judi Dench. She's currently being looked at through what must be around sixty phones, belonging to people standing gawping on the shoreline, dotted around in an uneven crescent.

The boat's motor has cut out for us to bob, leaving only the sounds of a sunny day and our Scandi tour guide's voice, monotonous and crackly through the PA microphone.

' . . . a violent storm hits, and the boat turns over, OK,' he tells us, as though he's telling it for the millionth time. 'And ven she sees the prince drowning, she svims him to a temple by the shore somevere. But before he can vake up and see who has saved him, she svims away.' A ruddy middle-aged woman in front of us puts her hand to her heart and chuckles to her male partner.

'What's wrong?' Bell says.

'What?'

'You've been wanging on about this statue since we booked this bloody thing.'

It's been six hours since His last response. I've sent Him short, unobtrusive messages. Long, sprawling declarations of pride and love. Casual, offhand messages that I drafted in my notes to sound as casual and offhand as possible. Sharp and spiteful accusations followed by terrified apologies and pleas. About twenty messages, about twenty different kinds of women, all of them me.

'Nothing's wrong.' I smile, and turn my head to the shore.

'There is, though, isn't there?'

'No! Well, yeah. No, a bit.' I hesitate. 'They're making the announcement this week. On *The One Show*.'

'And that's not good?'

'It means it's real. It means He can't pull out.'

I am ruining Bell's holiday, I know I am. For the last three days there has been dazed wandering in August heat beneath the Børsen with its green roof and dragon spires. There's been the ordering of swirly snail pastries for breakfast, and the getting of another for the road that had been eaten within the following ten minutes. There's been extreme gorging on lunches of open sandwiches that wouldn't look out of place on the Tate Wall, each one infused with consideration, gloriously technicoloured, and all the more satisfying to decimate and wash down with half a lager and a shot of schnapps if you're Bell and a glass of champagne if you're me because frankly schnapps tastes like cystitis feels.

There's been new tastes and heat on my bare shoulders and things I can't pronounce for almost seventy-two hours. I would say I had picked up about twenty minutes' worth, and only when Bell has fished my awareness out from inside myself. I honestly couldn't describe our Airbnb if you asked me. I could be anywhere. My world consists of around six inches, between my ears.

And when I'm not thinking about the catastrophe that I'm convinced is about to befall me, or about every step of what I would do in each apocalyptic scenario, I am furiously letting myself have it for not being able to just enjoy a holiday like a fucking sane person.

Esther Perel says the more we trust, the farther we're able to venture. But I do trust Him, I want to trust Him, I have to trust Him. I just have a massive problem with trust because I can't get over things, things like finding Facebook messages over four years ago.

'The Sea Vitch – who isss fabulous,' says the tour guide, who it turns out has a dry campness that only unfurls as he enters his stride, 'says that yes she'll sell the murmaid a potion that vill give her legs, OK. Yes, but – the payment for it is giving up hur voice, the most beautiful and enchanting voice in the vorld. The vitch tells the murmaid she vill only get a real human soul like she vants if she vins the prince's love and marries him, for then ven they are married a part of his soul vill flow in to hur. The Murmaid is like, "OK, yeah, sure, I'm happy to give up my voice and go and be vith him", because she vould have done anything for his love.

'The murmaid who is now a woman goes everywhere vith the prince, thrilled to be rid of the sea, her tail and her beautiful voice if it means being vith him, OK. But on the day it is announced that the prince must marry, he chooses somebody else.'

The ruddy woman gasps. Bell turns to me. 'I'm going to ask you something hypothetical all right, to get it out of the way so we can talk it out and then later we'll have a drink and a laugh.'

'OK.'

'What's the worst thing that could possibly happen, with this *Strictly* business?'

'Uh.' I take a deep breath.

'The Little Murmaid who is no longer a murmaid sits here and looks out to sea, voiceless, unvanted in this world, and unable to return to the home she decided to leave. She has lost everything, OK.'

I stare at the statue, all those people taking pictures. 'The worst thing would be He has an affair with his dance partner and it's all over the front pages of the papers. For all of my family to see, my friends. People I don't know. It would be my worst nightmare. I would be humiliated. It would absolutely destroy me.'

And I can just tell that wasn't what she was expecting. That she's taken aback at how easily that flowed from me, how it's as though my worst nightmare is always sitting inside my mouth waiting to be voiced.

'Right,' she says. 'Well, there you go.'

'OK, so who knows vat happens in the end?' I hear the tour guide ask through the mic.

A little girl's voice says, 'The, the mermaid, she gets her voice back and she gets married to the prince!'

'No. OK, so that's the Disney film version. In the Hans Christian Andersen version, she dies.' I look over at the little girl, who looks just like I felt when I first heard the real ending of 'The Little Mermaid' a couple of years ago.

*

That evening, Bell and I are at a chic, candlelit hole in the wall that sells fresh oysters and where the water carafes are in the shape of fish. Bell is squeezing a lemon into a half shell opposite me. She uses a satisfyingly tiny fork to prise her oyster from it.

'You know what, mate?' she says, as the oyster slithers around its shell sensually. 'The fact is He'll probably do the show, not be any good, and get kicked out. It may only last a couple of weeks.'

'I hope it doesn't, though. I want Him to do well! I just don't want Him to have an affair, I don't want to be shut out, I want to feel involved in some way so my weird paranoia doesn't kick in and this becomes fucking unbearable.' I take the lid off the tabasco and create a crime scene on my oyster.

'Listen – you're already living as though it's happening. This is not a fait accompli.' Trust Bell to put it better than I could, and in French, too. 'Just talk to Him, just be really clear what it is you need from this. Reassurance, or to be involved or whatever.'

'I have done, and it's not happening. I don't know how to remind Him without sounding like a nag, or bringing him down or making this experience a drag because it's amazing, everyone who ever does it says it's the best thing ever. I don't want to be the reason it's shit for Him.'

'Couples fight, mate. Me and Jim argue loads, on occasion I'd love nothing more than to kick him in the balls and run away. And vice versa.'

'Every day?'

'Almost,' she says. 'Yeah, there's more or less something we don't completely agree on on a daily basis.'

I nod. This is good. She carries on.

'But we love each other and we make up and it's OK really, because there's a foundation of good stuff. We enjoy each other's company, and can rely on each other, and I know full well he has my back.' She tips the shell over her mouth and the oyster slides in.

Do I know He has my back? Do I know He would defend me if I wasn't there? I'm not entirely sure that I would, but then again how does anyone actually know that for sure, how could Bell *actually* know that about Jim?

'You know, it's not a party, a relationship. It's a constant negotiation and you let one another develop. This could even be exciting for you, I mean it's *Strictly*! It's your favourite, and you get to go and be there every week and be His biggest fan!'

My God, she's right. And you know what, actually, I think to myself, Bell and Jim haven't been together as long as He and I have. It makes sense that our arguments are more intense and frequent because we know better what buttons to press. And, y'know, we're very fiery people in a way Bell and Jim aren't as much so that makes sense too, we will naturally always spark because he's loud and I'm crazy and we're fiery, we're just fiery, we're Cathy and Heathcliff, Burton and Taylor, Sid and Nancy. We're akin to the most intoxicating, wild love stories in history, riddled with hurt but raging with argumentative, screaming, 'don't leave me' passion. What is love without passion? God, give me fiery over boring any day.

The next day we go to Bell's über cool friend Sophie's summerhouse in the forest for a few nights. Sophie is soothing and sophisticated and looks like Alanis Morissette. She cooks us food and her husband takes care of their cherub-like toddler son who screams happily whenever he is naked. They take us to get smoked fish in baps from the local smoke house and sit us outside under the shooting stars with wine and when I go to bed at night all I can think is, *I have nothing to offer these interesting people.*

Bell decides to extend her trip, but I don't.

The last thing I see at Copenhagen airport before flying back to London is the replica statue of the Little Mermaid that sits at the terminal gate. I stand holding my duty-free bag, containing a minimalist set of salad servers we're in desperate need of, and look at her as people with briefcases hurry past.

I wonder what happened in that intervening time on dry land, after she presented herself to the prince as his saviour on legs, and before he disposed of her.

I wonder whether there had been moments he'd indicated to her that she was 'the one', and whether she'd kept coming back to those conversations to convince herself the relationship felt right. I wonder if he still liked her at all towards the end, or whether he was keeping her around to fill the gap in his own self-esteem.

I wonder whether the longer the relationship went on the more of her time and energy and self she felt she had invested in him. I wonder if that investment became the thing that made her endure the pain of walking on sharp knives every single day.

I look at her hunched shoulders, the curve of her back, and the metal eyes with no pupils, and wonder what she's thinking about. Whether she's silently diminishing herself, thinking cruel things about her own appearance and personality in order to normalise what's been happening to her. I wonder whether she started devaluing herself more and more until she disliked herself so much that she began to think she was lucky to have ever been looked at twice by a prince like him.

I think about those two versions of the same story, one with a wedding and the one with a death but both about the same mermaid. I wonder whether there's a version of 'The Little Mermaid' where the prince had given up *his* life to be with her. Whether instead of the mermaid having to slice her tail in two and walk on knives, the prince had gone to get gills and a tail of his own and joined her under the sea. I wonder why it never occurred to anyone to tell that version of the story for the last two hundred years.

But it didn't.

I stand staring at the woman from the story that I never really knew. She just sits there on the cusp of decision, unloved where she is but no longer fit for the sea.

Then I take my salad servers and I come back to London because my boyfriend is appearing on *The One Show* this week and I've decided to start being His biggest fan.

Because of pop culture

I'm going to step out of the narrative for a second to talk about Little Mo from *EastEnders*.

It's been difficult to know where and when to set my thoughts about this chapter, because actually they're thoughts that have cropped up in some shape or form way before, during *and* after the *Strictly* car-park break-up. So I'm sharing them as a conversation point, with you, the reader. Hi!

If you're not familiar with soap operas of the early noughties (and I'm sorry if you aren't because it truly was a golden age of television), I'll give you a quick round-up. There were four Slater sisters who arrived in Albert Square in the year 2000. They were: po-faced lioness Lynne; leopard-printed gobshite Kat; angelic family baby Zoe (those last two you may recall for having had the immortal exchange 'You ain't my muvva!' 'YES I AM!' which, in a golden age of television, was truly the jewel in the crown); and the fourth sister.

Little Mo.

Little Mo was timid. Softly spoken. Meek and passive. Little Mo had an abusive husband, you see, evil Scottish Trevor. I remember watching one Christmas as he poured gravy over her mashed potato and made her eat it off the floor like a dog. All her family knew something was going on because she used to tremble in their company whenever he was mentioned. One night she had enough, whacked him round the head with an iron, and went to prison.

Little Mo from *EastEnders* was probably my formative understanding of what abuse looks like, and despite my better judgement is still my inbuilt cultural benchmark of an abuse victim. And I have no doubt it was a well-researched, accurately written and sensitively portrayed character.

That, when all's said and done, I cannot relate to.

I also can't relate to Olivia Colman in *Tyrannosaur*, the best film I'll never watch again, because I was never covered in bruises. I wasn't Angela Bassett as Tina Turner in *What's Love Got To Do With It?*, being dragged across the floor. These images are blatant, outwardly violent. Pop culture taught me subtlety does not exist in these matters. There is no stealth, either – TV episodes last half an hour, films around ninety minutes. They can't represent years of nuance, or the daily gradual lowering of expectations until the best you can wish for yourself is for them to finish their drink with another woman on your birthday quickly. It wouldn't be possible to show that on screen. Or entertaining.

The media has taught me that abused women don't wear red lipstick, or sometimes dress like Stevie Nicks and put on *Rumours* because they feel like it or order mimosas at brunch and laugh, really laugh, laugh without it being visibly fraudulent. It's made it clear that abuse doesn't happen to women like me, confident women, who can crack jokes, can lead, can make decisions. I was that woman. Or, I was, at points.

In other words, pop culture told me that by identifying as an abuse victim, I am being dramatic. That I'm actually fine – those women have it much worse! It's unintentionally encouraged me to minimise my suffering as an overreaction; told me that I am not entitled to believe my experience, that I am an egotist to think what I went through is bad. An egotist, or just plain mad.

And here's the thing – if victims are being told they're not victims of abuse, does that mean perpetrators are being told that what they're doing *isn't* abusive? Because they can't see themselves in Little Mo's husband Trevor, or other onscreen domestic terrorists/expert predators that are physically violent or consistently cruel? It's likely, therefore, that in lots of cases offenders have never had their behaviour flagged, or even called into question. There's every chance they've been conditioned to genuinely think how they're behaving is normal.

It raises the question: are we all being gaslit via pop culture?

I am ...

Mending

Crouch End, 4 February 2019

Bell is having a baby boy. I said to her, 'You are growing a penis. How do you feel?' and she said, 'Predatory.' She touches her tummy all the time without realising.

Winston and I move to Shoreditch tomorrow. It's the right time. Earlier today there'd been yet another incident where I'd walked in on Bell and Jim snogging and punctured it.

'I'm compromising your intimacy,' I'd said to her.

'In English, please.'

'I'm a boner kill.'

'Nah, it's been hot having a peeping Tom around. You've been an aphrodisiac.'

Right now I'm sitting at the kitchen table, the same place I was sitting when I sent that statement out almost four months ago. It's dark outside, I can see the reflection of myself and Bell in the kitchen window. She's making bao buns at the counter, stuffing little clouds with what looks like Winston's food. From the living room next door I can hear the unmistakable sound of Bradley Walsh exuding charisma in front of a live studio audience, with the occasional contribution from Jim. 'Cayman.' 'Jane McDonald.' 'Milton Keynes, idiot!'

I have bought myself a kintsugi kit, because my little brown ceramic make-up brush pot got broken in the move. I've spread out newspaper all over the table so I don't get glue on it. Kintsugi is the Japanese art of piecing things like bowls and plates together with liquid gold after they have been broken. The idea is that the gold thread that sticks the broken pieces together makes the item not only stronger, but more beautiful than before it was smashed. It's a job that requires a great deal of calm and patience, which has truly been tested on the many occasions I have stuck my fingers together, to the newspaper, or to the pot itself.

Bell turns around with floury hands and a face full of trepidation.

'I can't stop thinking about when I told you in Copenhagen that all relationships are hard.' She shakes her head sorrowfully. 'That they take work, to take the good with the bad.'

'Where's this come from?!'

'I should have asked more questions.'

'Mate, mate!' I put the pot down on the paper and flap my hands to stop her from feeling sad. 'Please do *not* carry guilt about this. I doubt I would have answered any questions you would have asked. I worked my arse off normalising everything to everyone including myself. I wasn't about to break down over a plate of oysters on holibobs.'

'I dismissed you with trite bollocks. I kept trying to close the conversation instead of opening it up.'

'If you'd managed to get any closer to the truth, my defences would have flared up and I'd have pushed you away. Like I did Theo.'

'But honestly, is there anything I could have done better? To stop whatever was happening? I feel pretty convinced there won't be a next time in your case but, like, what if I see the signs with someone else?'

I've thought about this a lot – in fact, I've been asked it by people on social media almost daily since I put out the statement. I think everyone's case is different, in truth. But that's not helpful, so I'd suggest the following:

- Keep checking in with how things are going in your friend's relationships. Don't be shy to pry a little, in a nice way.
- Pay attention to changes in your friend's behaviour, stuff that feels inconsistent with who they are. If they're becoming withdrawn, suddenly difficult to get hold of, repeatedly calling you crying one minute and being 'absolutely fine' the next day.
- That said, don't make accusations about a friend's partner in a way that's judgey or attack-y, because if your suspicions are right and your friend is being abused they'll be in a place of constant defensiveness, and will always stand up for their partner or the relationship itself.
- You can get in touch with Women's Aid if you're worried about a friend, they don't just advise and help the people who are in the relationship.
- Be patient, understand you can't determine your friend's breaking point; they will leave an unhealthy relationship when they're ready and not when you're ready for them to.

'For me, personally,' I tell Bell, 'the thing that was a comfort was the certainty that you were always there. All those boozy nights at ours and tuna baguettes on your lunchbreak, discussing what shops we'd have if we had a mall underneath our home like Barbra Streisand does.'

'Boots, John Lewis, Robert Dyas.' Bell nods.

'Liberty's,' I add.

'Well, that's a given.'

'Anyway, all those little things totted up. It meant that on my birthday, when I felt the worst I've ever felt, I knew exactly who to call.'

'I feel the same. I would have called you, if it was me.'

'And PS: look, after the event you have categorically smashed it. You haven't once said, "At least you weren't married" or, "Thank God you didn't have kids". You accepted my pain for what it was, you never made me put it in perspective or feel guilt about people who have it worse. You've taught me how to treat myself.'

She nods.

'And you never once told me, "Chin up, you'll meet the right bloke in the end."'

'Well. You might not. And who cares?'

'Not me. Hey, do you like my shit pot?'

'Let's see.'

I go to hand it to her. She brushes the flour on her hands on her black dungaree-d thighs, takes it in her fingertips, holds it up to the light and twirls it around. Before she can say anything, I feel the urge to hold her shoulders and look her in the eyes. She clutches the pot before it re-smashes.

'Run away with me, Bell. I've got it all figured out. We'll take our savings, we could last about six months somewhere nice like St Lucia before turning to sex work.'

'You're skint.'

'I'll start turning tricks right away. Ego is the enemy.'

'And what about the baby?'

'Have him out there, fuck it. We can co-parent, teach him how to be a feminist and when he's brilliant send him off to be a world leader. He won't have a problem, he's a white guy.'

'It's a definite yes from me.' She smiles. 'The pot is very good, well done.'

'Thank you.'

'Lovelier for having once been destroyed, some would say.'

'Some would, yeah.'

She goes quiet. 'I'm going to tell you something that I can't tell Jim,' she says.

'OK.'

'I'm worried about having a baby. About my body being in pain, and what my belly and fanny will be like afterwards. I'm worried that I'm not done adventuring, that I haven't done all the things I want to do, and now I may never get to.'

'OK,' I say. 'I don't know much about this, but I hear your priorities shift, apparently?'

'Yeah, but then I think what if the people who say that are just trying to convince themselves? Babies seem really intense. I walked past a nursery the other day and looked inside, it was like a favela.'

'Oh my God.'

'Becks, what if I'm a horrible mum? I've never done it before, how do I know what I'll be like?'

'That I can answer without hesitation. You remember how good Freddie Mercury was in the *Stars in their Eyes* 2000 grand final?'

'He was unstoppable.'

'You and Jim are going to be the parental equivalent. Take it from me, your other child. Also – I mean, what do I know? – but I feel like your life having to be over once you become a mother is probably another patriarchal myth.'

She smiles.

'Call me please,' I say. 'I'll ring you too. I want to be there, want to help you. You really—' I laugh, and wipe a tear away. 'You really saved me, actually.'

'Well, I love you, mate, you see. You are my little kintsugi pot, and you're great.'

'I love you too.' We hug, her thighs cover mine in flour.

If heaven is real, then surely there must be a special section for the friends one makes in womanhood. It's probably some kind of well-lit pub playing Kate Bush not too loudly, that serves cocktails in delicate ribbed glassware and has really thoughtful touches in the toilets like expensive hand wash *and* cream and pleasingly forceful hand dryers. Nothing but the best for Bell, Queen mensch, who from the off made me feel great about myself, and who liked me for who I was, and dated me and loved me and asked me to move in with her. It's the healthiest, most adult romance I've ever had.

'Can I tell you my greatest worry, too?' I ask as we come apart. 'It's about falling in love again.'

'Sure.'

I take a deep breath. 'Thing is, mate, I've started to like myself a lot. And I'm really, really worried that no one will ever be good enough for me.'

And she doesn't say anything, because she can't, because she pisses herself laughing.

Brave

Ten days later I'm living in Shoreditch and I have a date. That actor I've only met once, Spencer, who was one of the first people to message me after I sent my statement out. I'd run in to him by chance one evening a few weeks ago, at the front of the Palace Theatre. *Harry Potter and the Cursed Child* is playing there, and he was just stood on his own in a sensible coat, woolly scarf and round glasses, looking vacantly at the theatre where lots of children were and eating a bag of Haribo.

'Hi!' I'd said.

'Oh hi!' he'd said.

'Do you know you look like a paedophile?' I'd said.

He'd asked me out later via text. The only date we could do was, mortifyingly, Valentine's Day.

'Sensational,' he'd written. 'I'll book a violinist.'

Spencer's older. He manages to be both suave and book-ish, though maybe the suaveness is something I've imposed on him so I'm less embarrassed by fancying such a nerd. Rich coming from me (internalised nerdaphobia?). Anyway he has his own flat and car, which in London is like being Elon Musk.

When I left the flat wearing my 'I'm being casual about this date' boiler suit that took me two hours to pick out, Theo was picking bits of orange sludge off themself. They weren't lying when they said they'd be here all the time, they even have their own key, although they were bloody coy about why. After years of vicious flirting, Theo has become Luca and Kyan's unicorn, which is when a woman or non-binary person joins a pre-existing couple. They asked Theo after the three of them had accidental sex behind the Biffa bins outside an after party. The night before, Luca and Kyan did MDMA, and one of them had cracked open a packet of Wotsits as the threesome were rubbing baby oil all over each other.

'It was somehow really sweet though,' Theo insisted, one of their legs over the bath and using the shower head to blast their upper inner thigh.

'Something like this happens to you every single week, and I am so afraid Spencer won't fancy me back I'm close to lying and telling him I'm celibate. Which isn't that much of a lie, really, except it's involuntary.'

'He does fancy you, he asked you out. What you gonna do, only go out with people you're not attracted to because it's not as fucking terrifying?'

Spencer and I met for our date in a proper 'bust on the bar' East London boozer. He was wearing a white shirt and maroon trousers; he looked like a manager in Pret. We spoke about theatre, he told me he'd seen a play I was in twice and the ego injection sedated me somewhat. He told me he had a love for classical music, and because I wanted to seem sophisticated I said 'Me too', and when he asked what my favourite piece was I had to confess all I could think of was the British Airways theme. He laughed and said not to worry, he was showing off anyway. I said, 'It's funny how on these things we send a representative instead of our actual selves.'

I confessed I'd just been accepted to train as a spinning

instructor when my agent called telling me I'd gotten a part in a new TV show. He said he couldn't imagine anyone more deserving. It felt like such a generous thing to say.

It was dark when we left the pub. He told me he'd been really nervous tonight, and I said so had I. We agreed to send our representatives home, and carry on the night as us.

'They do pizza by the slice at Voodoo Ray's in Dalston,' I suggested. We sat inside on a wooden bench with a slice each. I told him I'd cried with happiness when my agent told me about the TV show, and that earlier I'd pretended to take it in my stride to be impressive. He put his pizza down, leaned in and kissed me.

When they closed the restaurant, we stood opposite one another on the tiles outside, under a neon sign.

'I think I might have to be sensible, I've got a recall tomorrow morning.'

He walked home with me because I am a woman and Dalston is dodgy. When we got to the door of my building he told me he'd had such a great evening, truly. I told him I had too, and went to put the key in the lock.

'I mean . . .' he said.

'What?'

' . . . you wouldn't wake me up in the morning; I'm a very heavy sleeper.'

I felt hollow with fear. Of taking my clothes off. Showing a new person what my body really looked like. Of there being pauses while I remembered what to do, of seeming inexperienced even though I'm not really. Of his judgement, and of my own.

But the voice inside me said to be brave. That this was a good time to do this. That I was safe.

So I invited him in, and had sex with a new person for the first time in six years.

He stayed over, like he'd implied. I wasn't expecting that to have been the truth. My room was hot with another person, stuffy and a bit uncomfortable. When I went for a glass of water Theo was letting themself in after work, in drag. They pointed to Spencer's shoes and silently screamed.

'I'm not looking for anything at the moment,' Spencer had said in bed this morning.

'Oh, nor am I,' I'd answered truthfully.

We had sex again, and because I'd already done it once I could enjoy it. I thought my period was more over than it was, there were smears of blood on the sheets. I apologised, said it was gross. He said it really wasn't.

I'd always gone along with the idea that sex was the bit where you got penetrated. But it's more than that. It's the high alert before you even touch. It's in recalling afterwards, in the most inappropriate places, the heat of someone's breath on your skin, exactly like I did later this morning on the tube sitting next to a child, in my audition waiting room, in the audition itself. If I get that job it'll be a miracle. It's happening now, I can feel a mist swirling up and around me as I pay for my hummus wrap in Pret, their maroon and white uniforms having flipped a switch. I'm back there, under the bedsheets in broad daylight.

I have secretly been harbouring the belief that I might have been quite bad at sex, given that my ex did it with so many other women.

That I was the Madonna, not the whore. Built to mother, not for pleasure.

But it isn't true. I am built for whatever I like, whenever I like it. It feels liberating to realise you're everything.

I don't think it's possible to be bad at sex when you feel respected. When you're given the freedom to be who you want to be, understanding the more you are yourself the more it drives them wild.

My phone dings. Spencer. 'Still thinking about it. You?'

I reply, 'New number, who dis?'

'HAHA!'

Nah. There is nothing wrong with me and possibly everything right.

I Stayed

Because of my ego

New-build apartment, September 2018

The kitchen island is the optimum place. I can spy on the balcony while pretending to hoover crisps the way most of the others are hoovering other substances over by the leather sofa. I can spy my boyfriend and His dance partner standing against the London night skyline, dangerously close to one another. Dangerously close to the edge.

It's gone well so far, *Strictly*. He rehearses a *lot*, but I'm being His biggest fan like I told Bell I would. Supporting on social media, making carb-heavy dinners at night for energy, rallying round His friends and some of His actual heroes for letters of encouragement to compile in a thoughtful *Strictly* book to surprise Him with. But still, being careful to not be too much, you know?

He hadn't wanted me to come to the after party at hers tonight. In the end He'd yielded, but the instructions were firm: don't be clingy. So I haven't followed Him around like I'd wanted to, haven't cock blocked, haven't been too much. Instead, I've spent the last couple of hours performing nonchalance at their banter, their in-jokes, their mingling with the other attendees as a pair.

In actual fact, I'm obviously the opposite of nonchalant. I am chalant as fresh hell, am desperate to hiss '*STOPPIT!*' at them both, and have instead inhaled two sharing bags of crisps to keep my gob occupied.

One of the female dancers from the show comes to the island for a prosecco top-up, all legs and highlighter.

'Congratulations!' I tell her. 'What are you guys doing next week?'

'Salsa,' she says.

'Amazing!' I offer her the crisp bag. 'No thanks,' she says.

Silence. I plough through it.

'Ugh, I'm so happy the audience kept Him in. Think they must have seen how hard He's been trying.'

'Yeah.'

'Really happy for them, both.' I indicate the balcony, where the dancer is pointing out the Gherkin to Him.

'Yeah, that's the thing about her. Me as well,' the other dancer says. 'We're not like the other girls on the show. Other women, they know they can trust us with their husbands or boyfriends. I mean, she's married.'

I want to say, *Oh. I know she's married. I hear how she's married practically every day. I hear she's married so much that it has ceased to be a relief. Recently her marital status has begun to feel like a fortress conveniently built to keep me out of their business.*

'People don't get what it's like,' the other dancer continues, 'working this closely with someone. Girlfriends are gonna get jealous but it's our job.'

'No, I get it. I work closely with people as well, I'm an actress,' I say, feeling like a fraud, having now not worked in over a year. But my unworthiness at being at the party, and the success gap between me and everybody there – including my own boyfriend – clamps my mouth shut.

'Oh right,' she says to the Twitter app on her phone.

I watch her type her own name into the search bar and scroll the mentions thinking that, for the best part of ten years, pretending has been my actual job. The art of facade, that's my bread and butter. I thought I knew everything there was to know. Thing about facade is, the audience is at least aware that it's all a sham, they know the sword didn't really kill Hamlet, and she's not really Cinderella because she's also in *Hollyoaks*. But the next step after facade is altogether more sinister – a place that's entirely opaque, where the audience are made to think what they're seeing is the truth, and the reality is kept secret. And I couldn't have wished for a more striking introduction to that than at the television programme *Strictly Come Dancing*.

Strictly. My favourite show for the past ten years. A shimmering, foot-tapping, family-friendly den of iniquity that's papered over with sequins and rictus grins. The studio you see on television is in fact a four-sided MDF box held up with scaffolding – behind the walls there's just steel bars and murk. That's fine; it's how most television works. But the superficiality of the studio has nothing on some of the personalities that inhabit it.

Now look, I'm not talking about every single person. We'll bear in mind my humble experience at *Strictly* is exactly that – mine – and let's not forget that's the experience of someone outside of the Emerald City that was the inner circle. If all this sounds bitter, well, yeah, it is a bit. From the day my boyfriend became involved with *Strictly*, His life has been one big confetti cannon. The job of half these dancers is teaching the celebrity to dance, sure, but the other half is empowering the celebrities, rewarding their efforts with praise and fuss and ego stroking. The more confident the celebrity feels, the better they perform under pressure, and those dancers all want to win. It's easy to see why lots of participants say *Strictly* is the greatest experience of their lives. It's hard work, no doubt about that, but it's also like being thrown a party every day, where the occasion that's being celebrated is *you*, and *how great you are.*

They're savvy, too, those dancers. Not been paired with the next Gene Kelly? Easy. Create a storyline for you and your partner; a love story, or a torrid affair, a bit of *spice*. Column inches and public intrigue will follow, the kind that will get those phones picked up and keep you in the running for that all-important win as long as possible. There are even rumours of a few dancers being notorious for sleeping with their new celebrity partner every year, to imbue the novice with a swagger that means they will perform on live TV with more confidence.

'Hiiii!' a voice behind me squeals.

I spin around. 'Yaaay!' I exclaim delightedly.

The dancer throws her arms around me and we squeeze one another and dramatically sway from side to side screaming 'aaaarrrghhhhh!' and laughing and then we're jumping together and it's as though we're friends.

We do this a lot.

'Where's your husband?' I ask as she lifts two plastic cups from the stack on the counter. 'Haven't seen him in ages.'

'Pffft,' she shakes her head as she lifts up coloured bottles of alcohol, checking the dregs. 'Somewhere, I dunno. Bed, probably.'

'He taught me the waltz position earlier, said I was good!'

'Aaaaww, that's so sweet!' She selects a Jack Daniel's and pours a generous amount in each cup.

'I meant to ask you something actually.' *Oh no.*

'Yeah?' she says.

Oh fuck, think of something to ask, Rebecca, anything.

'What, um. What . . . hand cream do you use, again?' I ask, the 'again' denoting that I've asked it before, this banal question about the beauty industry's least stimulating fluid. Which I have, about an hour ago, when again I'd been flustered around her and felt I had to say something, anything.

She tells me that she's not sure what brand it is but that it's by the sink in her bathroom. Again. She does so with all the kindness and patience of Princess Diana talking to a sticky child handing her a posy.

'Oh God, duuurrrr, I've already asked that, haven't I?!' I laugh as she tops up the two drinks with a litre bottle of Coke.

She laughs back and screws the lid back on. 'Come outside with us!'

Us.

'In a bit,' I say. 'This is your time, tonight, y'know. He doesn't want me hanging around, it's too much.'

'Who cares what He thinks?' she says. 'Seriously, come.'

I watch her tiny toned body float towards the balcony with both drinks, and I think: *I don't like this woman.*

This woman who, since I was capable of conscious thought, every magazine, film, telly programme and advertisement has told me is better than I am. This woman that I've had to watch pressed up against my boyfriend on *Strictly*, or on the sofas of morning television, evening television, afternoon bloody television. That I'm watching right now, pressing her body against Him to get past and resume her position on the balcony as I stuff more salt and vinegar shards in my mouth.

I don't like how, when the *Strictly* partnerships were announced, a major newspaper put odds on each of the dance pairings to have sex, and I don't like how I remind myself about their relatively low odds every single day because I am paranoid.

I don't like the way He's cheering as she cha-cha-chas around the balcony, don't like the way he's looking at her. I don't like the way that I can see for myself, on telly and in real life, how she senses His eyes on her body and how it makes her hold herself like she's being painted, like Kate Winslet in *Titanic*.

And most of all? I don't like that I get it. That I can see what, according to Him, He doesn't see in her. She really is pretty, and small, and very nice. She knows she's pretty too.

People sometimes say that in a way that suggests knowing that you're pretty is something really terrible. I don't think it is; I think it's perceptive, and enviable. The first time we met was after *Strictly* one week, in a loud room, and the following exchange happened:

Me: Oh hi, the dancer, how are you?

The dancer: Oh my God, thank you so much!

Imagine being so gorgeous, compliments are the first thing you expect to hear. She has it all, and I know the need for nothing more, that stench of ambivalence, is what is luring Him in, like the curly smoke that wafts out of a pie in old Looney Tunes cartoons.

But the thing is, it's not just her that I don't like. I've stopped liking all women. When I see any woman, in that first second, I've begun to weigh them up so quickly it's like I'm using His actual eyes, feeling His actual feelings. I can instantly identify who is safe and who is a threat, friends or enemies. Years of catching His glances at some woman and His looking straight through others have given me an inbuilt chart of His preferences and turn-offs.

But it's the women who are most like my former self that feel like the biggest threat of all. I have begun to find those women oppressively inspiring and cannot stand beside one without considering how pointless my achievements, my shape, my opinions are. Those women, with the aspirations I used to have, the assertion, the confidence to admit the things they don't yet know – those women all seem to be moving on an upward incline as I spiral downward. I'm so scared that if I ever did take the effort to climb out of this hole and get as high as they are, I'd get the directions wrong and wind up alone on a shelf. And that's what it all comes down to. If I don't want to be alone for ever, I can't be around other women. Because if I opened my ears to what those women were saying,

I feel as though I would discover that I shouldn't be in this relationship. And there are so many reasons why leaving just isn't possible. Aren't there?

On the balcony, the dancer leans in to whisper something to Him and He laughs, laughs with such light-hearted freshness. I turn away from the pair of them and that's when I see her there, the woman trapped in the kitchen tiles, the one who follows me around. She's more a hazy outline than an actual woman, all shape no substance. I see her more and more often, and not just in kitchen tiles. Sometimes in the bathroom mirror in the early hours of the morning, sometimes on the tube in the windows opposite where I'm sitting. Occasionally she looks back at me from the glass jars in Tesco, where she stands as though perched on the edge of a precipice, a basket dangling at her side. Waiting in an aisle of tinned pulses for a response to her text of 'What should I get?', desperate for a message back so she doesn't get it wrong and buy all the wrong things.

There she is now, paralysed at 3 a.m. in the house of the dancer. Trapped between 'too much' and 'not enough'.

'There you are!' He says it like He's been looking for me for the last hour. The dancer is behind Him.

'Hieee!' I say.

'I told Him to come and get you.' She smiles.

'I think . . . I think I wanna go home?' I say, nodding at Him to take the hint. 'I'm really tired, it's gone three a.m.'

'Aaaah,' He says. 'OK.'

Five or so minutes later, in the Uber He got to take me home, I think that it's my birthday on Wednesday, that'll be good.

The next time I hear from Him is the following afternoon. He texts saying the three of them are chilling at theirs. I tell Him I've seen her husband is having a Sunday roast with another of the *Strictly* contestants on Instagram. He tells me to stop spying

339

on Him. I type a text into my phone – 'She isn't better than me' – but I don't send it.

They rehearse that Sunday until nine in the evening and I wonder at what point does a series of rough patches become a cycle.

But He comes home to me eventually. I always triumph, in the end.

I am ...

Wiser

'I've only got coconut milk.'

I try not to gag.

'That's fine,' I say, not looking away from between the blinds. Outside Debbie from number twelve is pulling the Dobermann, trying to get it indoors. The dog is facing the outside world, not fighting, just standing there being much stronger than she is. It doesn't look like it's taking much pleasure in what it sees, more as though it doesn't want to yield. Poor Deb looks knackered. She sees me through the window and her face instantly changes. She brushes the hair from her face and waves enthusiastically. I wave back.

'Do you remember how much I used to love Disney?' I ask Mum as she sits at her new and much cherished B&Q breakfast bar.

'Yeah. I've still got your old videos up in the loft.'

'Someone on Instagram sent me a story this week called "The Crane Wife".'

'Oh right.' She nods sagely.

'Have you heard of it?'

'No, can't say I have.'

'It's a Japanese folk tale.'

343

She makes a noise that means, *Well, la-di-da.*

'Shall I tell you it?'

'If you like,' she says, making a face to one side as though there's a studio audience there, and she's making them laugh with how daft I can be sometimes, telling fairy tales when there's coconut tea to be drunk and small talk to be made.

'Once upon a time, there was a crane who fell in love with a man.'

'A crane?!'

'The bird, not a building-site crane.'

'I was gonna say!'

'Anyway, this crane, right, she falls in love with this man but knows that he'll never marry her because she's a crane and he's a human. So she tricks him. Every night when he's asleep, she stays awake plucking out her feathers with her beak. She hopes that he'll never see her for the thing that she is, which is something that could fly, something that requires care and gentleness, that has needs. Every morning the crane is exhausted, but she is a woman again. To keep becoming a woman for when he wakes up is hard, painful work, but she keeps doing it anyway. Keeps plucking out all her feathers, one by one.'

A pause.

'Is that the end?' she asks.

'Yeah, that's it, Mum. It made me wonder what things would have been like if I'd heard it earlier, like when I was a kid. Instead of those other stories about mermaids and princesses.'

She makes a sound that covers two octaves, 'Hm-mmm', as if to say, *I don't really know what I'm meant to say to that.*

'I guess it's not as exciting a story as those others, is it?' I ask.

'Not especially, no.'

Nobody is entirely how you would want them to be, are they? I don't suppose I'll ever know the bits of me that my mum would prefer were different. I suspect she'd rather I didn't share as much as I do, for one thing. But you know what, we're both doing our best with the tools we've been given.

I wish I could say, *Mum, I am impressed by you. You stepped away from an unhappy relationship when nobody had done anything wrong. You intervened when you felt yourself shrinking and set yourself free.*

I wish I could say, *The concept of leaving a partner to be on your own was too abstract a thought for me up until six months ago, but now I get it.*

I want to say, *I'm proud of you for being OK with being a crane, for refusing to pluck out your feathers while literally living under the weight of those princesses and mermaids in the attic. And I can't believe it took all this palaver to happen to me to realise how brave you were for pioneering being a single woman out of choice, in a time and place where that just didn't happen.*

I want to say it even more because last week Maura told me that codependency thrives in families that don't feel comfortable talking about their problems.

But instead I just sip my coconut tea, which isn't that bad in fairness, and say, 'Have you ever seen that Cher clip where she's interviewed by Jane Pauley?'

'No.'

I get my phone out and click on the red and white You-Tube app.

'Did you know after Cher won her Oscar for *Moonstruck* no one would hire her and she had to do stuff for QVC to make money?' I ask Mum. 'It's because she was forty-two.'

'I quite like QVC.'

I've seen this clip a thousand times. I was sent it repeatedly by strangers on the internet six months ago. On the phone, 90s Cher is poured over a golden chaise longue, all brown lipstick and rock 'n' roll hair. She's speaking to a conservative-looking woman with a southern American accent.

JANE: You said 'a man is not a necessity, a man is a luxury'.

CHER: [unflinching]: Like dessert, yeah.

JANE: [laughs in surprise]

CHER: [not laughing]: A man is absolutely not a necessity.

JANE: Did you mean for that to sound ... mean and bitter?

CHER: Oh, not at all. I adore dessert! [smiles] I love men, I think men are the coolest. [serious again] But you really don't need them to live. My mom said to me, 'You know, sweetheart, one day you should settle down and marry a rich man.' I said to her, 'Mom, I am a rich man.'

And Jane Pauley laughs, Mum laughs, and so do I. My mum, with whom I have nothing in common.

It's on the tip of my tongue, the 'I love you'.

Baby steps.

Accepting

Shoreditch, March 2019

'Sex with one person,' says Theo, 'is like ordering lemon and herb spice at Nando's.'

'ONCE!' I exclaim, then look up from my phone at Pearl, whose lap my head is in. 'I ordered it *once* because I had a mouth ulcer and Theo will never let me forget it.'

Some of the furniture in our flat are real vintage finds, like the pink velvet sofa and the high-school lockers. Others – like the rusty light-up sign that says '24 hour cafe' they got in a car boot last week – are a constant reminder that tolerance is a virtue. A Terry O'Neill portrait of an elderly Bette Davis, sitting by a portrait of her younger self, glares at us from the living room wall ('the woman is an absolute mood' insists Luca). Kyan has an 'imposing plant' problem, it's like eating breakfast in Aqua's 'Dr Jones' video, which is niche but accurate. The shower rail in the bathroom literally hangs in the balance; the bloke we called to fix it and I had a 'discussion' last week about his decision to join NoFap, which is a group of men who are abstinent from porn and wanking after previous addiction. I had been fascinated until he told me that even though he now sees women as human beings, he still didn't believe they would have equality.

'Why?!' I'd asked.

'See?' he'd said. 'See how your tone changed straight away? We were having a nice discussion before now. And that's the reason. Women can't be calm about these things.'

So I kicked him out.

The flat has an invisible revolving door through which drag queens and trans artists and queer designers twirl at all hours of the day and night, and there is a smoke machine, a disco ball, disco lights and a cupboard full of wigs for emergency party time. Tonight it's Pearl's turn. The three of us are draped over the pink sofa, and one another, being careful to avoid the foam in Theo's hair from tonight's bleaching. I ghosted Pearl for a little while after New Year because it was much easier to label myself a coward than it was telling someone I wasn't into them. Then Theo pointed out that

1. People who ghost are pathetic or baddies, and
2. It's very up my own arse to assume anyone would be devastated that I wouldn't fancy them back.

So I let her know how I felt, and that I really do think she's cool and interesting, and we've been mates ever since.

'Monogamy is a bourgeoise scam, and Little Dorothy Gale finds that hard to get her head around,' Theo tells Pearl.

'I'm trying my best and one day will be progressive enough for you,' I say, though I'm back looking at my WhatsApp because Spencer and I are sexting.

'I can't help it if I'm not confined by heteronormative standards.'

'And you're sure – you're *sure* –' Pearl asks Theo, 'they're not tethering you to them so when they can't see you, you're not putting it about?'

'Isn't that basically any relationship?' Theo adjusts the raggy towel around their shoulders.

'Touché,' I say, as I tell Spencer I'm on my bed touching

myself. 'And can I also throw in that Theo isn't even supposed to be in a relationship. They tell you in recovery that you need at least a year sober before dating.'

'How long's it been?' asks Pearl.

'Three months,' Theo says proudly. 'I couldn't have done it without Sue over here.' They smile at me and my insides twinkle with pride.

Spencer messages saying he's hard.

'But look, as far as the relationship goes, the three of us have amazing, varied sex, and we're romantic and sincere. And there's not a red flag in sight.'

'A lack of red flags isn't a reason for something to progress,' Pearl says.

'But it sure makes a nice fucking change!'

I keep very quiet and ask Spencer what he's doing to me. It's great with me and him. We see each other about once a week. The sex just gets better and better. And yeah, sometimes I'm not completely clear on things. Like whether we are being private, or whether I'm being kept secret. Like why he answers my questions about how he's feeling with complex scientific analogies. Like how come when we're lying in bed after having great sex, he takes the opportunity to mansplain current affairs (a condition which Theo refers to as 'correctile dysfunction'). Like why when I haven't heard from him in a few days I put up honey trap Insta stories and obsessively check to see if he's watched them rather than just texting him saying hi.

But look, it's nice to feel liked, to have someone at the end of a phone when you're walking from the bus stop at 2 a.m. and a man crosses the road to walk behind you. And it's very nice to witness the animalistic effect that I am able to have as a smart adult woman on a smart adult man.

Also he's very different from Him, so I have high hopes of it going somewhere.

'I'm hooking my thumbs over your knickers and pulling them down slowly . . .' The screen reads.

I start replying – 'I'm laying back on the be—' But I'm interrupted. An unknown number is calling me. I click the red reject button and carry on.

'I'm laying back on the bed and pulling you on to—'

Another unknown number.

'I'm laying back on the bed and pulling you on top of m—'

Another one. What is happening? I click on my home screen. The numbers on my email inbox are climbing up up up. I click the mail icon. Lots of email addresses I recognise from last October: newspapers, magazines. I sit up and walk into the hallway to call my agent. Theo and Pearl have stopped talking.

'You're being asked for a comment,' he tells me.

'What about?'

'He's been on Jonathan Ross.'

'What?!'

But it makes sense. He and Jonathan have the same agent, Vinnie.

I hang up. 'Quickly,' I tell Theo and Pearl, who get up and gather either side of me. I click on the YouTube app.

On the screen, He's wearing a suit and sitting next to Samuel L. Jackson. For some reason I feel dejected about it, as though it means Samuel L. and I will never be proper friends. His voice is the same but different. It's louder, for the studio audience. It takes a lot of resilience to keep watching. Seeing His face and hair and gestures makes me want to hide.

A banner comes up at the top of the screen. 'Tell me you want my dick.'

'THAT'S SPENCER THAT'S NOTHING.' I swat it away.

My ex mentions me by name, for the first time since it happened. He says I was right about everything. He says, 'She's right, cheating *is* a form of abuse.'

'That's not what you were saying!' says Theo.

'No.'

'He's derailing.' Pearl shakes her head. 'Fuck that guy.'

I watch Jonathan Ross say 'Rebecca', like he knows me. I stand in my house of plants filled with second-hand things and watch these two men in sharp suits speculate on how I must have felt last October. How I must still be feeling. He says things are different now because He's given up booze.

'Derailment again,' says Pearl.

He announces He'll be doing a stand-up comedy tour about the incident. Theo hooks their arm around my shoulder and pulls me in. The audience give Him a round of applause at the end. I put my phone on airplane mode.

Theo says, 'Well, I don't know about you, but I believe him.'

I do a hollow laugh.

'You OK?' asks Pearl.

'Yeah.' I nod. 'This has happened to me before. Men absolutely love giving it the old "what I've learned from going out with Rebecca", "How I've become a better person since". Sometimes I think I'm not meant to ever end up in a relationship, I'm just a vessel men pass through to become fit for commitment on the other side. Max sent me a whole letter about how much I'd changed his life. In fact . . . ' I pause. 'Wait here.'

I walk out of the living room, down the corridor. Winston is lying flat out on my bed, the furry slug. I go behind my bedside table (actually an old crate stood upright) and pull out a piece of lined paper, torn from a jotter pad and folded in half.

During our relationship He rarely apologised to me about anything, insisting that He only says sorry 'when he really means it'. It ensured 'I'm sorry' carried substantial weight when it was deployed, which was mostly whenever I had gathered the strength and confidence to leave, and He became attracted once again to my strength and confidence. I was so starved of

351

kindness that an occasional 'I'm sorry' or even something as blasé as 'you OK?' – anything that acknowledged I was a person with feelings – would make it feel as though light was shining directly on me, like a sunflower that greedily tracks the journey of the sun, soaking up that warmth before the darkness falls again. Difference is, the sun *wants* the flower to grow. It doesn't want to keep the flower in the same place for when it feels like being reminded of its own greatness.

Pearl is still on the sofa, waiting for me in silence. Theo rushes in from the bathroom apologising, they just had to check the bleach. I sit and they huddle around me. I unfold the paper.

Last week I went for lunch with my former upstairs neighbour from Samstat Road. She handed me an old orange notebook I must have left behind when I moved out that night, and said, 'He gave me this to give to you.' I'd flicked through it later on the tube and found a piece of paper in it, in His handwriting. At the top it said 'Rebecca'. I'd never seen that word in that handwriting before, only ever 'Bun'. It wasn't long, a few hastily written lines. It said He was sorry, and it wished me luck with everything. I'd looked around after I'd read it, like I was expecting Him to be watching me in the carriage. I'd gotten out at the next stop and cowered in a corner of the station. I could hardly breathe.

None of us speak after I've read it aloud. I put my head on Theo's shoulder. Pearl takes my hand and massages my palm.

'It's such a shame,' I say eventually, 'that it ended in a media volcano. That we wound up as public property. I mean, at the time it was sort of brilliant, for me. The added layer, all the press and attention and support, it made it less difficult. It actually gave me a strange confidence, navigating something that massive on my own. But it's the aftermath that's the real bugger. Watching an apology made to me on television, followed by an announcement of yet another stand-up tour. How am I still ripe for another year's worth of material?!' I look at the letter. At the ink that ran from a pen his hand was holding. I wonder which bit of the flat He was standing in when He wrote it. I wonder if He did it before or after He'd been booked to apologise to me on TV. 'I really want to read decency between its lines,' I say. 'But given everything that's happened, I'm finding it difficult.'

'Come here.' Theo grabs the letter and leads Pearl and me onto the balcony, the grime of which has been glossed over with yet more Little Shop of Horrors plants, fairy lights and the odd crystal. We squeeze together to fit. The moon is full. Theo hands me back the letter, along with a lighter. I smile, lean over the edge, and torch the end of the paper. It's windy, so it takes a few attempts.

'Am I being a princess about this?' I ask them when it finally catches. 'I've been waiting all this time for an apology. And now I've got it, and somehow it's still not good enough.'

'What would have been acceptable?' Pearl asks.

'Pffft. Nothing, probably!'

'So maybe the apology isn't the problem, maybe the problem is "I'm sorry" comes with this intense pressure to forgive.'

I hold the paper between my thumb and forefinger. Twisting and turning it slowly above the streetlights of East London, working with the wind so the fire spreads. 'That makes sense. People ask me all the time whether I've forgiven Him yet, as though forgiveness is this desired end result, and the back cover of the book will close like in those dated Disney animations. Forgiveness sits weirdly with me, though. I'm not entirely convinced that, in certain instances, forgiveness isn't one of those 'pleasing feminine qualities' that serve to make women more palatable, like martyrdom or anal bleaching.'

'I don't forgive,' says Theo. 'I accept and move on. I find that much more actionable.'

The fire gets close to my fingers. I drop the paper on the balcony floor, and watch it curl and blacken under the flames.

I can't believe what I let my heart get used to. Accepting I would never get asked to dance when my favourite song was on, rather asked whether we could leave yet. Accepting I'd have to listen to Blink-182 every day, until one of us died. Accepting every opening night of mine would feature the question, 'Do I have to come?' Accepting there was only room for one career in the house, and it was His. Accepting my partner would never get to know my friends, or throw me a surprise party like some of my other friends' boyfriends did. I told my heart those were selfish things to want, rather than tell it 'you deserve them'.

I watch the letter burn. His name is the last word to disappear.

I Stayed

Because this is how my life is

Q: What's more depressing than picking at lukewarm mince at
   10:23 p.m.?
A: Picking at lukewarm mince at 10:23 p.m. alone, under the
   light of a greasy extractor fan, listening to Chris de Burgh's
   'Lady In Red' on repeat.

On your birthday.

The scene didn't start like this. If we rewound approximately
twenty-three minutes, you'd see the mascara/tear combo currently cascading down my cheeks trickle back up to my eyes,
my foundation, concealer, blush and highlighter smoothing
back over into a perfect peach. The shop-bought lasagne would
begin to bubble and it's rhythmic gymnastic ribbons of smoke
would cheerily float around the Lulworth-blue kitchen with its
grey and white marbled counter top. The same blue, grey and
white kitchen that twenty-three minutes later I will fucking
detest along with everything else about my useless life.

I don't usually listen to Chris de Burgh, let me be clear about
that. I thought it would be funny to have it blaring out the
speakers when He got home as I am wearing a red strappy silk
dress that's all wispy at the ends and that I never wear unless I

357

feel OK about my arms, which twenty-three minutes ago I did but I don't any more. Around my neck is a new chain. He'd been running late for rehearsals this morning as I had woken up, a car waiting for Him outside, so He'd had to chuck the unmistakable sage-green box of the jewellery brand I like at me as He ran out of the door. Inside the delicate green box was a delicate gold necklace on which hung the letter 'R', embossed with tiny leaves and flowers.

I could recount the details of the time when the lasagne went from hot to cold, when my arms went from tolerable to unacceptable. But suffice to say there was a text that read 'Going to have a drink. That all right?' followed by my dialling His number, followed by a phone call featuring repetitive accusations, tears, raised voices, and the following humiliating exchange when my heart spoke from inside me:

'Can I come?' it asked.

'No, Bun! You don't even *like* pubs!'

If someone else recounted that to me, I would think them a tragic weakling, like Beth from *Little Women* dying of scarlet fever. But the reason I *am* recounting it is that I could have sworn I *do* like going to the pub, that I am in fact a great big fan of the sesh. That I live for dinners of sauvignon with a Walkers crisp salad, love mopping the table dry for a quiz paper, then mischievously leaning in at a last order bell, and giving that sotto voce ' . . . one more?'

Not recently, of course; recently I am too knackered for the pub. Maybe that's what He meant.

Also in a sense He is absolutely right – that pub isn't where I really want to be tonight. Third wheeling. Ball and chain-ing.

He said all the usual stuff about being psychotic, which I appreciate. I have over the years tried asking nicely, convincing, seducing, giving Him space, emotionally manipulating (disguised as asking nicely), shouting, asking nicely while crying, and demanding while scream-crying. Tonight I was begging. It was a lot. It was desperate.

Chris de Burgh tells me he's never seen me looking so lovely as I did tonight again as Winston, a cloud with grey slippers and ears, pads silently across the counter, and bores his blue eyes into mine. Yes, my cat's colouring does match the kitchen. He sniffs at his weeping mother, then promptly slams his face into the lasagne. I watch him for a minute until it occurs to me that oh shit, I may have read that cheese gives cats diarrhoea, so I lift his fluffy cloud body up and lower him to the floor where he legs it.

Enough's enough. The dancer's a woman, and my pretend friend, she'll understand. More than He does, anyway. I open my phone to Instagram messages, our preferred avenue of communication.

'Hi Hun.'

Ick.

'I need you to know something and please don't tell Him. Today is my birthday and I have spent the day alone, with no idea what time you are finishing because He doesn't contact me and at 10 I got this text telling me you are going for a drink. I understand the need to unwind but I am on my own crying and absolutely devasta—'

Too emotional.

'I understand the need to unwind but I just need to express how difficult this is, in case He makes me out to be a monster here. I'm so sorry to message you but I'm not there to defend myself so thought it was fair I text you. xxx'

Send.

Good for me. Now what? None of this alters the fact I'm still standing here inhaling cold lasagne, face wet with wasted energy. I can't call Mum; presenting her with an emotional sharing would be like presenting her with the Large Hadron Collider, something far too big that she wouldn't know where to start with. Maura might be asleep. I look at the message from Theo on my phone, the first in weeks: 'HBD Celine x' and a picture of Celine Dion, but with my face photoshopped on. But how can I possibly tell Theo what's happened, after how I've behaved?

A banner appears at the top of my screen. The dancer's response.

'I'm so sorry!!! Oh no, He doesn't at all I promise!!! We practised till late and went for one drink. But on the way back now!!!!! I guess my husband just understands how hard it is. He will be with you shortly!!!!'

I place my hands on the worktop. Press them into the marble. Hard.

Fuck it, I'm going in.

'I'm sure your husband does understand. I also understand to a certain extent. I'm not as high maintenance as all that – just a text to say what time He'll be home as I have to let Him in (still no keys) and maybe to make sure I'm not alone on my birthday instead of being at the pub. He can act like that's so much to ask but, really, it's not.'

I run to the bathroom and grab the loo roll, then to our room and throw myself on the bed. I'm unravelling, breathing hard. It's pathetic, misdirecting my sadness and anger at the beautiful woman my boyfriend is clinking glasses with. I have to speak to a human being. I'm calling Bell.

'HAPPY BIRTHDAAAAAAA—'

I choke sob.

'—AAAAYwhatthefuck?'

I tell her what's happened. Or rather, make vowel sounds down the phone as I leak into bits of torn-off bog paper.

'. . . anIjustwannaknowisthisnormalBell?'

'Oh, mate—'

'Cos as well,' I continue, ploughing through the sound of her condolence, 'birthdays aren't really His thing, He just doesn't really give a shit.'

'Yeah, that's Jim as well.'

'What's me?' Jim's grizzly-bear-from-Grimsby voice sounds indirect, I can hear he's not taken his eyes off the telly.

'Birthdays.'

'Oh bloody hell, yeah, nonsense. Johannesburg.'

'HI, JIM.' I wipe my eyes with a tissue full of snot.

'Becks says hi.'

'YOU ALL RIGHT, MATE, HAPPY BIRTHDAY!' Jim yells back, then, 'The Nolans.'

'Are you watching *The Chase*?' I ask. They love *The Chase*.

'Well, it's five o'clock somewhere.'

'Just tell me I'm overreacting here, mate, please.' I pull my necklace taut, and swish the R back and forth along the chain.

'Look, He's fucked up!' Her voice is breezy, insistently breezy. 'He has royally fucked it up the arse. But the dancer's said they're on the way home so that's good news, how long ago was that?'

I check. 'Almost an hour.'

'Right, and how long does the journey take?'

'Twenty-five minutes.'

'The Miami Dolphins.'

'Shut up, Jim,' she says.

My phone dings at my ear. 'Fuck shit I've got a message.'

'There you go, see?'

'Hang on, I'll put you on speaker. It's from Him. Says . . . "Hey, just to get this out there before I get home. I went for a drink with a mate after work. I'm sorry it was on your birthday. I didn't think. I don't like discussing this sort of thing but fuck me, she has a husband who actually asked us to stay out later as he was watching the football."'

'Well.' Bell sounds uncertain. 'There you go.'

I check Instagram. 'There's one from the dancer too.'

361

'And?'

It says, 'I'm sorry! I'm on my way home now. I don't want to cause trouble.'

Neither of us says anything. Bell breaks it.

'That's a fucking weird thing to say.'

'I'm glad you said that, I thought it was weird but I don't know what's weird any more.'

'No, yeah. Fundamentally weird.'

'Why doesn't He want me, mate?' I grab a pillow and hug it to me. 'Why am I so useless?'

'It's not you.'

'I want it to be. If it's me, there's something I can do about it.'

I hear the outside gate creak; 5,000 volts shoot up my spine.

'He's here, oh God, I have to go, I have to let Him in.' I gather up the claggy tissuey bits.

'What d'you mean, where are His keys?'

'Uh, He lost them a couple of weeks ago.'

'And He hasn't got new ones cut?'

'He says He's too busy, He's got *Strictly*, hasn't He?'

'Hang on.' Her voice has changed. 'Is your choice to either go and get His key cut for Him, or just sit home waiting to let Him in every night?'

Or leave them outside when I'm asleep, I think, but don't say. On a street where strange men have followed me home on more than one occasion.

I hear Him swing the gate shut.

'Becks, we must remember that e. e. cummings line: "There is some shit I will not eat".'

'I have to go, mate, sorry.' I hang up. I run to the front door, open the latch before he can ring the deafening buzzer of death that sounds like an automatic lock release in a prison, and run back to the bed.

He walks past the doorway to the bedroom. He doesn't say

362

anything. I'm holding my breath, hearing his footsteps in the kitchen. Eventually he comes to hang his coat and fedora up on the hooks opposite the bedroom doorway. I can see he's wearing my favourite black and white striped T-shirt. He spins around. 'Hello.' He raises his eyebrows and says, 'Calmed down now?'

It may be the first time ever, in my entire life, that I have no idea what to say. I just look at Him, conscious I myself am looking like the pile of wet loo roll that I hastily shoved under my side of the bed. He sighs and walks away. I hear the fissle of foil, and when he comes back twenty seconds later, he's holding the plastic tub of lasagne in one hand and a fork in the other. He's being jaunty. He leans against the bedroom doorframe, cutting it into shards with the side of his fork. I am so sad I'm not even the littlest bit happy that the cat has been licking the lasagne with the same tongue that licks its own arsehole.

'What am I for,' I ask, but it's not a question.

'What?' His mouth is full.

I shrug. He shrugs right back.

I swallow down a sob. 'All you have to do, right—'

'You're doing that weird tick thing.'

I hold the sides of my head to stop it doing the sharp nod it's been doing lately. 'All you have to do is learn some dancing, and make your girlfriend think you're not cheating on her.'

'I just think,' He says, chewing, 'if you saw the two of us together earlier, it'd be obvious we're just friends.' He flicks the fork casually, a tiny splash of tomato sauce hits the doorframe. 'And you would see what a psycho you are.'

He goes and watches telly even though it's nearly midnight, and I can't help feeling that if this was a film, the camera would follow Him, like He's the protagonist even though it's my show. Follow Him as he launches Himself contentedly onto the sofa and turns on WWE wrestling, which I can hear pumping out now from the other room. He's watched it since He was a little

363

boy, it calms Him. I hear screams and slams of men pummelling each other like real men do, in Lycra swimming costumes like real men wear.

When He comes into the bedroom, it's in silence. I hear his clothes softly thudding on the floor (not the laundry basket, incidentally, but you have to pick your battles sometimes). He gets into bed. Edges closer. His arm snakes around me. I close my eyes and shrink away.

I know he expects me to kiss him.

No! A voice inside me shouts. I open my mouth for the no to fall out before he gets too close.

Once upon a time if someone had told me tearing apart the skin on my chest, reaching into my own ribs and pulling out my vital organs one by one would make Him want to kiss me, I'd have done it. I would have done yesterday. On holiday last month in Dorset, I'd have eaten hair clumps from the hotel bath plug if it meant being kissed in any way; on the mouth or the forehead or the neck or the inner thigh, deeply or fiercely or with love or even pity.

But now a voice inside me screams, *NO.* Tells me this kiss wouldn't be a kiss, it would be yet another line drawn under something bad. It would be a 'let's forget this ever happened'.

I don't want to gloss over the voice inside me that echoes, *No. You aren't what he says you are. You aren't what he says you are.*

But I sense Him giving up, of admitting defeat. And I can't help feeling my coldness has made Him feel less than He is. So I say:

'Come here.'

And I kiss Him, and then I lie there as He sleeps peacefully next to me, thinking about Bell's tone of voice when I told her about being locked inside the flat like an inmate.

I am thirty-two today. All those years have led to this.

I can't believe that this is my life.

The next day, Thursday, I get a text at around noon: 'Hey, I feel really bad about what happened yesterday. Thinking when the Saturday night show is over I could take you out all day on Sunday to make it up to you? Birthday fun? I've not looked after you and I'm really sorry. This will all be over soon. Love xxxxx.'

You know, when *Strictly* is over this will all be forgotten. I might get a new dress for the show at the weekend.

I am ...

No better than where I started

Shoreditch, April 2019

He's pretty attractive, if you're into manscaping. He's French as well; they're meant to be good at this, aren't they, or is that racist?

'Do you 'ave, uh . . . ?' His hands make a twisty motion on the top of the Yellow Tail shiraz we got on the way here.

'Sure.' I open the drawer beside him. It would be easy to brush his shoulder with my own. I don't. I give him the corkscrew and quickly draw back my hand.

Spencer has been sleeping with other people. When he said he'd stopped using dating apps, I'd made romantic assumptions. But they were wrong. I guess we'd both said we weren't looking for anything serious. I mean, he'd saved it for *after* he'd had sex with me, which leaves a slightly bitter taste now I remember it.

I'd tried getting over it and carrying on, tried thinking what Theo would say, that no one is really wired for monogamy. But I would think of the way Spencer seemed soothed when he walked through my bedroom door, the way I'd feel him looking at me as I made coffee in the morning. And the idea he had been doing those things elsewhere to other women, the idea that those things could have been tactics to make me feel special, made me feel so powerless that I had to break it off.

We weren't right together anyway. I had tried and failed to turn our encounters into something significant, my determination rising from the fact that we were 'more compatible than me and my ex', which in hindsight was a very low bar to leap over.

But it feels like the 'tried and failed' that broke the camel's back.

And now there's this French guy in my kitchen.

He comes over, brushing past the massive plants. Hands me a glass of red wine, and looks me in the eyes as he takes a sip.

I went on Tinder at around six this evening. Matched with a few guys. Was clear about what I wanted. And when I wanted it, which was tonight. Wanted to meet in the pub round the corner, so it would be quicker to get back to my flat. The French guy was the only one who could make it. *He'll do*, I'd thought.

He's wearing a black shirt, he's tried too hard. So have I, in my tiny leather skirt and a black strappy top with no bra. I came deliberately dressed like an inevitability. We haven't spoken much, his English isn't great. He doesn't get my jokes. Or doesn't find them funny, which is worse.

'I can change . . . ?' He points to my laptop where Spotify is playing Amy Winehouse.

'Yeah.' I nod. He goes over to it and searches. I gulp my wine and try to stop my head from nodding. It's a nervous tick I haven't had in a long time.

Kyan and Luca are in Mykonos, and Theo is at a party taking drugs. I saw them put a clear packet with white powder in their jacket pocket before they left the flat. I told them not to sabotage themselves. They said it's fine, that in NA they expect you to relapse, that it's part of the journey.

I said to them that they are in self-destruct mode, with everything. They asked what the fuck that was supposed to mean.

I said they are seeking relationships that sound progressive

370

on paper but that don't make them happy, that Kyan and Luca don't care about their sobriety because I've seen them offhandedly offering Theo coke. That I know it's not what Theo wants because I've sat with them and Bell on that sofa where Theo's said all they want is a baby. And *I'm* supposed to be the unconventional one?

Theo said it's none of my fucking business.

I said they say the harshest things to me sometimes, and I never complain.

Theo says that I am being controlling. That I only don't want them to take drugs because it would mean I hadn't managed to fix them.

I told them fine, do the drugs then, but I won't be consoling them when they wake up feeling like a failure and an addict. That was when I got their pronoun wrong.

Theo said see? I don't respect them at all, and there's the fucking proof, bye. And they left the house with the drugs.

The French man chooses a song. It's 'Boogie Wonderland'. Right, OK.

I should want to be promiscuous. Shouldn't be a one-man woman. It's the right thing for a single woman in her early thirties to be doing this stuff. I want to represent the liberation of my generation. I want to be one of those women; free and sexually voracious.

The French man comes up to me. He strokes his hand down the length of my bare arm.

Fuck. Oh fuck. I don't want this.

'This is OK?' he asks.

'Yes,' I say. He pulls me to him. My arms hang by my sides.

NO, shouts a voice from inside me. I open my mouth. The 'no' sits there, in the back of my throat. His face is so close to mine. I think what would happen if I told him to leave. His expression would change. He'd be confused. Or angry. He could call me a bitch. Could push me. Say this was my idea anyway, and he'd be right. I made my bed, and now I have to have sex in it. To 'Boogie Wonderland'.

He kisses me. The voice inside screams. He asks if we should go in the bedroom.

PLEASE! the voice begs.

'Yeah, sure,' I say.

He hesitates, and I realise I haven't been enthusiastic. And I can't help feeling my coldness has made him feel less than he is. So I take his hand, say, 'Come on', and lead the way so he'll feel less uncertain.

I have sex with this man. I perform willingness. He asks me at one point to look at him so I do, but I don't see him at all. My eyes have clouded over.

Afterwards, I go outside on my own to smoke. He joins me. I smile and agree with him that it was good. His Uber takes six minutes.

He leaves and I sit at the kitchen table. I have been violated, and not by him. I see it now. I would rather have my body invaded than risk offending a stranger. I would rather stay in a situation that hurts me than risk making a mess.

I rub my fingers over my eyelids, feeling mascara flake underneath them. My face is wet.

I see it now. That the thing that has always been standing between me and a happy life was never anybody else. It's not useful any more to consider how He was a prick, or that Spencer had no capacity for emotional language, or that Max wanted to have his cake and eat it, or that all of them were cowardly. Maybe they were, and maybe that's all right, y'know, they're at liberty to be whoever they want to be. But the problem has come with not valuing myself enough to steer clear.

It doesn't matter how I was taught to be compliant, or to ignore my intuition. It doesn't matter how many fairy tales or romance novels I ate up, how their unhealthy messages have informed my choices.

Whenever I feel sad, or unattractive, or weak, I've gone into retrograde. Gone and found a man so I don't need to fully find myself.

I don't have the energy any more.

I can't see any benefit to love. I only feel the pain.

And the longing, God. Longing, and the shame of longing, is what hurts the most.

Theo gets back at around 6:30 a.m. I'm in bed, naked. I hear them throw their bag on the floor. Hear them go through the kitchen cupboards. Sit at the table. Get up and begin to cry. Fall on the ground, sobbing. I get up from my bed, clamp a towel to myself, and run to join them. I throw my arms around them. The towel falls away, redundant.

'I'm so sorry,' they say.

'So am I,' I say.

Their cries scratch their throat, like something is being ripped from their insides and out through their mouth.

'I hate myself!'

'It's not your fault. You're doing your best,' I say, to both of us. 'I'm here.'

I am ...

Powerful

Allow me, if you will, to flip the lens for a moment and place you, person reading this, outside on a cold night at the beginning of October. Behind you is the entrance to a VIP gazebo that's bleeding light on to the wet tarmac at your feet. Above you, the lip of the tent provides a little awning, protecting you from the drizzle. Perhaps you huddle back to get completely under it. All around you, the muffled sound coming from inside: clamour and clinks of glasses and bass from the Black Eyed Peas' 'I Gotta Feeling'. Smells of dull evening damp, of smoke being blown from mouths still tasting of lemon, salt and tequila, and of the slightly sterile top note that unfortunately arises when expensive perfume is too liberally spritzed over warm sticky bodies.

And in front of you, around fifteen feet away in the dark car park, something intriguing is happening.

Two silhouettes are standing in profile opposite one another in the rain, barely decipherable were it not for faint slivers of glare from the gazebo cradling parts of their form; outlining the sleeve of his overcoat, the delicate curve of her bare calf, occasionally dappling the hem of her dress (if you can call it a dress, more like a cobweb) as it flutters in the chill. *She must be freezing*, you think. There's a foreshadowing in the dark space that exists between the pair of them, a tension that says, *This is private, don't look*, but a mischievous force whispers to you, *Don't turn away, something is about to happen.*

Mischief is right. An animalistic bellow is let out from the male silhouette, then gets swallowed by the night so that all is quieter than before. Stiller, too. Even the slivers of gazebo glare no longer want to touch them. Even the wind has stopped fiddling with the cobweb.

A moment. Then, something happens to the female silhouette. Despite staying the exact same height and size, something about her seems to unfurl. She slowly steps forward. You lean in to hear what she's saying, and can just about make out the words 'I am'.

And then – you whip back in astonishment. Because out of nowhere, from four distinct parts of her being, this woman is radiating pure, white, powerful light.

Now, OK, look. I can't be sure this is exactly what it looked like. I wasn't on the outside looking in. But speaking as that woman on the inside, that's how it felt. Four parts of me lighting up, all at once, for a split second. One sonic boom.

They are the four parts of me that have been so important in telling this story (in fact, it's my belief they are important to any human story). Rest assured that if any of the following comes across as trivial, or a bit ... meta ... it isn't to me. It helps to make things simple, especially when things have been tough.

My Brain

My brain is a part of my anatomy that contains a soft mass of tissue and a lot of fat, which I can't help. It's not the boss of me but try telling it that.

My brain is the house of both my imagination and my memory. My imagination is the most far-reaching part of me, going way beyond the boundary of my skin. I find it so hard to believe it exists in such a small brain, in such a small person, in such a small world. My imagination has won Oliviers, Oscars, and arguments long after they've happened. Most of the time it looks like a mood board of an MGM musical put together by somebody on psychedelic drugs, and around the late 90s my imagination almost exclusively contained scenarios featuring Leonardo DiCaprio.

But sometimes my imagination can turn on me. The pictures it creates can be grave, and feel so real it's more like a memory, as though I've seen a nightmare happen right in front of me. My imagination sometimes makes me want to stick pins in my eyes so as never to see anything ever again.

My actual memory is more like Blockbuster Video, shelves of titles in different sections: drama, comedy, horror, etc. The most prominently placed section is romcoms, with titles like *Slow Dancing to Savage Garden on my 13th Birthday*, *Hand up my Skirt on the Tiger Tiger Dancefloor* and *The Actor who begged to be Pegged* (a pretty famous actor at that).

My memory is also my weak spot. There came a point during a five-year span that some of the videos on the wall went missing, and I couldn't be sure they were ever there in the first place. This has to do with discovering that my mum's mum, and her mum, and her mum, and every woman on that side of the family, had fallen victim to a pretty fucking intense neurological disease.

The more my memory failed me, the more it seemed people jumped to fill in the gaps. Like 'I didn't drink the last of the wine, you did' or 'It wasn't Savage Garden, it was Boyzone' or 'I never actually *promised*, stop lying'. And even though my brain would try to rationalise that the best person to recount the events in my life was me, its voice would always get drowned out by my impulsive, rowdy, and oh so dumb heart.

My Heart

I keep getting told by friends, my therapist and social media to be kind to myself, so I won't say my heart is an idiot, I'll say it's not very bright.

My heart performs charms. It can take a sliver of romance – a candle in a restaurant, snow in London, the sweet tingle of somebody's toe touching my foot arch under a table – then multiply it and whirl it up till romance is all I can see, until it's shrouded all around me like a pink mist. I hold Walt Disney and Richard Curtis accountable for this.

My heart is vast and ready to receive. Wide open, like Julie Andrews' arms on the mountain in *The Sound of Music*.

Or like a wide-open target.

On many occasions my cartoon-bunny heart has gone hopping up to people who look sad, not noticing their sharp fangs are dripping with the blood of hundreds of other bunnies just like it. Like Audrey Hepburn, my heart has an enormous need for affection, and a terrible need to give it.

My Vagina

Feels quite abrupt, that. Feels like I should ease people into the idea of my vagina. But, that's my vagina for you. When it wants to have its say there's no stopping it.

My vagina lies dormant most of the time, but when it sparks up it's less like a match being struck and more like I've been hosed down with gasoline then had a lit firework popped in my pocket. All or nothing, on or off. Electric.

Electricity can be hazardous, though. For all its might, my vagina is also the part of me that's the most fearful. Here's a list of things that my vagina is afraid of:

- Being useless
- Being told 'no'
- Being laughed at
- Being not tight enough
- Being too hairy
- And, for some reason, being too good for anyone who wants it.

I can't explain that last one but I never said my vagina was rational. It's hungry for sweaty, dripping, pulsating peril, but not rational. It's chased after some of the most bizarre people while knowing full well what a waste of time it is/they are. Thing is, where my heart is too dim to register red flags, and my brain clearly and sensibly points them out, to my vagina red flags are like – well – a red rag to a bull. Like in a paso doble, now I think about it.

My Body

So I don't mean my body, I mean my Body. With a capital B. There's a difference. My body (lower case) is merely the flesh-and-bones wrapping paper with what keeps me alive inside. It is something that wants so much to be looked at, but not until it's better than it is.

My Body (capital B) has for the last three years been my enemy.

I can't liken my Body to anything glamorous, anything out-side of myself because it isn't fancy or sparkly and neither does it desire to be. It is connected to something deeper, something ancient in the air. My Body has a kindly but formidable voice, which echoes softly from a place at my core.

It's a quiet voice, which means it's easily drowned out by my brain, heart and vagina. Those are wittier, sweeter, hungrier, much louder. My Body isn't like them, it's steadfast and above all patient. It sits in the corner and waits until the party is over. Then it speaks.

I try so hard to shut it up. I try to distance myself from that inner voice of my Body by focusing on my surface, holding myself together with make-up, manicures, blow dries, tans and dresses I couldn't afford but that I would take back the following Monday. And to prevent my Body's reverberating echo from knocking me off my feet, I hold on tight to the opinions of other people, on social media and in real life, who think my life is perfect because that's exactly what I've told them.

Since around 2015, my brain, heart and vagina have obsessed over one thing: my love life. For three years I've carried around their arguments, their competitiveness, their struggle for my attention and eventually their screaming agony everywhere I've been. All three have become exhausted. Over the last few months my brain has set itself to self-destruct, and my heart has broken, and my vagina has begun to starve. It's meant that I have consistently heard the soft, firm, steady voice of my Body saying, *This is wrong, my darling. This is all wrong.*

And over these last few months I have been living in abject terror, as my Body's voice is always right.

I say all this because in that moment in the car park, standing opposite the person that from 2013 I had claimed was co-star of my great love story, something incredible happened.

'The *Sun* have got pictures of me and the dancer kissing.'

'Oh.'

'And I have to get the fuck out of here before her husband hits me.'

Right there, was the first time in my entire life that my brain, heart, vagina and Body were unanimous.

And they all said, *You have everything you need.*

And in that moment, I saw the light. Knew they were right, of course they were. And I knew they didn't just mean there, in that moment in the car park either. They were telling me I have always been, exactly, who I needed to be.

Elstree Studios, September 2019

Almost a year later I am back.

'All good back there?' Mick the driver asks me.

'Yeah.' I pull my coat to cover my bare legs. 'I'm fine.'

The wrought-iron gates slide open, and in we glide at 5mph. Alone in the back seat this time, first thing in the morning.

I got a good job, a really good job. *The Crown*. It's a small role, and I don't say that modestly but realistically. I've gone about mopping up a few toxic spillages these past few months. Work and I are working through a few things. It behaved pretty badly, I said some things out of resentment. The truth is I let my job be too big a part of the person I am, so when the work started disappearing so too did chunks of me. Work is never who you are, it's what you do.

Still, what I'm doing is pretty cool.

I've already filmed one TV series this year. I've written for *Vogue* and *Elle*, and moved to where I've always wanted to live. I am self-reliant financially, and not a single bank account has to be a secret from anyone. I am providing my own security, and my own adventures, too.

I moved in on my own, away from Theo. It was difficult, but I'm trying to break my habit of saving people, which is a huge codependent trait. It was like recovering from alcoholism and living above a Wetherspoons. I'm thrilled to say my moving has saved our relationship.

Oh, there've been major slip-ups, though. The 'real life ghost'

Hugo, who left me drunk in Soho? He started sending me flirty messages when I was in the House of Commons giving a speech about gaslighting. And pretty soon after, I agreed that yeah, it *had* been too long and we *should* go out again, which we did – to London Pride of all things – where we got pissed in about forty-five seconds, sexy danced a bit to Kylie Minogue, and then he completely disappeared. Fool me once, shame on you, fool me twice – you must be really really fit.

But in general I'd say this is the most confident and attractive I've ever felt, except perhaps when I was five and told twin boys to strip in the bushes. I've learned to navigate a complex relationship with sex, and my sexuality. I must caveat the following by saying I'm not sharing out of exhibitionism but to illustrate for anyone who feels, like I used to, that they are undesirable and won't ever have sex again. Trust me: you are, and if you want it, the opportunities are there. With men and with women. I've had incredible sex, 'neither here nor there' sex, 'might as well not have been there at all' sex, and dangerous sex with a guy at a Hen weekend right before the rest of the bridal party arrived, in the Airbnb we had booked. I've driven to meet someone in a country cottage wearing nothing but a trench coat, lingerie and high heels, which is something I've always wanted to do but never dared in case my car broke down and I had to call the AA (I didn't, but I did have to refill my petrol just off the M20 and got a few second glances in the M&S Simply Food). I've learned to ask for what I want. I've come during sex, and sometimes I haven't, and sometimes that's mattered but other times it hasn't because I've had a really good time. I've been astonished at how many men think I've never heard the 'condoms just don't work for me' line before when one is presented to them. And there's other stuff I'm not telling you as well, following Iman's advice to women: 'There is power in mystery. Keep a little bit to yourself.'

Then came a breakthrough moment, when I discovered I find

it difficult to have sex without romance. I either don't enjoy it much, actively dislike it, or project a connection on to it that suits me but isn't necessarily there ... the latter leading to a vulnerability hangover that makes me fragile and needy when all they were after was a shag. So I started having less of it, and didn't miss it as much as I thought I would.

'Do you mind if we take a detour, Mick?' I ask him.

'Where to, love?'

'Do you know where they film *Strictly*?'

'Oh, not another *Strictly* nut! My wife is too, she loves it.'

'Yeah, I am.'

And I am, you know. I still watch it, which some people are surprised to discover. Because it's fabulous, and I'm fabulous, and none of this was the fault of a programme about dancing.

Mick does the slow slalom around the network of giant metal sheds. Past the 007 one. He drives us past an exact replica of Downing Street, where I'll be filming later on, and the gates of Buckingham Palace with a giant green screen behind them.

I've only been able to reclaim my life by considering what my part in all this crisis was. Not because I'm not entitled to anger, to sadness, to grief, or even a slice of self-pity – everyone is. But when you've walked out of a prison, to choose victimhood, to keep blaming others, is to keep your mind behind bars. Taking responsibility will set you free. I've said it before – I am no victim. And it's funny, y'know, because in my experience victimhood is a terrain most often laid claim to by the least worthy travellers, who will bark at you the reasons they're putting their towels on all the sunloungers before anyone can question whether they have the right to.

'Here we go, love. They film it in that one there.'

Wow. It's so ... bland.

'Is it OK if we stop here for two minutes? I think I'm early anyway.'

'No problemo, I'll turn the car around.'

I step out of the car.

There's a version of me that exists somewhere that stood by Him. Another version of me never found out about those photos with His dance partner at all, and continued on ignoring my Body, sitting in the audience at *Strictly* week after week like a pea-brain. In one version, God forbid, I degraded myself and begged for him to choose me, scared as I was of having no money, no home, of jumping off the female trajectory and starting from scratch.

I walk and try to figure out the exact spot where just over a year ago everything changed. I face away from the *Strictly* building. To my left is a space big enough for a gazebo, currently home to a dirty great skip.

I mean, there's obviously a chance I'm in the wrong car park, everywhere looks the same here.

My left hand reaches for my right forearm. There's a tattooed circle on it. I always thought actors weren't allowed tattoos, they always need covering up when you play roles, but in the read-through I discovered that Gillian Anderson has them. And what's good enough for Gillian . . .

I get embarrassed when people ask me what it means, and I have to say it's about being whole. And that the 'O' for October will always remind me of what I'm capable of. I feel uncomfortable being earnest. Which is why I did it – I want to practise taking myself seriously. I want to open up conversation, especially with other women, who are ever-ready to share their experiences and wisdom when I offer up my own.

I unbutton my coat. Underneath, I'm wearing a cobwebby dress from All Saints. Something about it was just too neat to pass up. It's more snug than the last time I wore it. I care less about that now because after years of trying to be perfect, I've given up to focus on other pursuits. A couple of months ago I was asked to run a 10K through London in my underwear for body positivity. There's something about running past High Holborn, St Paul's and Buckingham Palace in your knickers that makes you give far fewer fucks what other people think once you get your kit back on. And yeah, I squirmed a little when I saw the knicker pictures, but some toxic relationships take longer to untangle yourself from and that's OK too.

People in North Face jackets begin to bomb around, but ignore me as I stand on the tarmac, facing nothing.

There's also another version where this bit of car park doesn't mean anything to anyone. I have been sorely tempted once or twice to indulge in the 'I wish I had never set eyes on Him' narrative. But it's futile. And it's not true either.

I stand, smarter, richer, fatter, and happier. Then I smile to myself and get back in the car. I've got a job to do.

As we drive away through Elstree, I think that losing love was hard. But it was much easier than losing myself.

Enough

I thought my last chapter would be just that, but a few things have happened recently – like last-night recently – that felt too significant not to share.

I'm in Devon. I'm big on the countryside nowadays, ever since my encounter with the Norfolk Broads. It's autumn here. The trees are all on fire, the sunsets are hot pink, it's wildly glamorous. Nature is putting on a show.

It's been just over two years since the rainy *Strictly* car park, and the moment I consider to have been my romcom meet-cute with myself. I've been told that I had PTSD several times since then. I've had recurring nightmares where I see the flashing lights of the cameras outside Elstree. I've had that nightmare when I'm awake as well. In others I'm back in Samstat Road, crying on the floor because I thought it was all over. And some very graphic, very frightening ones where people have come after me for releasing that statement, nightmares that have made me wake up riddled with fear and guilt, shaking because I have ruined somebody's life by saving my own. I still felt responsible for that up until very recently. That is the lasting impact of emotional abuse.

Maura tells me it's because everything that happened was

388

traumatic. I've also been told that trauma may manifest itself when I least expect it. I've tried to coax it out in safe spaces, tried to cry in therapy, at home watching *Ghost* on my own. During the beginning of the first lockdown I found a bunch of notebooks, random diary entries from when he and I were still together, words bursting with pain and self-loathing. I didn't recognise the woman who wrote them at all. And still I couldn't coax out the trauma from within me, just read them in a state of numbness.

I haven't seen him since that night in the *Strictly* car park, which both amazes and doesn't surprise me. When we were still together, I had thought that if I left we'd be constantly running into one another on tubes, in Tesco, at parties. I thought I'd see him on the TV constantly. I always had the impression his reach extended much further than it actually did. In fact, I'd thought he was the centre of the actual Universe for a long while, a thought propagated partly by his narcissistic behaviour. For reference, *Psychology Today* states that:

Narcissism is characterised by a grandiose sense of self-importance, a lack of empathy for others, a need for excessive admiration, and the belief that one is unique and deserving of special treatment.

You don't have to be famous, hot, rich or on the telly to be a narcissist. You just have to believe that the world only exists as far as you can see it. It's so, so common. And, as far as relationships go:

Narcissists may show passion and charm in the early stages of dating. But for most narcissists, relationships are transactional. They provide positive attention and sexual satisfaction to bolster a narcissist's ego and self-esteem. Most narcissists lose interest in the relationship as the expectation for intimacy increases or they feel that they've conquered the challenge of securing a relationship.

On a more practical level, I would add that you can tell if you're the partner of someone with narcissistic tendencies if your symptoms include feeling trapped inside your own body, extreme helplessness, and as though you are slowly bleeding out.

Notice how I've worded my accusations, however. 'Narcissistic behaviour'. Because I believe to diagnose someone as being a full-blown narcissist is a bit like saying affairs with dancers are a curse. It makes everybody involved less accountable for their actions.

I really do believe that our relationship was built on the foundation of something pure, and that we loved one another in the beginning. I want to honour that, because it's my hope at least that both of us had every intention of loving the other well, we just didn't know how. This isn't a story about how a monster corrupted a princess, and is intended to question the cause, not the symptom. It's about how a relationship began to change as a result of two people's sense of self-worth, and I have empathy for both parties. It's about how all those fairy tales and films almost screwed me over with their unrealistic portrayal of love and how those stories were, in the end, the thing that prompted me to step into my power and claim my own narrative. To put a story out into the world about a woman who repeatedly got love wrong, who found a masochistic pleasure in going out with someone who hurt her because it fed her own sense of not being good enough. A woman who was never encouraged to put herself first, so had to learn. And whose life changed purely for the better the second she did.

I had been properly single, which is to say not sort-of-dating anyone at all, for around a year, helped massively by a global pandemic. I had always seen being single as a bit of a holding pen, a limbo, somewhere I would tolerate but get out of eventually. It isn't. I've loved every second of it. I've been lonely, at times. But I am often lonely when I'm in company, too, so I can't put loneliness down to being on my own. Being single is an opportunity for growth, one free of compromise, and we should cherish it when we have it.

Sure, I've had the odd chat on an app whenever I felt like an ego boost, which didn't always work. Doing the 2 a.m. death swipe on a dating app is a bit like being pissed and hungry when nowhere is open; you'll wind up with something greasy eventually, but you'll wake up with a foul taste in your mouth.

The last straw was when I went out with a guy who was straight in with a 'Better outfit than in your pictures!' neg the second he clapped eyes on me, then when I asked where he'd travelled from said 'Pretty far, but we'll split the fare on the way back, yeah?', then when I texted Poppy saying how shit it was and sent a picture of him at her request received a message from her saying 'ABORT ABORT' and on my way home found out he'd once messaged her on Hinge on a Sunday morning saying 'I'm in your neck of the woods' and she'd reluctantly let him round. He'd arrived still pissed carrying a bag of croissants, tried to grope her the second she'd let him in, then asked if she could order him an Uber cos he lost his wallet the night before.

Then, in the break between lockdowns I started talking to someone on Hinge, and we arranged to meet.

'I reeeaaally wanna caaaanceeel,' I'd moaned at Theo over the phone on the day, lying on my bed with my hand over my face. 'I haaaate Hiiinnngge.'

'Don't flake.'

'Everyone's *horrible*, though.'

'The losers were all a lesson; some people are there to show you what you *don't* want,' they'd said.

'ALL RIGHT,' I'd said. 'But as God is my witness, this is the last one.'

I've been full of unease over the past two years in matters of the heart. Each time I have tiptoed up to love, I've felt as though there is something sticky and tar-like clinging to me. 'That-relationship' residue. Some strangers I've dated have even made the delightful decision to bring it up – always vexing as I don't use my last name on apps. I once laughed at a joke a man told me, and his response was, 'I must be well in here, I know you've got a thing for comedians.'

And then by complete accident, I listened to Theo that night, didn't cancel, and within five minutes of the date thought, *Oh, for fuck's sake. I think he might be wonderful.*

For the three months I've been seeing this new man I've had to live patiently and non-judgementally alongside my own pessimism around love. Esther Perel says in her book *Mating in Captivity*, 'Love rests on two pillars; surrender and autonomy.' I spent thirty-two years being all surrendering, and the last two all autonomous. I know more about myself now than I did, thanks to a great deal of therapy and a determination to get curious. Some of me has been fun to discover, some of me hasn't. But I've worked very hard to accept all of it, and to not get too attached to anything in particular because I'll keep changing as I carry on living.

What I know for sure is that, for me, love can arrive with enough force to destroy. So I need to go carefully.

I'm sure it won't surprise anyone to know that when this new man is nice to me, and he is so nice to me so often, my first thought tends to be, *What's his ulterior motive?* I have to smash through it, like I'm smashing my fist through a pane of glass, every time, before I start to relax into being treated well. Before I can feel the warmth that his kindness warrants. I think they call this 'having trust issues'. I have loads of issues, as it goes.

There's also suspicion, defensiveness and overthinking. These probably won't go away, given what I've experienced. But you do get better at spotting them, and at gently reminding yourself that this new relationship isn't the same as that one.

I've done a lot of reading up on love, in case that wasn't obvious. But reading about being in love can only get you so far. It's like thinking about Nesquik chocolate milk powder, which is something else I often do. The taste of it, its deliciousness, the way it's the world's most perfect drink, how it tasted the last time I had it. I'm able to recall some of the sensations. But if I don't go out to Londis and get some, I'm denying myself the true experience.

When you know you are ready for Nesquik, you know. Also, love.

This man, he's not like anyone I've ever dated. I was wary when we first met because he didn't have a list of achievements to dazzle me with. But the thing is, he *does* have them, he just doesn't feel they are what's important in getting to know someone. Instead, he talked about what he values, and he asked me about what I value in people, and I realised when we did that I'd never clearly known that about a person I've gone out with before. I've only known how successful they are, or how hot, or revered, or who they know. Because in some way I've felt that by attaching myself to those things, other people will think I'm important by association.

I really, really didn't want to end this book with me falling in love with a different man. Although it involves Him, this isn't that. As a warning, there's a chance the next bit will feature too much information. Trust that I'm telling it for a reason.

He came to visit me in Devon last night. He brought margarita ingredients as he'd noticed that's what I always order. We took our cocktails and a speaker into the fields at sunset, then took our tops off and ran around in our underwear as fast as we could to the bit where Robbie yells 'aaaaaaallll' in 'Angels', freezing and laughing. Back at my Airbnb (actually someone's garage covered in William Morris wallpaper), I must have lit around a hundred candles. After the initial shy suspense – which I happen to properly enjoy – it got sexy, what with all the tequila and candles and him being so sexy and everything.

And, this thing happened during the sex that ensued. My body started trembling. And I started crying. I panicked. 'Please God, not the trauma, not now.' My body went from trembling to shaking violently as I tried to stop the emotion escaping. I closed my eyes.

And I can't say whether I saw it in front of me, or heard a voice saying it, or what. All I know is that the words 'You've been through so much, and you deserve this' arrived.

I knew it was my brain, my heart, my vagina and my Body speaking at the same time, the first time since the car park. And there was that light again. It was so powerful, I had to surrender. The tears just would not stop.

I have never had a dialogue with myself that was entirely compassionate, understanding, loving. It was how I would speak to a friend. I worked so hard to forgive myself for being the person that I am, and it was starting to happen.

But Jesus Christ, I was scared about what He would do. What anecdote this would become. That time He screwed someone and they lost their mind (and not in a good way).

'I'm really sorry,' I said through my quiet sobs, 'I need to stop.' At college Abigail Wilson deep-throated Jimmy Fuller in Mercy nightclub toilets in Norwich and gagged and threw up on his penis, and the fact that I'm even recounting that anecdote goes to show people remember shit like this, and laugh about it, and take the piss.

But he didn't.

He lay next to me as I cried, and asked whether I was OK.

He told me I didn't have to explain myself if I didn't want to.

He just put his arms around me and let me cry.

So I told him everything, from beginning to end. And he shared with me too, so that I wouldn't feel things were unequal.

'You're so decent,' I told him as we lay next to one another, in a tone of complete disbelief.

I've learned that passion doesn't need to be dangerous. It can be safe.

That adult relationships aren't a matter of urgency.

That healthy doesn't mean unsexy. Because there is nothing sexier than somebody who has their shit together.

I really love my life as a single person. Love the *possibility* in it, how the future looks like a series of options that are mine and mine alone. My life is so vibrant and exciting, I don't want to give up anything about it. But I know that I won't lose anything about my life by inviting this person in. In fact, I think his presence could enhance it.

I love me, and I won't let anything happen to her.

All because once upon a time, my worst nightmare came true.

Epilogue

When I'm upset and people try to give me advice, I often would like to punch them in the face. So let's just say the following are some learnings that I am offering to share with anyone that has been hurt, or feels trapped, or is trying to cope with a wildness in them they were never prepared for.

- All functioning humans will, at some point or other, be heartbroken. The good news is, to be heartbroken is to know for sure that you are not psychotic. The bad news is it hurts a tremendous amount.
- I was *desperate* for true love, and desperation is not a good fertiliser. When it happened, I daren't change a thing – daren't grow – in case he stopped loving me. And he stopped loving me anyway. So never stop unfolding into your own thing, it's pointless.
- 'Selfless' is bullshit trussed up like a compliment, and it's a word for the most part glamorised in women. Even just those words, 'self' and 'less'. As in, being less than who you are. No.
- The world will find ways, subtle and un, to tell you that by being a confident woman who is aware of her talents, who wants big things and isn't afraid to use her voice, you are either deluded or malfunctioning.

People will wrinkle their noses, or laugh, or brand you an egotist, or try to flatten you to elevate themselves. Have patience with them. They haven't yet learned that they're acting out of fear.

- The life in front of you does not consist of a set of empty boxes to get ticked off. It's OK to want marriage, and children, and a mortgage. And it's OK to not. But whatever it is you do want, know there is no rush.

- On that note, try not to hold on to your mistakes just because you've spent a long time investing in them. You can change your mind, you know.

- Having therapy doesn't mean you are mad. It means you care enough about yourself to intervene in your own suffering. It's difficult and joyous and can make you angrier before you get happier, but it works. You don't have to go with the first therapist you find, shop around. Lots of them offer discounted rates for people in financial difficulty, and counselling is available on the NHS.

- At the risk of coming across woefully humourless – the word 'gaslighting' is garnering a reputation for being over- and misused, and I've even heard this observation being used for comedy. I'm all for having a laugh – *hello obviously* – but this is a case of punching down not up. We're in danger of the word becoming distilled, leading to people who are experiencing gaslighting dismissing themselves or not speaking out for fear of scepticism. Believe me they're in a self-dismissive/fearful enough place as it is. Be smart about how you use it, don't stop (kindly) correcting people who are using it in the wrong context.

- I tell this to everyone – go on a solo holiday. It will

confront you with your own sense of agency; you will *have* to make choices, and you'll see how much fun it can be. Myself, I wound up in a Brooklyn live-music salsa bar, where I kissed a millionaire I never saw again.

- Write your feelings down. Your anger, fear and sadness will find a way out of your body, and putting them on paper is a safe and private place to work them through. In time, it will be your document of what you overcame. One day you will read the story of what you are capable of.
- Your Body wants what's best for you, trust it when it speaks. Ask it questions. The answers will only arrive when you are calm, so find your ways to achieve that.
- I don't know who needs to hear this today, but being sexually submissive doesn't make you less of a feminist. See also wearing make-up, enjoying attention, and wanting to feel desired.
- Perhaps you're not insane. Perhaps it's not your period, or your gender. Perhaps you don't 'always do this', and you *did* remember it right. Perhaps your actions didn't cause their reaction, and you're not too sensitive, and you *can* take a joke, and you *can't* be more like someone else's girlfriend and nor should you need to be. Perhaps they're a bit of a dick.
- The best day of your life hasn't happened yet, and you haven't met everyone that will love you.
- Emotions don't get in the way – they *are* the way.
- You will be OK. You will laugh again. You will burn again. Just not as quickly as you will want to.
- If you have found yourself in any toxic relationship – be it a romance, a friendship, a job, whatever – chances are you will come up against the

question: 'Why did you stay?' You have no obligation to answer it. What I have found the most helpful in all of this, however, has been to take the question at face value and ask it of myself. 'Why did *I* stay?' It could gently encourage you to consider how you learned about love, about shame, about self-worth. It could help you identify the patterns. 'Why did *I* stay?' could help you confront the shadows in you, the ones that are in all of us, and accept them. Doing so will mean that you accept every single bit of yourself, not just the bits that the outside world deem admissible.

'Why did I stay?' has been difficult. But it has helped me look at my life with understanding and forgiveness for everything it has been, and move forward with the mantra 'never again'.

Never again.

Never again.

- Care, affection, recognition, respect, commitment, trust and open/honest communication.

In the book *All About Love* by bell hooks, she attempts to give love one concrete definition. She makes the excellent point that if we all knew what love truly meant the word would be better understood, and better used. She concluded that in order for something to be called love, it *has* to comprise of seven things. I'll say them again:

- care, affection, recognition, respect, commitment, trust and open/honest communication.

Now, most people receive care and affection at times in a relationship. Overwhelming amounts of it, sometimes, and it feels great. Sex, for example, can make a person light up with the receiving of care and affection. But it's possible to let that great feeling make up for the other five things that are missing.

The more hungry you are for love, the more your brain, heart and vagina will convince yourself that all seven of those things are present, even when your Body knows they aren't. Your Body will try to tell you there are things missing. *That person doesn't respect you*, it will calmly say. Or, *You don't trust them*. Your brain, heart and vagina will shout louder. *But you love them*, they will exclaim. *And they love you, they told you so!*

It blew my mind when I read this because it means an abusive relationship of any kind cannot possibly coexist with love. In an abusive relationship there isn't responsibility, trust, respect or communication that's open and honest, and not just from the perpetrator. From the victim, too.

Most people find this difficult to hear, about the seven things. Because if it's true, if we definitely need all seven for it to be deemed love, it means that an overwhelming number of people are currently in loveless situations.

The good news for anybody struggling with the love in their life, or for anyone who is afraid of losing what they deem to be love, is this.

It was only when I stepped out of what I deemed to be my great love story that I saw care, affection, recognition, respect, commitment, trust, and open and honest communication had always been there for me. I had just been focused in the wrong direction.

This is for my friends Sam, Theo, Naomi and Tim. For Polly, Phoebe, Lucy and Daniella. For Ben, Paul, Diana, Oonagh, Lena and Emma.

And especially for Claire, Sean, and baby Louis Rigby.